STUDIES IN HISTORY, ECONOMICS
AND PUBLIC LAW

Edited by the
FACULTY OF POLITICAL SCIENCE OF
COLUMBIA UNIVERSITY

NUMBER 506

THE MÉLINE TARIFF: FRENCH AGRICULTURE AND NATIONALIST ECONOMIC POLICY

BY
EUGENE OWEN GOLOB

THE MÉLINE TARIFF: FRENCH AGRICULTURE AND NATIONALIST ECONOMIC POLICY

BY

EUGENE OWEN GOLOB, Ph.D.

Instructor in History, Columbia University

NEW YORK

COLUMBIA UNIVERSITY PRESS

LONDON: P. S. KING & STAPLES, LTD.

1944

PRINTED IN THE UNITED STATES OF AMERICA

To

E. B. G.

FOREWORD

Historical method and historical evidence are essential to all the social studies. Ricardian classical economics, resting on excessive faith in rational investigation, seems, on the surface, to be one of the few significant exceptions to this general statement. Most of the data employed in the social studies are historical in nature, records of the past, tested by the historian's canons of reliability. It is small wonder, then, that history, which pervades its fellow disciplines, should attempt to encompass them all, to synthesize the story of the development of society. Synthetic history, which has alternated between professional scorn and favor, is of two principal types. One constitutes an attempt to treat, historically, all the categories of the complex of society. The other does this and more, for it endeavors to apply to these categories the methods and techniques of the other social studies. The first runs the risk of failing to penetrate the surface of events, of relying for understanding on mere juxtaposition of the different subjects or categories. The second may bog down in a mass of details, in the welter of different types of data yielded by the different methods.

Both kinds of synthetic history have dealt, in the main, with broad subjects and relatively long periods of time, for breadth and generalization have seemed to be in their very nature. But successful achievement on this plane of great complexity would require a clear, well-developed philosophy or canon of history, and there has been general reluctance to return to this type of thought. Despite their great influence, Hegel, Marx and their fellows have discouraged philosophical analysis among scholarly historians. Recent efforts, like that of Spengler, to write general, philosophical history, have merely tended to confirm the seeming wisdom of ignoring the philosophy of history.

The development of true synthetic history, societal in scope and analytical in character, must therefore be a slow and difficult process. One step in this direction, however, might well be the writing of synthetic histories of limited, particular subjects, and the present brief study represents such an effort.

The Méline Tariff is one of the major pieces of economic legislation of the nineteenth century. It is hardly an exaggeration to say that it was part of the fundamental economic law of the Third Republic, and the life preserver of French agriculture. It may be examined and tested as a tariff law, its incidence and effectiveness studied. It may be analyzed from the standpoint of theoretical economics. It may be looked upon as the culmination of a long protectionist campaign. It may be viewed in the light of French political history, or as one phase of the development of French commercial policy. While any one of these approaches would be legitimate, synthesis requires that all be undertaken, and, it must be confessed, more besides. It cannot be claimed that all these facets of the subject have received equal treatment in this book, or that they have been fully explored. To have done so would have been to exceed the practical limitations imposed upon this work.

One of the most interesting aspects of the Méline Tariff is its enactment of agricultural protection, which brings it under the heading of nationalist economic policy as distinct from mercantilism or simple protectionism, and this study has been restricted to the agricultural side of the trends and institutions from which the Tariff of 1892 arose. In considering agricultural protection against the background of French agricultural history and developments under the Third Republic, it may be possible, at the same time, to shed some light on French society from the focal point of agrarian protection.

Agriculture, in France, did not fall before rising industrialization to the extent that it did in England. While France accepted the new techniques and institutions of industry, and even played a significant rôle in developing them, she did not permit agriculture to be eclipsed, or to suffer revolutionary change. For the first three quarters of the nineteenth century there was no fundamental change in the methods, crops, institutions or general economic situation of French agriculture. During part of this period, from the Restoration to the Second Empire, agriculture benefited from tariff protection which resulted from an alliance with industry. The liberal policy of Napoleon III swept away many agricultural duties, and lowered others. Agriculture remained unruffled, however, for the long period of stability did not close until the early years of the Third Republic.

In the late 1870's and in the decade of the 1880's, during what has been called the "Great Depression," agricultural prices and incomes fell as world communications improved and new, fertile lands overseas began effective competition with old world production. French agriculture attempted a twofold solution of the problems which thus shattered its tranquility. On the one hand it turned toward association, in the Social Catholic sense; on the other hand toward protection, justified on grounds of nationalist economic theory. As before, the success of agricultural protection depended on an alliance with industry, and this was arranged before the legislative elections of 1889. But the agrarian leaders were for the most part recruited from the royalist opposition to the Third Republic. They were among the Boulangist coalition which went down in defeat. For agricultural protectionism to succeed, therefore, it had to be divorced from the constitutional question, the leadership had to be given to republican statesman, compromises had to be effected.

The Méline Tariff was the compromise that resulted from this situation. It went far toward satisfying the demands of the agrarian leaders, although it failed to meet them completely. The succeeding years saw the enactment of further protectionist measures. Considering its objectives, this structure of nationalist economic policy, built on the foundation of the Tariff of 1892, was generally successful. It was designed to save French agriculture from the fate that had befallen English agriculture, to increase French production so that food prices would not rise unduly. French agriculture was saved: and while the cost of living may have risen, burdening the French people, their sacrifice was not excessive on the scale of nationalist economics, for an essential part of the economy was preserved, diversification maintained, independence safeguarded, and the peasantry kept as a sturdy social group.

This, in brief, is the story to be told in the pages that follow. The first chapter treats of the historical background of French agricultural conditions and institutions, organizations and tariffs. The second deals with the depression that engulfed French agriculture in the 1880's. The third and fourth are concerned, respectively, with agricultural association and nationalist economic thought, the fifth with the union of these factors in the drive for the Méline Tariff, and the sixth with the elaboration of the law itself. The last chapter, carrying the story to 1910, attempts to evaluate the Méline Tariff in the light of its sponsors' intentions. It might seem regrettable not to have continued to the present, but the War of 1914-1918 and its aftermath so changed the situation as to destroy the continuity of the categories used: 1910, the date of the first major tariff revision after that of 1892, seemed an appropriate point at which to close.

My greatest hope is that this work may, in some small way, contribute to a better understanding of some of the problems that have faced and will continue to face the people of France.

I wish to express my gratitude to the scholars and friends who have been of aid and inspiration to me: to Professor Carlton J. H. Hayes, whose seminar introduced me to the problems of historical scholarship; to Professor Shepard B. Clough, who suggested and guided the preparation of this study, and Professor Charles W. Cole, under whom it was completed; to Professor Harold Barger, whose painstaking criticism was of inestimable value, especially with respect to the economic materials; to Professor Jacques Barzun, for his careful reading of the manuscript and his many helpful suggestions, and to Mr. Donald W. O'Connell, for his advice and assistance on the economic aspects of the work. I also wish to thank

M. Louis Mila, of the *Société des agriculteurs de France;* M. Louis Salleron, of the *Association générale du Crédit Mutuel et de la Coopération agricoles;* Dr. Robert Valeur; Mr. Nelson H. Eddy; Mr. Robert E. Tschan; Professor Frederick E. Croxton; my wife; and Mr. Joseph Brahdy, who generously prepared the charts and maps. The staffs of the Columbia University, Amherst College and New York Public Libraries, and of the pre-war *Bibliothèque nationale* and *Musée social* in Paris were most helpful. Research abroad was made possible through the award of the W. Bayard Cutting Traveling Fellowship by Columbia University.

EUGENE O. GOLOB.

COLUMBIA UNIVERSITY,
JULY 14, 1943.

CONTENTS

ABBREVIATIONS USED IN NOTES

AC . . . . *L'Association catholique*

BSAF . . . . *Bulletin de la Société des agriculteurs de France*

CRSAF . . . . *Comptes rendus des travaux de la Société des agriculteurs de France*

DR . . . . *La Démocratie rurale*

JAP . . . . *Journal d'Agriculture pratique*

JEC . . . . *Journal des économistes*

TN . . . . *Le Travail National*

JO . . . . *Journal officiel de la République française*

- CD . . . . . . *Chambre des Députés: Débats parlementaires*
- CDP . . . . *Chambre des Députés: Documents parlementaires*
- SD . . . . . . *Sénat: Débats parlementaires*
- SDP . . . . *Sénat: Documents parlementaires*

CHAPTER I

AGRICULTURAL HISTORY, ORGANIZATIONS AND PROTECTION PRIOR TO 1880

Agricultural History

The fertile land of France was well endowed and well situated to become the home of a rich civilization which was to give of its light to the rest of mankind. The fame and glory of France are in her arts and literature, the products of her craftsmen, the achievements of her thinkers. At times the halo of political and military triumph has rested over the spires of her cathedrals and the mansards of her cities. She has seen days of tragic defeat, and crushed, has arisen. But the foundation of her brilliant urban culture was always in her fields and farms, in the pastures of Brittany and the vineyards of the Bordelais.

Population

Agriculture, once the calling of all but a few of the people of France, had to yield before the rise of industry and urban civilization, but it fell back gradually enough for its traditions and vitality to be preserved. The story of this development must be told in several ways, with reference to population, tenure, production, prices and trade. Two methods of classification are employed in French population statistics. On the one hand population is divided into rural, including persons inhabiting communes of 2,000 or less (3,000 up to 1866), and urban, composed of those living in communes of over 2,000. This method is open to the criticism that farmers living in communes of over 2,000 are classed as city dwellers. Because of changes in methods of taking the census it is inadvisable to consider this series before 1846.[1]

1 Maurice Block, *Statistique de la France comparée avec les divers pays de l'Europe*, 2nd ed., 2 vols., Paris, 1875, vol. I, p. 35; vol. II, p. 22. Agricultural *enquêtes*, or investigations, occurred in: 1839-40, *Statistique de la*

(Thousands)

	Total Population	Rural Population	% of Total	Urban Population	% of Total
1846	35,400	26,754	75.6	8,647	24.4
1851	35,783	26,648	74.5	9,135	25.5
1856	36,039	26,195	73.2	9,885	26.8
1861	37,386	26,597	71.1	10,790	28.8
1866	38,067	26,372	69.5	11,595	30.5
1872	36,103	24,889	68.9	11,214	31.1
1876	36,906	24,934	67.6	11,971	32.4
1881	37,672	24,576	65.2	13,097	34.8

Under the second method, first used in 1861, the active or earning population is classed according to occupation. Dependents are grouped with earners, and servants are assumed to follow their masters' callings:

> at this rate, if the replies had always conformed to the questionnaires, they would have had to enter as many Presidents of the Republic as there were servants at the Élysée Palace.[2]

Further, farmers who engaged in trades or home crafts on the side might have been classed as artisans.[3] Nevertheless, this

(Thousands)

	Agricultural Population	% of Total	Non-Agricultural Population	% of Total
1861	19,873	53.1	17,513	46.9
1866	19,598	51.5	18,469	48.5
1872	18,513	51.3	17,590	48.7
1876	19,969	51.4	17,937	48.6
1881	18,249	48.4	19,423	51.6

France: agriculture, Paris, 4 vols., 1839-1842; 1852, *Statistique de la France: agriculture*, Paris, 2 vols., 1858-1860; 1862, *Statistique de la France: agriculture: résultats généraux de l'enquête décennale de 1862*, Strasbourg, 1868; 1882, *Statistique agricole de la France: (Algérie et colonies): Résultats généraux de l'enquête décennale de 1882*, Nancy, 1887; 1892, *Statistique agricole de la France: résultats généraux de l'enquête décennale de 1892*, Paris, 1897. *Enquête*, 1882, p. 366.

2 Alfred de Foville, *Le morcellement: études économiques et statistiques sur la propriété foncière*, Paris, 1885, p. 79.

3 CRSAF, vol. XXIV, 1892, pp. 121 ff.

second series reflects occupational trends more accurately than the first.[4]

While we must bear in mind the possibility of bias rising out of the cession of Alsace-Lorraine, both tables illustrate the absolute and relative decline of the farm population.[5] The difference between the terms " rural " and " agricultural " undoubtedly explains the great disparity between these sets of figures: village storekeepers, fuctionaries, clergy, professionals, *rentiers*, etc. are considered " rural " in the first set and are classed as " non-agricultural " in the second. The explanation for the decline must be sought in either or both of the following factors: 1) falling rate of natural increase (births minus deaths) in the farm population, 2) migration to the cities. The first may be ruled out. A correlation in which departments are compared as to rank in urbanization and rank in natural increase yields the inconclusive coefficient of —.16.[6] In 1877-1886 the average annual rate of natural increase in the fifteen most urban departments was 1.3 per thousand, and 4.6 per thousand in the fifteen least urban departments. The birth rate was 26.2 per thousand in both groups. It is clear that we must turn to the second factor for an explanation of the decline of the farm population, bearing in mind that migration to the cities tended to raise the urban birth rate by increasing the proportion of lower age groups to total population.[7] The following table makes the picture clear: [8]

4 *Enquête 1882*, p. 367 ; Bureau de la statistique générale, *Résultats généraux du dénombrement de 1876*, Paris, 1878, p. xlix.

5 The population of the ceded territories amounted to 1,549,738 in 1871, *Statistisches Jahrbuch für Elsass-Lothringen*, Strasbourg, 1907, p. 3.

6 *Dénombrement de 1876*, p. xxiii. Émile Levasseur, *La population Française: histoire de la population avant 1789 et démographie de la France comparée à celle des autres nations au xixe siècle*, 3 vols., Paris, 1890-1892, vol. II, pp. 23, 156.

7 Joseph J. Spengler, *France faces depopulation*, Durham, N. C., 1938, pp. 83-84.

8 *Dénombrement de 1876*, pp. 74-75. The figure of 191,215 is assumed to represent foreign immigration. *Ibid.*, p. xxv.

NET INCREASES FROM 1872 TO 1876 OWING TO IMMIGRATION AND EMIGRATION

	Urban Population	Rural Population	Total Population
15 Most Urban Depts.......	357,589	— 57,188	260,401
15 Least Urban Depts......	22,356	— 81,730	— 57,374
All France..................	608,523	—417,328	191,215

Increase owing to immigration was above all true of Paris. In 1866 the French-born population of the capital was composed of 592,763 born in the department of the Seine and 1,098,818 born in other departments or colonies: in 1876 the figures were 758,110 and 1,099,646 respectively, and in 1881 807,060 and 1,265,454 respectively.[9]

The storied life of the cities, increasing industrialization which created many jobs and new vocations, the spirit and mythology of the nineteenth century, combined to make the cities more attractive to many than the hard, even and unchanging course of the countryside. So much has been written on this subject, and so dark a picture painted, that one is left with the feeling that rural France was almost deserted.[10] Yet it is clear from the figures given that the movement, while serious, never assumed mass proportions. It was not a Great Migration, and, indeed, was actually weaker in France than in other nations at comparable stages of industrialization.[11]

Division of the Land

One factor frequently invoked to explain this trend was the division of land among increasing numbers of owners, and the decline in the size of farms—*le morcellement.* Medieval France

9 *Ibid.*, p. 256. Émile Levasseur, *Les populations urbaines en France comparée à celles de l'étranger*, Paris, 1887, p. 57. See Spengler, *op. cit.*, ch. II.

10 A long list of works on this subject is given in Spengler, *op. cit.*, p. 36, note 15. In addition one may cite René Bazin's well-known novel, *La terre qui meurt*, Paris, 1899, and Jules Méline's *The return to the land*, Justin McCarthy trans., New York, 1907, and *Le salut par la terre*, 2nd ed., Paris, 1920. See Michel Augé-Laribé's comment, *L'Évolution de la France agricole*, Paris, 1912, p. 123.

11 Spengler, *op. cit.*, pp. 27 ff.

"had no Domesday Book," and land statistics were scattered and local until the *cadastre*, or land register, was begun in 1807.[12] We must start therefore with the statement that land ownership was more widespread in the eighteenth century than a formal exposition of the *ancien régime* would lead one to believe, although the Revolution did greatly democratize landowning.[13] Decrees of the Constituent and Legislative Assemblies abolished feudal privileges and dues, expropriated Church lands and the lands of emigrés and provided for their sale.[14] The changes in the law of inheritance after 1790 which substituted equal division of property among heirs for primogeniture likewise had the effect of increasing the number of those who owned land.[15] The strength of this tendency, however, should not be exaggerated. "It is true," says Henri Sée,

> that the sale of the *biens nationaux* brought about the total disappearance of the former Church properties, and seriously cut into the holdings of the nobility, but not as much as one might believe: many properties of emigrés which were improperly sold could be restored to their owners; under the Directory, Consulate and Empire there were repurchases, retrocessions, sometimes buyers' forfeitures. The indemnity of one billion [francs] granted emigrés in 1825 also helped to rebuild the landholdings of the nobility.[16]

There are no direct figures as to the number of landowners before the agricultural *enquête* of 1862, and estimates for pre-

12 De Foville, *op. cit.*, p. 39.

13 Henri Sée, *Esquisse d'une histoire du régime agraire en Europe aux XVIIIe et XIXe siècles*, Paris, 1921 pp. 18-19. "How then could certain historians . . . deny all proprietorship to the peasants? Because peasant proprietorship was not clearly autonomous; it was burdened with seignorial rights."

14 P. Sagnac, *La Révolution (1789-1792)*, vol. I of, E. Lavisse, ed., *Histoire de la France contemporaine depuis la Révolution jusqu'à la paix de 1919*, Paris, 1920, pp. 138, 143, 336, 408.

15 De Foville, *op. cit.*, p. 52.

16 Henri Sée, "Les progrès de l'agriculture en France de 1815 à 1848," *Revue d'Histoire économique et sociale*. Paris, 1921, vol. IX, p. 69.

ceding years are based on the *cotes foncières*, the individual assessments due in accordance with the land tax law of December 1, 1790.[17] Unfortunately, any such estimates are necessarily inaccurate, for the *cote foncière* refers to the holdings of a person in a given commune. A farmer whose lands lie in several communes will have as many *cotes*. Thus the number of *cotes* is higher than that of actual landowners. An added difficulty is that until 1883 no distinction was made between unbuilt properties and those upon which buildings had been erected.[18] Nevertheless we may present the following figures:[19]

Year	*cotes foncières*
1826	10,296,693
1835	10,893,528
1840-1844 (average)	11,524,066
1856-1860 (average)	13,133,590
1878-1882 (average)	14,267,232

This increase in the number of *cotes foncières*, when compared with the decline in rural population from 26,753,743 in 1846 to 24,934,334 in 1876, would seem to indicate a notable rise in the number of landowners and a corollary tendency to parcelling or *morcellement*. Using proportions of 63 and 59.4 landowners per 100 *cotes*, the *Administration des contributions directes* estimated the number of proprietors at 7,584,901 in 1851 and 8,454,218 in 1879.[20] Alfred de Foville, noted agricultural economist, estimated their number at about 4 million before the Revolution and, using the coefficient 63, at over

17 Ministère de l'agriculture; office de l'enseignement agricole, *Principales mesures législatives et administratives prises en faveur de l'agriculture sous le gouvernement de la 3e république*, Paris, 1914, p. 29. See also Augé-Laribé, *op. cit.*, p. 185.

18 Ministère des finances; administration des contributions directes, *Annuaire des contributions directes*, 1911, annex, p. 63.

19 *Loc. cit.*; *Enquête 1882*, tables, pp. 275 ff.

20 *Annuaire des contributions directes*, 1911, annex, p. 234. General revaluations of the *cotes foncières* occurred in 1814, 1851, 1879-1881 and 1908-1911. See *Principales mesures*, p. 29.

6½ million about 1825, from 7 to 7½ million about 1850 and around 8 million toward 1876.[21] These figures are flatly contradicted, however, by those of the official *enquêtes* of the Ministry of Agriculture, gathered by direct observation, which give 3,799,759 landowners in 1862 and 3,525,342 in 1882, which seemingly would indicate concentration of ownership.[22]

Neither set is really accurate. The figures based on the *cotes foncières* are undoubtedly exaggerated, because of the very nature of the *cote*, because the tax collectors were paid per entry, because consolidations of properties were frequently ignored, because increase in the number of urban parcels was not taken into account.[23] The *enquête* data, directly gathered, might be expected to be reliable, but many objections can be raised against them. The questionnaires were extremely complicated and before 1892 were answered by the secretaries to the mayors of the communes, who, in rural areas, were usually the village teachers.[24] There are significant contradictions among the figures: for example, 4,835,246 landowning and non-landowning farmers are listed in 1882, and at the same time 5,672,007 *exploitations* or farms are recorded.[25] If we turn to authority for some clue as to the comparative accuracy of these sets of data we find that while Michel Augé-Laribé, a leading contemporary agricultural economist, uses those of the *enquêtes*,

21 De Foville, *op. cit.*, p. 58.

22 *Enquête 1882, tables*, p. 188.

23 De Foville, *op. cit.*, pp. 66-67.

24 Michel Augé-Laribé, *Grande ou petite propriété*, Montpellier, 1902, p. 190. Also, by the same author, *L'évolution de la France agricole*, p. 101. For a general criticism of French agricultural statistics, including the *enquêtes*, see René Musset, "Les statistiques agricoles officielles françaises," *Annales d'histoire économique et sociale*, vol. V, 1933, pp. 285 ff.

25 *Enquête 1882*, pp. 283, 321. These figures are lower by 70,102 than the total for owners, tenant farmers, sharecroppers and day laborers who also own land, *Enquête 1892*, tables, pp. 248-249. On this point see Henri Sée, *Französische Wirtschaftsgeschichte*, vol. II, Jena, 1936, p. 381.

Emile Chevallier, in his *Rapport* for the Exposition of 1900 follows de Foville.[26]

If we multiply de Foville's figure of 8,000,000 landowners in 1875 by the average number of persons per houshold, 3.65,[27] we obtain the total of 29,200,000, which alone is higher by 10,213,395 than the total *agricultural* (as distinct from *rural*) population of 18,986,605 in 1876. Applying the same method to the figures of the *enquête* of 1882, we obtain 12,887,498; adding to this the households of the 1,415,945 day laborers, sharecroppers and tenant farmers owning no land at all, amounting to 5,148,199 persons, we reach the total of 18,035,697, sufficiently close to that of the agricultural population, which was 18,249,209 in 1881.[28] It would therefore seem advisable to follow the data of the *enquêtes agricoles*.

It is hard to generalize, on the basis of these figures, about the trend in land ownership during the first three quarters of the nineteenth century. Because of the decline of the agricultural population, it is impossible to determine a shift to other forms of land tenure. The first useful data on these forms appear in the *enquêtes* of 1862 and 1882.[29]

(Thousands)	1862	1882	1862	1882	1862	1882
					—Totals—	
Landowners also farming as		Non-landowning:				
Tenant farmers	647	500	387	468	1,035	968
Sharecroppers	204	147	202	194	405	342
Day laborers	1,134	727	868	753	2,004	1,481
Totals	1,985	1,375	1,456	1,416	3,445	2,791

Increase is evident only in the class of tenant farmers owning

26 Augé-Laribé, *Évolution*, pp. 102 ff.; Émile Chevallier, *Exposition universelle internationale de 1900 à Paris: rapports du jury international: classe 104– grande et petite culture– syndicats agricoles– crédit agricole*, Paris, 1902, p. 34.

27 *Statistique générale de la France: résultats statistiques du recensement générale de la population effectué le 7 mars 1926*, Paris, 1928, p. 67.

28 *Enquête 1882*, pp. 342, 367, 369.

29 *Ibid.*, tables, p. 188; *Enquête 1892*, tables, pp. 248-249.

no land, but this may represent a rise in status to tenancy, as well as a fall from ownership.

In turning to the question of land division from the standpoint of the *exploitation* or unit of land worked, we are again faced with difficulties. Where should the limits of "small," "medium," and "large" farms be set? Extent and value are the obvious criteria, but a very small wheat farm would make a sizable vineyard, and there are no adequate figures as to the revenues of individual farms for this period.[30] Taking into consideration the limitations of the standard, let us consider the following figures drawn from the *enquêtes agricoles*.[31]

NUMBER OF FARMS (Thousands)

	Small 1-10 ha.	Medium 10-40 ha.	Large over 40 ha.	Total
1862	2,435	636	154	3,026
1882	2,635	727	142	3,504
Total area (Thousand hectares, 1882 only)	11,366	14,846	22,296	

Unfortunately, it is impossible to compare the total areas, but it is clear that the small and medium groups gained at the expense of the large. Thus we are confronted with the paradox that while the number of owners fell, according to the *enquêtes*, between 1862 and 1882, the number of smaller farm units rose. The increase in farm tenancy, as we have seen, does not explain this discrepancy. It must be borne in mind, however, that the loss of the major part of Alsace-Lorraine following the War of 1870 introduces an element of exaggeration into all the changes recorded.[32]

30 Augé-Laribé, *Grande ou petite*, p. 11. De Foville's analysis applies to *propriété* rather than *exploitation* and therefore has little significance, for one owner might have a large tract of land divided into several completely independent farm units.

31 *Enquête 1892*, pp. 363-364. 1 hectare = 2.47 acres.

32 The figures for the ceded territory cannot conveniently be subtracted from the 1862 totals because parts of the four departments affected remained in French hands: the territory of Belfort (Haut-Rhin) and the new department of Meurthe-et-Moselle composed of the sections of the departments of the Meurthe and the Moselle which were not ceded.

It is evident that no conclusion can be reached, except the negative one, that there was no strong trend in operation with respect to either land tenure or the size of farms. French agriculture entered the 1880's with a structure in respect of size and type of ownership not greatly changed from that of the first part of the nineteenth century.

Crops and Livestock

The same relative stability may be observed in the way in which the land was used, although notable technical progress was made. The inaccuracy of nineteenth-century French statistics is such that there was much disagreement as to the area of continental France.[33] According to the *enquête* of 1882 it was 53,028,463 hectares in 1840, 54,307,690 after the annexation of Nice and Savoy in 1860 and 52,857,199 after the loss of Alsace-Lorraine.[34] In the following table areas devoted to various agricultural uses and production figures for certain crops are listed. The data are not strictly accurate, and classifications and methods of compilation changed so from one *enquête* to another that only a rough comparison is justified.[35] In addition we must again take into consideration the fact that owing to the cession of Alsace-Lorraine, increases in 1882 over 1862 are actually greater than the figures indicate and decreases are either smaller or non-existent.[36]

33 De Foville, *op. cit.*, p. 110, note 1.

34 *Enquête 1882*, p. 6. If the ceded territory given as 1,450,941.8 hectares (*Enquête 1892*, p. 243) is added to this figure the result is greater by 3950 hectares than that recorded for continental France in 1862, 54,305,141 hectares (*Enquête 1862*, p. v). In 1882 (*Enquête 1882*, tables, p. 101) the 1862 area is given as 54,307,690 hectares.

35 Augé-Laribé, *Évolution*, pp. 102-103.

36 The data on areas and production were drawn from the tables of the *enquêtes* of 1862 and 1882. It was not possible to make corrections for the annexation of Nice and Savoy, or for the loss of Alsace-Lorraine (see note 32 above). In 1883, the ceded territories were composed as follows: (*Enquête 1882*, p. 170) cultivable lands 674,119.8 hectares, truck gardens 18,662.0, pastures 210,325.6, vineyards 32,686.5, woods and forests 443,844.9, waste lands 13,405.5, buildings 8,115.0, waterways and roads 49,782.5, total 1,450,941.8 hectares.

Area (in 1,000 Hectares)[37]

	1840	1852	1862	1882
Wheat	5,592	6,985	7,473	7,191
All Grains	14,552	15,366	15,621	15,090
Garden crops [a]	523	...	714	774
Potatoes	922	829	1,235	1,338
Sugar beets	58	111	136	240
Other indus. crops [b]	382	...	552	275
Vineyards	1,972	2,191	2,321	2,197
Woods, forests [c]	8,806	...	9,035	9,455
Fallow land	6,763	5,705	5,148	3,644
Orchards, parks [d]	...	...	1,037	842
Fodders, pastures [e]	6,024	7,621	8,180	10,188
Wastes, marshes [f]	9,191	6,580	7,346	6,512

Production

	1840	1852	1862	1882
Wheat (in 1,000 Hectoliters)	69,592	95,262	109,796	129,339
All grains " "	190,884	226,339	263,822	295,254
Wine " "	36,783	38,060	48,630	33,582
Sugar beets (in 1,000 quintals)	25,741	32,249	44,268	88,504
Fodders [g] " "	152,464	213,897	263,759	286,409
Hemp and flax " "	1,044	978	1,097	750
Potatoes " "	69,288	41,719	102,733	100,994

There were few great changes in the division of the land among the various crops. Truck-garden crops, potatoes and sugar beets gained in importance. More land was devoted to fodders and pastures. Vineyards decreased in area and pro-

37 a. The figure for garden crops in 1840 is an estimate (*Enquête 1882*, p. 169) for which no explanation is given.

b. This includes flax, hemp, colza, tobacco, hops, etc. The 1840 figure is again an estimate (*loc. cit.*)

c. Nice and Savoy are not included.

d. This is an estimate based on the percentage of total land listed for this category. *Enquête 1892*, p. 244.

e. An estimated 249,000 hectares growing annual forage crops, roots, beets, etc., are included.

f. Sub-marginal pasture lands are included in this figure. Some 800,000 hectares were apparently lost in 1862 and found again in 1882. *Enquête 1882*, p. 102.

g. The figure for 1882 is lower than the total of fodders given by the *enquête* of that year. Because several crops were listed for the first time in 1882 they were omitted to make the *enquêtes* comparable. 1 quintal = 100 kilograms or 220 pounds, 1 hectoliter = 100 liters or 26.4 gallons.

duction, owing to disease. Mildew (*oïdium*) attacked the vines in the 1850's; phylloxera first made its appearance in the department of Bouches-du-Rhône about 1865, but the full weight of its blow was not felt until after 1875. In the sixty-five years 1835, 1840, 1845 and 1849-1910, the average annual wine production was 42.8 million hectoliters and, with the plague years subtracted, was 50.8 million hectoliters. The extent of the ravages is indicated by the fact that in the mildew period production fell to a yearly average of 29.8 million hectoliters, and that in the years 1876-1892, when phylloxera was prevalent, it was 32.7 hectoliters.[38] The decline in production owing to phylloxera was " never as great in any one year as had been that caused by *oïdium,* but it was spread over a period of many years." [39] The only really significant decline in area and production, however, is that under the heading of " other industrial crops," comprising oleaginous seeds, flax, hemp, etc., which may be explained by secular trends.[40] The decline in land lying fallow and the great increase in grain production on a relatively stationary amount of land indicate improvement in agricultural technique which is made clear by the following figures of yields per hectare.[41]

	1840	1852	1862	1882
Winter wheat (hectol.)	12.45	13.64	14.69	17.98
Rye (hectol.)	10.79	11.51	12.91	16.38
Sugar beets (quintals)	273.00	290.00	324.00	368.00
Clover, alfalfa, etc. (quintals)	29.97	33.00	37.46	43.40

The steady increase in land devoted to fodders and pastures gives evidence of progress in animal husbandry which is illus-

38 Direction de la statistique générale et de la documentation, *Annuaire statistique,* 1937, pp. 62*-63*. *Enquête 1882,* p. 146.

39 Arthur Louis Dunham, *The Anglo-French Treaty of Commerce of 1860 and the Progress of the Industrial Revolution in France,* University of Michigan Publications: History and Political Science, vol. IX, Ann Arbor, 1930, p. 291.

40 Increased use of sesame oil, rising importance of American cotton, etc.

41 *Enquête 1882,* tables, pp. 4, 5, 37, 59.

trated by the following table.[42] Unfortunately, information on dairy products and poultry is unavailable before 1882.

(Thousands)	1840	1852	1862	1882
Cattle	9,937	11,921	12,812	12,997
Sheep	32,151	33,282	29,530	23,809
Pigs	4,911	5,246	6,038	7,147
Horses	2,818	2,866	2,912	2,838
Goats	964	1,338	1,726	1,851
Meat Production (1,000 kilograms)				
Beef, veal	309,656	339,538	479,961	685,006
Mutton	63,773	....	101,495	149,137
Average Weights (kilograms)				
Bulls, oxen	413	437	456	465
Cows	240	275	324	321
Sheep	26	30	35	35

Rising numbers, weights and meat production are evidence of better care and breeding, and greater meat consumption. Sheep declined in importance as wool producers, owing to the severe competition offered by Australia,[43] but became increasingly valued for food.

On the whole, the first three quarters of the nineteenth century showed no sharp changes in the use of farmland. Agricultural techniques improved slowly,[44] and the relative importance of products remained essentially the same. Grain crops (which occupied over twenty-eight per cent of the total area of France, thirty-four per cent of the cultivable land) and wheat especially,

42 *Ibid.*, pp. 104 ff.; *Enquête 1862*, pp. 130 ff.

43 Even a firm protectionist such as Henri Lavertujon, reporter to the Chamber on wool and other animal products, admitted that it was useless for France to attempt to compete with Australian wool production. CDP, 1891, p. 585.

44 It would be very interesting to trace the increase in agricultural equipment and machinery during the nineteenth century, but unfortunately there is very little information on the subject. In 1852 there were 2,577,713 plows, in 1862 3,206,421, in 1882 3,267,187. In 1852 there were 59,981 threshing machines, in 1862 100,733, in 1882 211,045. *Enquête*, 1882, tables, pp. 196–197.

which alone accounted for almost half the grain acreage, remained predominant in French agriculture. France's agrarian economy therefore tended to be extremely sensitive to fluctuations in the price of wheat.

Prices, Land Values and Wages

For the purposes of this study two aggregate price indexes, designed to indicate changes in agricultural income rather than in the cost of foodstuffs to the consumer, were constructed for the years 1820-1857 and 1857-1881. The first is based on market data, gathered from many sources, published by A. de Sauvy in the *Bulletin de la Statistique générale de la France;*[45] the second, on import prices of the *Commission des valeurs en douane*, which set official prices in 1826 and revised them yearly from 1847 on. The latter have the disadvantage of being arbitrary and approximate, but they do indicate price trends, and have often been employed as the basis for indexes.[46] The year 1857, closing the first series and opening the second, furnished base prices for both; the arithmetic averages of production in the *enquête* years 1840, 1852, 1862 and 1882 were employed as weights. The number of commodities represented varies: ten in 1820-1839, eleven in 1840-1846, sixteen in 1847-1857, fifteen in 1857-1871 and sixteen in 1872-1881. The aggregate for the base year was varied accordingly. In addition, the export price of non-Bordelais ordinary wine of the *Commission des valeurs en douane* was used for 1847-1881, with

45 A. de Sauvy, "Indice annuelle des prix de gros en France de 1820 à 1857 et aperçu sur le mouvement des prix depuis 1790," *Bulletin de la statistique générale de la France*, vol. XVII, 1927-1928, pp. 309 ff.

46 *Tableau décennal du commerce de la France avec ses colonies et les puissances étrangères 1877-1886*, 2 vols., Paris, 1888, vol. I, pp. xxii ff. See, for example, the indexes of de Foville, Flux and H. D. White in the latter's *The French International Accounts 1880-1913*, Harvard Economic Studies, vol. XL, Cambridge, 1933, pp. 242 ff. For a discussion of the prices of the *Commission des valeurs en douane* see White, *loc. cit.* No written instructions appear to have governed its methods of setting prices. Meat prices, 1857-1881, were taken from the *Statistique agricole annuelle*, 1918, pp. 338-339.

the reservation that the export quotations are even less reliable than the import.[47]

The upward trend of agricultural prices is evident. Three peaks preceded major political and social changes, the Revolutions of 1830 and 1848 and the *Coup d'état* of December 2, 1851. One coincided with the military disaster of the Franco-

47 The 1820-1839 list includes: wheat, rye, barley, oats, beef, veal, mutton, sugar, rape seed oil and olive oil. The 1840-1846 list includes, in addition, pork. The 1847-1857 series comprises sixteen commodities including, in addition to the above, potatoes, butter, cheese, flax and hemp. The same list was used for 1857-1871 with the exception of rape seed oil, which reappears in 1872-1881. The 1857 values (PQ) used as a base for 1820-1857 are as follows (1857 values for base for 1857-1881 in parenthesis): wheat, 2,913 (2,960); rye, 374 (397); barley, 227 (193); oats, 648 (364); beef, 488 (488); veal, 194 (194); mutton, 160 (160); sugar, 259 (110); rape seed oil, 63 (34); olive oil, 342 (254); pork, 374 (374), potatoes, 699 (551); butter, 131 (176); cheese, 178 (161); flax, 55 (55); hemp, 50 (50). The wine value for both groups was 3,141, 1857 having been the last of three high price years for wine.

Narrowing the list of commodities seemed preferable to the use of substitutes of questionable similarity. Although this tends to increase the importance of grain prices prior to 1847, the resulting bias is not excessive when we consider that an *enquête* conducted in 1820 would probably have resulted in proportionately higher production figures for grains. Sharp differences between de Sauvy's prices and those of the *Commission des valeurs* after 1857 made it inadvisable to adjust one set to the other. No greater continuity is warranted than that provided by basing both series in 1857. The 1852 *enquête* does not give production figures for rape seed oil and mutton, and the weights for these commodities are averages of the data of the other three *enquêtes*. The pork weight is the 1882 figure reduced by the average percent difference between the 1882 figures and the means of all the *enquête* figures for beef, veal and mutton. Production figures for olive oil, butter and cheese are first given in 1882, but it is probable that overweighting results only in the case of the dairy products.

An aggregate index was also constructed from the *enquête* data, prices being weighted by the quantities produced in 1862. It is composed of twelve items, chosen as most representative of the categories used in the *enquêtes* for which there are comparable data: wheat, rye, oats, potatoes, alfalfa, etc. (Alfalfa, clover, sainfoin and a *mélange de legumineuses* are given a common per quintal value before 1882. The 1882 price used was a weighted average of the four items.), flax and hemp, sugar beets, wine, beef, veal and mutton. With 1840 as a base year = 100, 1852 is represented by 108, 1862 by 153 and 1882 by 165. As it covers only four years, with from ten to twenty years between them, this index has, of course, but very limited significance.

Price Index, 1857 = 100 (Column B, wine included)

			A	B		A	B
1820	85	1841	81	..	1862	104	101
1821	78	1842	83	..	1863	91	90
1822	71	1843	86	..	1864	97	92
1823	79	1844	80	..	1865	83	80
1824	71	1845	81	..	1866	96	85
1825	72	1846	98	..	1867	112	100
1826	74	1847	118	90	1868	108	91
1827	78	1848	79	61	1869	92	82
1828	89	1849	74	57	1870	98	84
1829	93	1850	70	56	1871	115	94
1830	92	1851	71	57	1872	97	86
1831	88	1852	78	63	1873	112	94
1832	88	1853	92	78	1874	107	90
1833	74	1854	113	113	1875	98	81
1834	71	1855	118	116	1876	102	83
1835	72	1856	113	117	1877	103	86
1836	77	1857	100	100	1878	108	88
1837	82	1858	82	86	1879	111	96
1838	80	1859	85	82	1880	108	93
1839	89	1860	104	98	1881	105	93
1840	89	1861	114	105			

Prussian War. The steadiest rise in the index excluding wine occurred after 1865, a rise that was eliminated by the inclusion of wine prices (which varied, roughly, inversely with production) from 1847 on. With the exception of vine growers, then, agricultural producers benefited from rising prices, although a recession had begun in 1880 and 1881.

An upward tendency is discernible in land values and wages of farm laborers. There are two principal sources on French land values and revenues in the nineteenth century, the *enquêtes agricoles* and the *enquêtes* of the *Administration des contributions directes*, which formed the basis for tax assessments. The following table is drawn from the latter source, for the years 1851 and 1879.[48]

48 Ministère des finances, direction générale des contributions directes, *Évaluation des propriétés non bâties prescrite par l'article 3 de la loi du 31 décembre 1907: Rapport de M. Charles Dumont, ministre des finances, sur l'ensemble des opérations (3 novembre 1913)*, Paris, 1913, 2 vols., pp. 292-293.

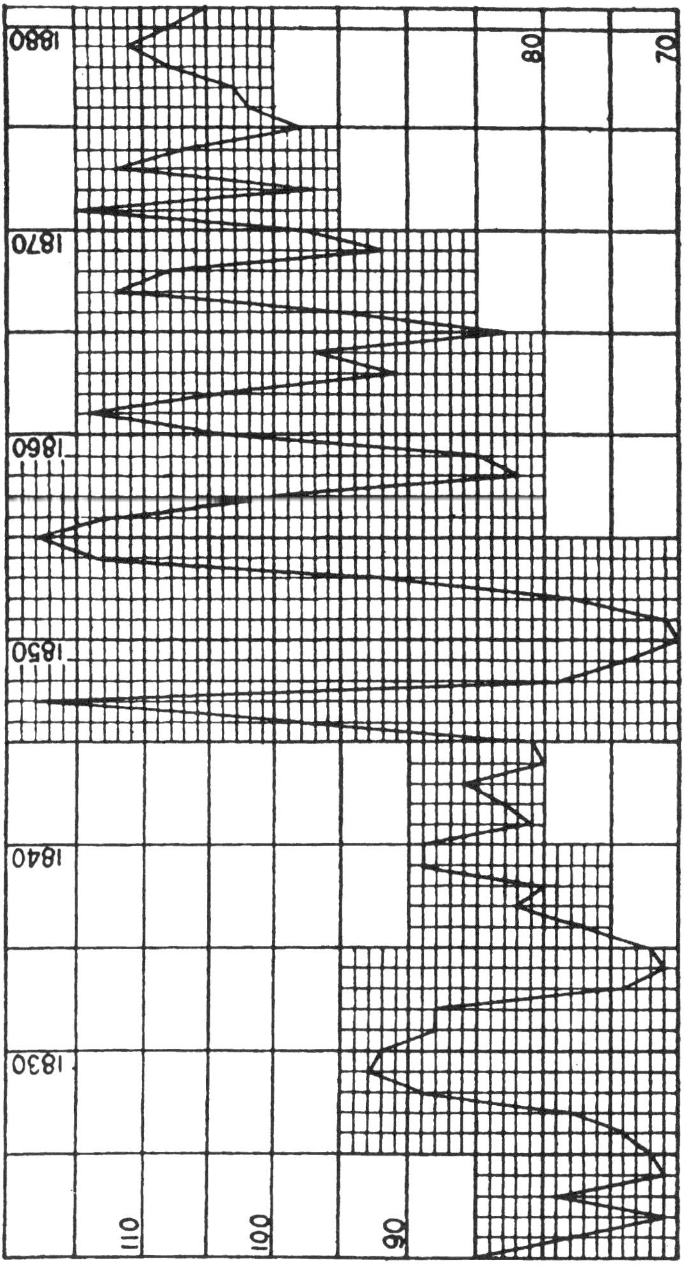

FIG. 1. PRICE INDEX (wine excluded), 1820-1881. Base 1857 = 100.

	Gross value per hectare (in francs)		Rent per hectare (in francs)	
	1851	1879	1851	1879
Lands of superior quality and various cultures......	2,815	3,382	81	104
Cultivable lands and non-agricultural land [49]	1,479	2,197	42	57
Pasture lands	2,256	2,961	73	97
Vineyards	2,067	2,968	69	130
Woodlands	642	745	20	23
Wastelands	155	207	5	6

Turning to the *enquêtes agricoles* we find that data are given for three qualities of land in each category in 1852 and 1862 and for five qualities of land in 1882, the only comparable figures being for the two highest qualities.[50]

GROSS VALUE PER HECTARE
(in francs)

	1852		1862		1882	
	1st	2nd	1st	2nd	1st	2nd
Cultivable lands	2,282	1,559	3,066	2,175	3,442	2,644
Pasture lands	3,282	2,267	4,151	3,958	4,467	3,374
Vineyards	2,521	1,768	3,564	2,638	3,818	3,003

RENT PER HECTARE
(in francs)

	1852		1862		1882	
	1st	2nd	1st	2nd	1st	2nd
Cultivable lands	55	46	96	69	104	80
Pasture lands	113	79	152	104	151	120
Vineyards	87	62	139	98	158	120

The distinguished agricultural economist, Daniel Zolla, estimated that the value of the land increased over two and one-half times between 1821 and 1851.[51] The rise from 1851 to 1882 is made clear by the figures given.

49 Unfortunately, the inclusion prior to 1908 of non-agricultural land under this heading greatly lessens its significance.

50 *Enquête 1882*, p. 388, tables, pp. 180-184.

51 Daniel Zolla, *L'agriculture moderne*, Paris, 1913, p. 282.

This rise in land values was accompanied with an increase in wages of agriculture workers. The average daily wage in winter of a farm laborer, without board, was 1.41 francs in 1852, 1.61 in 1855, 1.85 in 1862 and 2.22 in 1882.[52] From 1862 to 1882 there were the following increases in annual wages: foremen (*maîtres valets*) francs 361 to 465, laborers and wagoners 256 to 324, adult shepherds 230 to 290, female farm servants 130 to 235.[53] "The cities and industries attract the young farm girls more than the men . . . ," with a resultant shortage of farm servants.[54] No definite conclusion can be drawn as to whether or not wages kept pace with land values. With 1852 = 100, wages were 131 in 1862 and 157 in 1882. For the same years estimated average gross land values per hectare, based on the *enquêtes agricoles*, were 100, 147 and 159, which would seem to indicate a slightly more rapid growth in land values.[55] On the other hand, following the *enquêtes* of 1851 and 1879, the relatives are 100 and 143 respectively, indicating a more rapid rise of wages. The likelihood is that land values rose more rapidly than wages through the 1860's but that the gap was closing as the decade of the 1880's opened.[56] This does not necessarily imply a lower margin of return to farmers, and higher rents do not prove increased costs. It will be remembered that many landowners also farmed as tenants, sharecroppers and day laborers, and that they might gain from higher wages and lose from higher rents. It is clear, however, that the large proprietors would

52 *Enquête 1862*, p. cxxv. *Enquête 1892*, p. 419.

53 *Enquête 1882*, p. 397.

54 Pierre Régnier, *L'ouvrier agricole*, Paris, 1924, p. 30.

55 The averages were computed by weighting the figures for each quality by their percentages of the total land in 1882, 17%, 22%, 25%, 20%, 16% (*Enquête 1882*, tables, p. 180). The 3rd quality figures for 1852 and 1862 were weighted by the percentages assigned to 3rd, 4th and 5th qualities in 1882, which tends to produce an upward bias. The average value of the three types of land (cultivable, pasture and vineyard) was computed by weighting the value of each by the area involved.

56 Zolla, *op. cit.*, pp. 281-282; Régnier, *op. cit.*, p. 31.

benefit most from rising land values and rents, and lose through an increase in wage rates. Hence, for this group, which would normally provide the agrarian leadership, the 1860's and early 1870's were a period of prosperity, which was receding as the 1880's approached.

Foreign Trade

A consideration of foreign trade in agricultural commodities is of special significance, for it sheds light on the relative positions of the rural and urban elements of the French economy. Despite greater agricultural production, agricultural imports increased, indicating more rapid growth of industrial city society. Unfortunately, a change in methods of classification in 1880 destroys the value of the official summaries, and it was necessary to prepare import and export lists of appropriate commodities.[57]

Such figures would furnish much ammunition to an exponent of crude balance-of-trade doctrine, and arguments of this nature were prominent in the campaign for the Méline Tariff.[58] Agricultural products accounted for all of the commodity import surplus in the first four periods, and over two-thirds in the

57 *Tableau décennal . . . 1877-1886*, vol. I, pp. xcix, ci, cv, cvii. Import list: wool, grain, cattle, hemp, oleaginous seeds, foreign and colonial sugar, butter and cheese, table fruits, seeds, fresh, salt and otherwise preserved meats, horses, wines, olive and vegetable oils, flax, dried vegetables and their flours, cocoons, hops.

Export list: wines, grains, raw sugar, butter, cheese, wool, horses, cattle, eggs of fowl and game, table fruits, seeds, potatoes and dried vegetables, oil-cakes, olive and vegetable oils, fresh, salt and otherwise preserved meats, hemp, flax.

Daniel Zolla (*Études d'économie rurale*, Paris, 1896, pp. 293, 304) uses similar lists, including in addition: common woods, brandies and spirits, rice, silks, raw skins and furs, fats of all types. He declares, however (p. 292), that it would be preferable to omit some of these items.

"Special," as distinct from "general," commerce may be defined as imports for French consumption or manufacture, and exports of French products and manufactures. "General" commerce comprises all imports into and exports from France, including goods in transit. *Tableau décennal . . . 1877-1886*, p. xiii. See table, p. 38.

58 See chs. V, VI below.

last. After remaining relatively the same from 1827 to 1876, the proportion of agricultural to total commodity imports rose sharply in 1877-1882, while agricultural exports were maintained at approximately the level that had been reached during the middle of the century. The increase in the proportion of total agricultural trade to combined total imports and exports was entirely accounted for by the rise in imports of farm products.

Five commodities were responsible for eighty-seven per cent of the increase in agricultural imports between 1867-1876 and 1877-1882: grains, from 244.6 million francs to 574.3, wine, from 16.5 to 200.4, oleaginous seeds, from 71.3 to 142.8, cattle, from 137.3 to 185.5, and wool, from 270.8 to 319.4. The principal export drops were in grains, from 119.6 to 84.0, raw sugar, from 41.8 to 25.2, and wines, from 244.1 to 237.4. Exports of butter and cheese, wool, table fruits, potatoes and dried vegetables, vegetable oils and meats rose in the last period.

The importance of wheat to French agriculture calls for a closer examination of France's international trade in this commodity. The following table of annual averages for ten-year periods is in thousands of hectoliters.[59]

	Imports	Exports	Import Surplus
1832-1841	865	426	439
1842-1851	2,218	1,649	569
1852-1861	4,461	2,511	1,950
1862-1871 *	5,206	1,932	3,274
1872-1881	13,322	2,661	10,661

* Excluding 1870

Of the forty-nine years included, twenty-eight showed import surpluses and twenty-one export surpluses. In the last ten years, however, only two years presented export surpluses, and the import surpluses were of ever greater volume as "needs of consumption rose more rapidly than production." [60]

59 *Enquête 1882*, p. 66. France continued to export fine wines, but imported larger quantities of cheap wines.

60 *Ibid.*, p. 67.

Special Commerce in Millions of Francs

	1827-1836	1837-1846	1847-1856	1857-1866	1867-1876	1877-1882
1. Agricultural imports	153.2	224.5	356.9	692.8	1133.8	1931.9
2. Agricultural exports	76.1	98.0	214.2	512.0	771.0	769.4
3. Agricultural import surplus	77.1	126.5	142.7	180.8	362.8	1162.5
4. Total imports	479.9	776.4	1077.1	2200.5	3407.5	4526.6
5. Total exports	521.4	712.9	1223.7	2430.1	3306.4	3408.5
6. Total import surplus	—41.5	63.5	—146.6	—229.6	101.1	1118.3
7. Proportion of (1) to (4)	32	29	33	31	33	43
8. Proportion of (2) to (5)	15	14	18	21	23	22
9. Agricultural imports and exports	229.3	322.5	571.1	1204.8	1904.8	2701.3
10. Total imports and exports	1001.3	1489.3	2300.8	4630.6	6713.9	7935.1
11. Proportion of (9) to (10)	23	22	25	26	28	34

In respect to livestock France was a net importer of horses, cattle, pigs, sheep, goats and donkeys, and a net exporter of mules. In the period 1872-1881 net imports of horses, cattle, pigs and goats began to decline, marking the beginning of a trend to self-sufficiency. Net imports of sheep continued to rise. In the light of increased production of beef, pork and mutton, these imports may be taken to indicate an increase in meat consumption, a corollary of the trend toward industrialization.[61] As this was more rapid than technical improvement and the rise in domestic consumption, foreign sources of supply became necessary.

Summary

Despite the apparent rapidity of tempo and the often contradictory and revolutionary changes in French political life, the nation's economic development was relatively slow and un-

61 *Ibid.*, pp. 67, 234, 268, 269. Official consumption figures are estimates based on domestic production plus net imports.

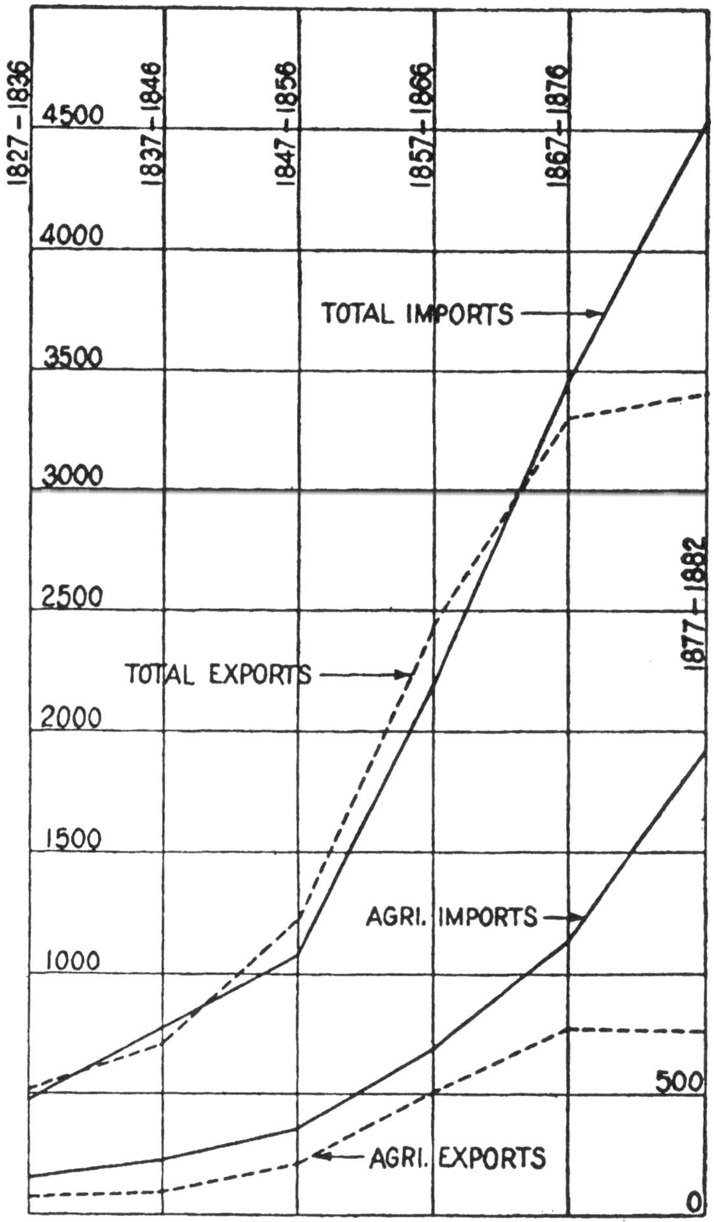

FIG. 2. SPECIAL COMMERCE (000,000 francs), 1827-1882

spectacular. In general, France did not seize on capitalism as the doctrine of a new day.[62] In agriculture, where tradition was stronger and older, change was even slower than in industry. Writing of the July Monarchy, Henri Sée remarked that if one considered "agricultural processes and the productivity of cultivated land, it would not seem that there had been any basic change since the end of the *ancien régime*."[63] From the first *enquête agricole* in 1840 to that of 1882 the pace quickened somewhat. Yields increased, livestock rose greatly in number, fallow land declined, land values and wages of farm laborers rose. Prices had mounted, and although they had begun to level off, there could be little danger of their collapse in a land where consumption increased more rapidly than production. And yet, the farm population was slowly declining, and the very food imports which were evidence of higher consumption betokened the fusing of French agriculture with the international economy as the world grew smaller. In this regard we must bear in mind the importance of grains, and of wheat especially, in French farming (and diet), and the diversified character of the crops grown on most farms.

The keynote of the first three quarters of the nineteenth century was that "French agriculture was striving to keep pace with industry,"[64] but was slowly falling behind. It had improved technologically, but had lost ground relatively to urban life and industry. As French agriculture entered the decade of depression in the 1880's, it was fairly prosperous, but it had passed the peak, and, as if to predict events that were to come, the ravages of phylloxera had created a crisis in one major phase of agricultural production.

Agricultural Organization

While French agriculture of the Third Republic thus possessed an economy well grounded in the *ancien régime*, it

62 Sée, *Französische Wirtschaftsgeschichte*, vol. II, p. 291.

63 Sée, "Progrès de l'agriculture . . . ," p. 72.

64 Shepard B. Clough, *France: A History of National Economics, 1789–1939*, New York, 1939.

did not inherit any noteworthy organizational structure. Urban guilds and agrarian feudalism were swept away by the Revolution, and in both industry and agriculture association was a development of the late nineteenth century. This does not connote the complete absence of agricultural organization prior to 1870, but rather an important difference of character.

The oldest French agricultural organizations still extant in 1870 were the *fruitières* of Franche-Comté which date back to the thirteenth and fourteenth centuries. They were, in a primitive form, milk cooperatives connected with the manufacture of Gruyère cheese. Early in the eighteenth century cattle owners of the Landes grouped together for mutual insurance against loss of livestock.[65] But the first regularly constituted and recognized agricultural association was the *Société d'agriculture, de commerce et des arts de Bretagne*, founded by the Estates of Brittany in 1757-1759 at the suggestion of Vincent de Gournay for "*la perfection de l'Agriculture, du Commerce et de l'Industrie de Bretagne.*" Between 1760 and 1789 similar groups were created in many parts of France.[66] Among them was the *Société Royale d'agriculture de Paris*, created by the Council of State in 1761 and soon elevated to the rank of *Société Royale d'agriculture* for all the kingdom. After a brief suppression in 1793, it was reconstituted, and, with changing titles to fit the changing governments, survived the vicissitudes of French politics, finally becoming the *Société nationale d'agriculture.*[67]

The national and various provincial societies were basically "agricultural academies," however, whose function was to encourage technical improvements by study, publicity and the awarding of prizes. A new type of organization, first suggested in 1819, came into being around the beginning of the July

65 Comte de Rocquigny, *Les syndicats agricoles et leur oeuvre*, 2nd ed., Paris, 1900, p. 5.

66 Émile Justin, *Les sociétés royales d'agriculture au XVIIIe siècle (1757-1793)*, Saint-Lô, 1935, pp. 36-38, chs. ii-iv.

67 Antoine Lecomte, *Les associations agricoles professionnelles et mutuelles*, Paris, 1907, p. 4.

Monarchy. This was the *comice agricole*. In general the *comices* exercised the functions of local academies, limited as the case might be to the commune or arrondissement. "Less dignified and perhaps more accessible to the small peasants," they held contests, "solemn distributions of prizes to loyal old '*serviteurs*,'" and endeavored to popularize new and advanced processes.[68]

After issuing regulations in 1851 designed to promote the development of the *comices*, the government of Napoleon III decreed in 1853 the formation of *Chambres consultatives d'agriculture* for each arrondissement, to provide some basis for agricultural representation and a means of contact between the state and the farmers. It is generally agreed that they never functioned. In the same year the Emperor created the *Conseil supérieur du commerce, de l'agriculture et de l'industrie* to act in an advisory capacity.[69] The next step in the development of French agricultural organizations was the formation of *syndical* associations in accordance with a law of June 21, 1865. Their functions were strictly limited to the promotion of specific projects, such as dike building, drainage of swamps and marshes, irrigation, etc. "They are much more similar to associations of capitals than to professional groups."[70]

Common to all these associations was their limited, nonpolitical character.[71] The *Société des agriculteurs de France* was entirely different. In 1867 M. Lecouteux, editor-in-chief of the *Journal d'agriculture pratique*, organized an international exposition of steam tillage, and some of the landowners present,

68 Augé-Laribé, *Évolution*, pp. 169, 170; Lecomte, *op. cit.*, p. 5; Rocquigny, *op. cit.*, p. 2.

69 Gabrielle Lécolle, *Les associations agricoles, syndicats, coopératives, mutuelles, et les nouvelles lois sociales agricoles*, Paris, 1912, p. 10; Rocquigny, *op. cit.*, p. 4; Sée, *Französische Wirtschaftsgeschichte*, vol. II, p. 411.

70 Augé-Laribé, *op. cit.*, p. 194.

71 According to Augé-Laribé, *ibid.*, p. 170, the *comices* were used during the Second Empire to promote peasant loyalty to the régime. They had no independent political initiative, however.

> struck by the results obtained by private initiative, decided to form a society whose annual general assembly would be a sort of central congress which would unite at Paris the delegates of the agricultural societies and the *comices,* to pool their ideas on improvements of rural interest.
>
> This was the *Sociéte des agriculteurs de France.*[72]

In his opening address as general secretary of the new society, Lecouteux proclaimed its aim to be "individual and collective initiative substituted for governmental action in agricultural matters." At the first general assembly in December 1863 there were 1,782 members; in 1878 there were 3,662 and by 1890 the membership had risen to about 10,000.[73] The *Société des agriculteurs de France* was and is essentially a club of distinguished landowners, members of the old nobility or conservative upper bourgeoisie who had acquired estates.[74] "Its authority rises primarily from the personal influence of its leaders," and while, as we shall see, it played a dominant rôle in protectionist politics, to use a distinction peculiar to French affairs, "*elle ne fait pas de politique*"[75]—it stayed aloof from party or constitutional politics.

The aristocratic nature of this organization led Gambetta to promote the *Société nationale de l'encouragement à l'agriculture* in 1880. Its purpose was the furtherance of agrarian interests by republican leaders, with the hope of gaining peasant support for the republican régime. Its economic policies closely resembled those of the *Société des agriculteurs,* and many members were common to both organizations. The first was "that of the dukes, as at the Academy," the second "that of former ministers."[76]

72 *Les agriculteurs de France,* Paris, n. d., pp. 5, 6.

73 Comte de Luçay and Paul Sénart, *Voeux de l'assemblée générale de la Société des agriculteurs de France,* 2nd ed., Paris, 1894, pp. i, xxviii.

74 Sée, *Französische Wirtschaftsgeschichte,* vol. II, p. 412.

75 Augé-Laribé, *Syndicats et coopératives agricoles,* Paris, 1926, p. 81.

76 *Ibid.,* p. 82; Sée, *loc. cit.*; Augé-Laribé, *Évolution,* p. 220.

By 1882 there were therefore many agricultural associations. Nevertheless it cannot be said that they were sufficiently numerous or popular, adequately centralized or for the most part designed to furnish a basis for a mass agrarian movement, whether "political" or "professional" in character. The Le Chapelier law of June 14, 1791 had forbidden associations based on common economic interests. The law of May 25, 1864 granted freedom of association, but this right was in practice so limited as to depend completely on extremely benevolent ministerial interpretation.[77] Thus the legal foundation for effective pressure politics was lacking, and it was only in 1884 that this was provided.

Agricultural Protection

With protection, as with organization, agriculture of the Third Republic was faced with the necessity of building its own structure, but in this instance the foundation was already laid. When France began to settle down after the upheavals of the Napoleonic era, the long established tradition of protection and state intervention in industry and commerce stood fortified by the policies recently pursued by the Emperor.[78] French commercial policy aimed at favoring the importation of foodstuffs while reserving for French industry raw materials produced by French agriculture. While export of farm commodities might be prohibited, the export of manufactured articles was held highly desirable.[79]

77 Étienne Martin Saint Léon, *Histoire des corporations de métiers, suivie d'une étude sur l'évolution de l'idée corporative de 1791 à nos jours et sur le mouvement syndical contemporain*, 3rd ed., Paris, 1922, p. 614 ff., 651.

78 For the historical background of French protectionist policy see Clough, *op. cit.*, chs. I-III; Charles Woolsey Cole, *Colbert and a Century of French Mercantilism*, 2 vols., New York, 1939; Eli Heckscher, *Mercantilism*, London, 1935, 2 vols., and the same author's *Continental System, an Economic Interpretation*, Oxford, 1922; J. Morini-Comby, *Mercantilisme et protectionnisme: essai sur les doctrines interventionnistes en politique commerciale du XVe au XIXe siècle*, Paris, 1930, book I; Émile Levasseur, *Histoire du commerce de la France*, 2 vols., Paris, 1911-1912.

79 Auguste Arnauné, *Le commerce extérieur et les tarifs de douane*, Paris, 1911, p. 162; Morini-Comby, *op. cit.*, p. 50.

The Restoration

The Restoration at first veered partially from this tradition. In April 1814 the comte d'Artois issued an edict greatly reducing duties on raw cotton and sugar, and on June 6th sent a letter to the Chambers of Commerce indicating that the government intended to adopt a policy of only moderate protection. Threatened with competition to which they had become unaccustomed, the manufacturers protested, and a debate on protection was in full swing. Under the severely limited suffrage of the restored monarchy the government was controlled by the wealthy classes, but the political situation was such that they were divided into three groups: the Ultra Royalists, mostly great landholders, a Moderate group following the lead of Louis XVIII and a bourgeois Liberal group which favored the economic policies of the Empire.[80] Out of the different economic interests of the Ultras and Liberals came agreement between them on protection for both. "The increasingly prohibitive tariff legislation, begun in 1814 and completed in 1826, was the work of this coalition" of industrialists and landowners.[81]

In 1814 duties on cloth products and iron were raised, and a long list of prohibitions originally aimed at England in 1806 was restored and made applicable to all nations.[82] In the same year the prohibition of grain export was abolished; the country was divided into three zones, and export was allowed when prices fell respectively to 23, 21 and 19 francs per hectoliter. This policy was retained in 1816 when the Ultras, in control of the *Chambre introuvable*, added an import duty of 50 centimes per 100 kilograms on grain and equally moderate duties on livestock, meats, eggs, hay, etc. In 1817 butter, flax and hemp were placed on the list of dutiable products.[83]

80 Clough, *op. cit.*, pp. 93-98.

81 S. Charléty, *La Restauration (1815-1830)*, vol. IV of E. Lavisse, ed., *Histoire de la France contemporaine depuis la Révolution jusqu'à la paix de 1919*, Paris, 1921, p. 273.

82 Clough, *op. cit.*, p. 97.

83 Percy Ashley, *Modern tariff history: Germany—United States—France*, New York, 1904, p. 277; Charléty, *op. cit.*, p. 91; Arnauné, *op. cit.*, p. 163.

Agricultural protection was as yet in its early stages, however, but in 1819 the *échelle mobile* or sliding scale of grain duties was established. A fixed tax of 25 centimes per hectoliter was set on wheat in grain, and 75 centimes per quintal of flour, one franc being added to each duty when imports were made in foreign bottoms (*surtaxe de pavillon*). When prices dropped to the zone export limits set in 1816, the duty was increased by a franc, and if prices fell further it rose by " 1 franc per hectoliter and per franc of fall " in price. When zone prices declined to 20, 18 and 16 francs respectively, imports were prohibited.[84] Abundant crops and low prices led to demands for further protection, and the system was reorganized in 1821. The country was divided into four zones instead of three, and the base prices were changed to 24, 22, 20 and 18 francs. The following year the duties on fattened oxen and bulls, cows, calves and sheep were raised to 50, 50, 25, 5 and 5 francs respectively from the 1816 uniform rate of 3.30. The tariff on fresh meat was increased from 50 centimes to 8 francs per 100 kilograms.

The Restoration structure of agricultural protection was completed by the act of 1826. This law sanctioned a duty of 40 francs per 100 kilgrams on raw wool which had been decreed in 1824, after an increase from 10 francs in 1820 to 30 francs in 1823. The distinction between fattened and unfattened oxen was removed, the rate on the latter being raised to 50 francs a head. The same duty was applied to horses. From 15 francs per quintal in 1816 and 45 in 1820, the tax on hops was elevated to 60 francs per quintal.[85]

Thus the Restoration broke with tradition. The policy of supply, born in the Middle Ages, partly continued under Mercantilism, yielded, as in eighteenth-century England, to protection for group interests. Agricultural protection was raised to the level of, and linked with industrial protection. From this time on its fortunes were to vary with the strength of the alliance between landowners and manufacturers.

84 Adrien Moras, *La crise du blé*, Paris, 1902, p. 11.

85 Levasseur, *op. cit.*, vol. II, pp. 120-121, 122, 131 ; JAP, ser. 6, vol. XVI, 1890, II, p. 155.

The July Monarchy

The July Monarchy wished to purify the protectionist system of some of its abuses, but did not question the bases of the policy. The result was that downward changes of only secondary importance were made, protection remained secure and some significant increases in duties occurred. High wheat prices following the July Revolution led the government to propose that the prohibitions retained in the sliding scale be abolished, that two zones be substituted for the four created by the law of 1819, and that the price of bread replace that of grain in applying the tariff. Only the first suggestion was adopted in the law of 1832. When the zone prices fell to 22.01 francs, 20.01, 18.01 and 16.01 respectively, the import prohibition was replaced with an increase of the duty of 1.50 for each franc of decline in the price of wheat. The law was to remain in effect only till July 1, 1833, but before its term arrived it was extended till the next general revision of the tariff law.

In 1836 the duty on castor beans was raised, but the taxes on other oil-bearing seeds was lowered. The reduction did not survive long, however. In 1845 the duties on sesame, poppy seed and colza were increased from 2.50 per hundred kilograms to from 4 to 14 francs for the first, and to from 2 to 9 francs for the second and third, depending on the origin and mode of shipment of the imports. The linseed duty was likewise raised to from 1 to 9 francs. These new tariffs were "fought by the refiners and soap manufacturers of Marseille, and supported by the farmers of the Nord and the olive growers of the Midi, both of whom feared the competition of sesame. . . ." [86]

The July Monarchy's two principal attempts at reform failed. In 1840 the government proposed a series of reductions in duties on livestock, but the manufacturers hesitated to risk agrarian anger by giving their approval. They came to the support of

86 Clough, *op. cit.*, pp. 127-128; Arnauné, *op. cit.*, p. 167. The next general revision occurred in 1881, but the sliding scale was abolished by the conventional system of the Second Empire. See p. 49, below.

the cattle owners and the measure was defeated. In 1847, after securing a one year's suspension of the sliding scale on wheat, the government introduced a bill which would have abolished fifteen prohibitions and transferred nearly half the dutiable articles to the free list. The measure was tied up in committee, and the July Monarchy came to an end before it could be considered.[87]

The Second Empire

The short-lived Second Republic maintained the tariff structure intact,[88] but very early in its existence the Second Empire manifested its desire for a change in policy. Acting under a broad construction of a law of 1814 which permitted lowering by decree, in cases of urgency, duties on raw materials and foodstuffs, subject to later legislative confirmation, the government in 1853, diminished tariffs on many agricultural products. The duties on cattle were reduced to 3 francs a head on oxen and bulls, to 1 franc on cows and to 0.25 on calves and sheep. The sliding scale was suspended, the *surtaxe de pavillon* on grain was abolished, and the 1845 rates on oleaginous seeds were lowered. In 1856 the *Corps législatif* reluctantly gave its assent to these measures, and shortly thereafter the government introduced a measure to replace all the remaining prohibitions with protective duties. A violent outcry followed: a Committee for for the Protection of the National Endeavor (*travail national*) lobbied successfully in the *Corps législatif* and the proposal was withdrawn, with the promise that it would not be revived before 1861. In 1858 the sliding scale was again suspended, the government hoping thereby to abolish the system indirectly. Once again the *Corps législatif* protested, and the following year the *échelle mobile* was restored.[89]

87 Amé, *Étude sur les tarifs de douanes et les traités de commerce*, Paris, 2 vols., 1876, vol. I, p. 206; Noël Beaurieux, *Le prix du blé en France au XIXe siècle*, Paris, 1909, p. 52; Clough, *op. cit.*, p. 130.

88 Dunham, *op. cit.*, p. 10.

89 Pierre Perreau, *La révision du régime douanier de 1892*, Paris, 1910, p. 7; Levasseur, *op. cit.*, pp. 9, 289. A list of articles prohibited until 1860 is given in H. O. Meredith, *Protection in France*, London, 1904, p. 8; Dunham, *op. cit.*, pp. 21-25.

From the first the administration of the Second Empire had stated its opposition " to free trade on the one hand and to prohibitions on the other. It believed . . . that only infant industries should be strongly protected, and that adult industries should receive just enough protection to enable them to compete on equal terms with the industries of other countries." [90] Checked along the legislative salient, the imperial government was persuaded to attempt tariff revision by other means. A *sénatus-consulte* of December 1852 had confirmed to the Emperor the power granted the Prince-President by the Constitution of January 1852 to " sign all treaties of peace, alliance and commerce. . . . " [91] It was under this power that the negotiations initiated on an unofficial basis by Michel Chevalier were brought to official fruition in the Treaty of Commerce with England, January 23, 1860. Under this accord the system of prohibitions was swept away, and France agreed to admit British goods " within two years at duties that were not to exceed 30%, and within five years at a maximum rate of 25%." [92] The treaty was implemented in October 1860 with convention setting specific duties, and " in nearly every case, the French government granted reductions in its tariff that greatly exceeded what England had expected. . . . " [93] In 1861 the sliding scale was abolished and replaced with a statistical tax (*droit de statistique*) : in 1863 the *Corps législatif* ratified a number of previously issued decrees which admitted flax and hemp, oleaginous seeds and hides free.[94] While the Cobden-Chevalier Treaty, extended by other commercial agreements containing the most-favored-nation clause, did not approach

90 Dunham, *op. cit.*, p. 133.

91 *Ibid.*, chs. III and IV, p. 38.

92 The only export prohibitions to survive were "copyright violations [*contrefaçons de librairie*] and munitions of war." Arnauné, *op. cit.*, p. 264. Dunham, *op. cit.*, p. 98. Most of the reductions were to take effect on October 1, 1861, in keeping with the pledge of 1856.

93 Dunham, *op. cit.*, p. 139.

94 Perreau, *op. cit.*, p. 15.

free-trade in the sense in which the term is employed by classical economists, it is true that "Napoleon III brought France as close to free trade as she has ever come." [95]

The treaty was not popular in France. It was considered by many to have been the result of an "economic *coup d'état.*" [96] The government held firm, however, and it was not until May 1868 that the Methuselah of French politics, Adolphe Thiers, and Pouyer-Quertier, who was to play an important rôle in shaping the trade policies of the Third Republic, were permitted to interpellate in the *Corps législatif* on the "consequences of the economic régime of France." Despite the fact that it held a majority, the government decided on one of the inevitable *enquêtes*, to begin in March 1870 and to be conducted by a parliamentary committee which was heavily weighted in favor of protection. The outbreak of the war with Prussia in July 1870 brought the *enquête* to a premature close.[97]

The Third Republic

The return of peace saw Thiers established first as head of the Executive and then as President of the Republic, with Pouyer-Quertier as Minister of Finance. In order to reestablish French finances Thiers immediately turned to protection. In 1871 he proposed and secured approval for increased duties on sugar and coffee, a rise in harbor dues, and restoration of the *droits de pavillon et d'entrepôt* which had been abolished in 1866.[98] When he suggested import duties on raw materials,

95 Clough, *op. cit.*, p. 188. Commercial agreements were concluded with Belgium, the Zollverein, Italy, Switzerland, Spain, Austria, the Hanseatic towns, the Netherlands, Sweden and Norway.

96 Dunham, *op. cit.*, p. 320.

97 Perreau, *op. cit.*, p. 18.

98 Charles Seignobos, *Le déclin de L'Empire et l'établissement de la 3e république (1859-1875)*, vol. VII of E. Lavisse, *Histoire de la France contemporaine depuis la Révolution jusqu'à la paix de 1919*, Paris, 1921, p. 326. On Thiers' policy see Arthur L. Dunham, "The attempt of President Thiers to restore high protection in France (1871-1873)," *The Journal of Economic and Business History*, vol. I, 1929, pp. 302, 324.

however, the industrialists who had most bitterly attacked the régime of 1860 turned about and refused their consent.[99] After Thiers had offered his resignation, which was refused, a compromise resulted. By the law of July 26, 1872 a raw-material duty of about 3% was enacted, with compensatory drawback provisions. Since this law was in contradiction with the treaties with England and Belgium, a special emissary was sent to London to secure the British government's consent to its application. Britain refused, and Thiers, with legislative authorization, denounced the Cobden-Chevalier Treaty and the Treaty of 1861 with Belgium. A new convention was concluded with England in November 1872, admitting the French raw-material duties and granting England most-favored-nation status and exemption from harbor dues. Sentiment in the National Assembly soon shifted, however. Thiers fell from power in May 1873 and the new treaty was never ratified.[100] As regards the *droits de pavillon et d'entrepôt*, they were found to violate the Franco-Austrian agreement of 1866, and while Austria would in all likelihood have consented to a modification of the treaty which would have permitted their operation, Bismarck persuaded Vienna to refuse, and these taxes too fell by the wayside.[101]

In July 1873 the government of President MacMahon concluded new agreements with England and Belgium which in effect restored the régime of 1860 until 1877, the date of expiration of the treaty with Austria. Thiers' policy had thus been completely discarded. While the agriculturalists would have approved the maintenance of the raw-material duties, " liberals and protectionists were united in the [ballot] urn, the former desiring to maintain the régime of the conventional tariffs, the latter not wishing to pay duties on their raw materials." [102]

99 Amé, *op. cit.*, vol. II, p. 276.

100 Dunham, *op. cit.*, pp. 316-321.

101 Levasseur, *op. cit.*, vol. II, p. 563.

102 *Ibid.*, p. 564.

In 1875 the government began consideration of the legislation that was to replace the existing system in 1877. It decided to revise the old general tariff, which dated back to the Restoration, and bring it into harmony with the conventional régime. The opinions of the Chambers of Commerce were requested and a great majority replied favorably to the tariff structure of the commercial treaties.[103] In February 1877 Teisserenc de Bort, the Minister of Commerce, introduced a bill based on the conventional tariffs, and providing for important increases only in the case of cotton thread and goods, but the constitutional crisis of the *Seize mai* prevented its consideration.[104]

The new chamber found the liberal majority reduced, and Teisserenc de Bort's second bill, introduced in January 1878, provided for specific, rather than *ad valorem* duties, which were on the average 24% higher than the conventional tariffs. Further increases were proposed on cotton thread and goods. The tide of protection was beginning to run strong, however. A bill renewing the commercial treaty with Italy was rejected by the Chamber of Deputies, and in March 1878, following the lead of the Senate, the Chamber appointed a commission of thirty-three members to conduct an *enquête*, which lasted a year and a half.[105]

Ample time was thus provided for protectionist propaganda. The *Société des agriculteurs de France* devoted the larger part of its general assembly of 1879 to the tariff, and after considering the recommendations of its various sections, passed the following resolutions:

1. That in the forthcoming general tariff agricultural and industrial interests be treated according to the same principles.

103 Perreau, *op. cit.*, p. 22.

104 Seignobos, *op. cit.*, pp. 23 ff.; Levasseur, *op. cit.*, p. 568; Gabriel Hanotaux, *Histoire de la France contemporaine (1871-1900)*, vol. III, Paris, 1906, pp. 582 ff.

105 Meredith, *op. cit.*, p. 14; Levasseur, *op. cit.*, p. 169.

2. That in preparing the duties to be inserted in the general tariff, the financial and economic conditions to which the dutiable goods are subject, the influence of drawbacks, if any, on the competition these articles offer to those of our national production be considered.
3. That reciprocity should form the basis of commercial treaties, if any are concluded.
4. The committee which prepared the preceding resolutions will be charged with presenting them to the tariff commission [of the Chamber] or to all others occupied with these matters.[106]

There was no unanimity among the various sections on the value of commercial treaties. They were condemned by some and ignored by most. Only one section, under the presidency of the society's leading free trader, Raoul Duval, approved generally of the régime of 1860. One section demanded that all competing agricultural products be subjected to "compensatory duties representing the sum of all taxes paid by national agriculture." [107]

As in the past, however, it was clear that the success of the protectionists depended on alliance between landowners and industrialists. The *Société des agriculteurs* claimed that all it wanted was equality. In the words of its president, the marquis de Dampierre,

> we do not ask for protection, but we do not wish anyone, within the country or without, to be protected to our detriment; and if some French industries obtain protective duties in any form whatsoever justice demands that agriculture, which too is an industry, share equally in this protection. . . . [108]

Pouyer-Quertier declared that "we cannot have two weights and two measures in France. . . .[109] Meetings between deputies

106 Luçay and Sénart, *op. cit.*, p. 47.

107 *Ibid.*, pp. 47-52.

108 CRSAF, vol. VII, 1880, p. 32.

109 *Ibid.*, p. 95.

representing agricultural and industrial interests were arranged. A member of the *Société des agriculteurs,* the deputy comte de Roys, declared that "the agricultural deputies have undertaken to vote for the tariff desired by their industrial colleagues, and the latter will do justice to their [the agrarians'] demands."[110] At a session of the *Société des agriculteurs* the deputy Kerjégu stated that the meeting of the deputies had had as its aim

> agreement between agriculture and industry; we wished to find in a common accord all that could be done for the one without thereby harming the other. It is a great undertaking, which has brought forth many interesting discussions and profound studies. But rest assured; if the conditions demanded for the farmers are not granted, agriculture's deputies will no longer be in the same position in respect to industry, and will thenceforth have the right to refuse industry the protection it demands.[111]

The *entente* did not hold. The *Société des agriculteurs* had asked for duties equivalent to 10% *ad valorem* on all agricultural imports: the agricultural deputies were forced to compromise on 5%, and the compromise was very poorly received by the members of the *Société.*[112] The industrialists on their part found much cause for complaint. The sixth section of the *Société des agriculteurs,* headed by Raoul Duval, demanded reductions in the duties on agricultural machinery and on "the raw materials used by French mechanics and builders in order to maintain fair competition with foreign producers in the interest of French agriculture."[113] When M. de Monicault, vice-president of the *Société des agriculteurs,* argued their case before the tariff commission of the Chamber, the president of the commission, M. Malézieux, remarked that while the agriculturists denied

110 *Ibid.,* p. 282.

111 *Ibid.,* p. 291.

112 *Loc. cit.*

113 *Ibid.,* p. 51.

any desire to combat industry, here was a concrete case of hostility.[114] Further, while industry was not opposed to the commercial treaties, the position of the *Société des agriculteurs* stiffened, and in 1881 it resolved " That the commercial treaties previously concluded should not be renewed, and that in the future France should have only a general tariff . . .[115]

The net result was that despite the determined opposition of Pouyer-Quertier in the Senate the government had its way. Its principal concessions to the agricultural protectionists were first, that conventional tariffs were never to be more than 24% below the general tariff and, of cardinal importance to agriculture, that grain and cattle would not be included in any trade agreements with foreign countries.[116] The latter concession, by preserving France's freedom to modify the duties on these commodities, was " the starting point of the evolution in legislative tariff politics which was prepared in the course of the 'eighties and completed in the tariff reform of 1892." [117]

Under the law of May 7, 1881 oxen were made subject to a duty of 15 francs the head, bulls and cows 8 francs, calves 1.50 francs, sheep 2 francs, fresh meat 3 francs per kilogram and salt meat 4.50 francs. A duty of 60 centimes per quintal was set on wheat and wine was taxed at 4.50 francs per hectoliter.[118] In 1881 and 1882 treaties with Belgium, Italy, Switzerland, Spain, Portugal, Sweden and Norway were drawn up and rati-

114 BSAF, vol. XI, 1879, p. 339.

115 Luçay and Sénart, *op. cit.*, p. 54.

116 Sée, *Französische Wirtschaftsgeschichte*, vol. II, p. 539; Levasseur, *op. cit.*, vol. II, p. 574. On the attitude of industry, see the comments of Foreign Minister Ribot to the Tariff Commission of the Chamber in 1890, JAP, ser. 6, 1890, I, p. 622. Meredith, *op. cit.*, p. 15. The authorship of the tariff of 1881 is usually ascribed to Tirard, Teisserenc de Bort's successor as Minister of Commerce. Tirard, however, declared that it had been prepared by his "friend, M. Teisserenc de Bort,—for it is not I, as is always said, but he who drafted these tariffs." SD, 1891, p. 820.

117 Wellimir J. Bajkić, *Der fransösische handelspolitik 1892-1902*, Stuttgart and Berlin, 1904, p. 2.

118 *Principales mesures*, pp. 97-99.

fied, to run until 1892. Negotiations for an agreement with England failed because of British objection to the specific duties provided for by the new law, but in February 1882 the two governments granted each other most-favored-nation status. This had already been secured to Germany by article 11 of the Treaty of Frankfurt in 1870—the " industrial Sedan." [119]

> The treaties concluded by France in 1882 seem to have been governed not so much by the desire of obtaining concessions from other nations—though this, of course, was always present, as by the desire (felt by the executive) of opposing a firm barrier to the protectionist reaction in France.[120]

Rates included in an international agreement could not be changed without prior denunciation of the treaty or consent of the other nation.

The system inaugurated by Napoleon III was on the whole maintained, to the bitter disappointment of the *Société des agriculteurs de France.*[121] Their resentment was heightened by the fact that industry faired much better than agriculture. The high Restoration rates were, of course, lowered, but the conventional duties were generally maintained or increased. Nevertheless, an opening had been left in the defense against agricultural protection. The ink on the trade treaties was not long dry when the omission from them of agricultural products was used to get under way the protectionist campaign of the 1880's.

The Sugar Question

Before finishing this review of French tariff policy in the first three quarters of the nineteenth century it will be well to consider briefly the related questions of sugar and colonies.

119 Arnauné, *op. cit.*, pp. 298, 299; Edgard Allix, *Les droits de douane: traité théoretique et pratique de législation douanière*, 2 vols., Paris, 1932, vol. I, p. 56.

120 Meredith, *op. cit.*, p. 59.

121 CRSAF, vol. XXIII, 1881, pp. 110, 111.

The beet sugar industry was a by-product of the Continental System,[122] and with the return of peace, the early days of the Restoration saw reduction in the duties on imported raw sugar and lifting of the prohibition on refined sugar.[123] As we have seen, however, protection rapidly regained favor, and in 1814 and 1816 a system designed as a compromise between domestic beet-sugar and refining interests and colonial producers of raw sugar was established. An export subsidy on refined sugar was granted, the prohibition of refined sugar imports restored, and differential tariffs placed on raw sugar to favor the colonies.[124] The beet sugar industry prospered, and public interest, completely ignored insofar as the consumer was concerned, entered the picture only when the treasury began to suffer from declining customs receipts. In 1833, therefore, the export bounty was replaced with a drawback, "which excluded beet sugar from collecting anything because it paid no import tax," and the duty on foreign sugar was reduced sufficiently to enable it to compete with colonial and beet sugar. In the face of the continued success of beet sugar, colonial producers and domestic refiners pressed for taxation of beet sugar and reduction of the duty on colonial raw sugar, and secured these concessions in 1837.[125] The anticipated benefits to the colonies failed to materialize, and after a proposal for expropriation and suppression of the beet industry had been defeated, a compromise resulted whereby the tax on beet sugar was to be raised gradually till it would equal the duty on colonial unrefined sugar in 1847. A further diminution of the duty on colonial sugar occurred in 1851, but in 1856 it was provided that the differential between taxes on colonial and foreign sugar should gradually decrease and disappear in June 1880. The tariffs were

122 J. Charles-Roux, "La question des sucres," *Revue politique et parlementaire*, vol. II, 1894, II, p. 248.

123 Clough, *op. cit.*, p. 93.

124 E. Boizard and H. Tardieu, *Histoire de la législation des sucres*, Paris, 1891, pp. 13 ff.

125 Clough, *op. cit.*, p. 130; Boizard and Tardieu, *op. cit.*, pp. 35 ff.

abolished in 1861, but the following year, in order to meet budgetary difficulties, sugar was again made dutiable, and in 1864 differential rates were established for sugar produced in French colonies.[126]

Colonial Policy

There are three basic ways of regulating economic relations between colonies and mother country; subordination of the colonial economy to home needs (the colonial compact), colonial autonomy, and tariff union.[127] The first principle governed the policies of the Restoration and July Monarchy, the second those of the Second Empire, and after continuing the liberal régime for over a decade, the Third Republic adopted the third principle.

The Restoration

The Restoration applied the colonial compact, with certain modifications based on a decree of 1784 and the Navigation Act of 1793,[128] to the six colonies which remained under the French flag following the Napoleonic Wars. Trade between colonies and mother country was reserved to French shipping. Except for certain enumerated goods foreign commodities could not be imported into the colonies in either French or foreign bottoms. A differential tariff favoring French shipping was placed on the importable articles. Raw materials could be exported only to France, and the market of the sugar growers of Martinique and Guadeloupe was thus automatically limited. Because of the necessity of maintaining commercial relations between the French island of Réunion (Bourbon), and Mauritius which had passed under the English flag, the local administration was authorized to modify the basic regulations. Certain ports of French Guiana were open to foreign shipping and trade,

126 Charles-Roux, *op. cit.*, pp. 251-252.

127 Arthur Girault, "Le nouveau régime douanier des colonies et ses résultats," *Revue d'économie politique*, vol. VIII, 1894, p. 854.

128 Girault, *The Colonial Tariff Policy of France*, publication of the Carnegie Endowment for International Peace, Division of Economics and History, Oxford, 1916, pp. 25, 49.

but tariff differentials in favor of French goods and ships were established. In Senegal a small number of foreign articles were admitted at the same rates as similar French products, provided they had been carried by French ships. In St. Pierre-Miquelon a tax of 1% was applied to foreign goods shipped under foreign flags, and exports to France, principally consisting of codfish, were granted bounties. Only in India were the French colonies exempted from the colonial compact, for the trading-post character of the French establishments precluded such a possibility.[129]

The July Monarchy

Under the July Monarchy the severity of the system was modified to some extent. In 1845 and 1846 lists of foreign commodities which might be imported into the Antilles and Réunion were greatly extended, and exports to France from the colonies were relieved of export duties. Differential rates favoring French goods and shipping continued to exist, however, and the principle of the old system was maintained.[130]

French policy toward Algeria, the conquest of which had commenced in 1830, followed the colonial compact on the whole. In 1835 it was provided that French products, with the exception of sugar, should enter the colony free, and that foreign merchandise would be subjected to import duties. While Algerian exports to France were free of export duties, they were subject to taxation if destined for foreign countries. Until 1843, however, Algerian products were subject to full French import duties. In that year a reduction of 50% was granted on a few articles, and at the same time Algerian tariffs on foreign commodities were raised. This double tendency of tightening relations between France and Algeria on the one hand, and raising barriers between the colony and the world at large was continued and strengthened in 1851.[131]

129 Fernand Sémars, *Rélations économiques des colonies avec la métropole*, Nancy, 1905, pp. 31-35.

130 Girault, *op. cit.*, p. 60.

131 *Ibid.*, pp. 62-65.

The Second Empire

The liberal trade policy of the Second Empire was applied to the colonies. In 1854 they were divided into two groups: the first, consisting of Martinique, Guadeloupe and Réunion, was granted councils-general, and it was provided that these colonies' tariffs were to be set by law, rather than by decree of the home government, as was the case with the second group, consisting of all the other colonies. The law of July 3, 1861 greatly liberalized the tariff structure of the Antilles and Réunion. Foreign shipping was admitted to the trade between France and these colonies on payment of a special tax. The differential rates favoring the import of French products were abolished. Colonial products might be exported freely, and with the exception of sugar, coffee and several other commodities, were admitted to France free of duty.[132]

In 1866 the Antilles and Réunion received tariff autonomy. The councils-general were given the right to enact tariffs, subject to the approval of the Council of State at Paris, but in addition they were permitted to vote wharfage fees, *octrois de mer*, entirely on their own authority. The result was that Martinique in 1864, Guadeloupe in 1868 and Réunion in 1873 abolished their customs duties, and by increasing the wharfage fees placed French and foreign imports on equal footings.[133] A decree of July 9, 1868 formally suppressed the colonial compact and provided that all products might be imported to all colonies under any flag and exported with equal freedom. Imports into the colonies lacking councils-general, however, were subject to tariffs set by decree of the French government. A decree of 1863 and laws of 1866 and 1867 provided that Algerian imports into France should either be duty-free or subject to the conventional tariff, that French and foreign imports into Algeria should receive equal treatment, and that with the exception of some important items, including iron, steel, machines, etc., imports into Algeria were to be duty

132 *Ibid.*, pp. 70-71.

133 Girault, "Nouveau régime douanier des colonies . . . ," p. 855.

free.[134] Hence the Second Empire broke completely with long-established tradition and governed economic relations with the colonies according to principles of autonomy and, to a great extent, economic liberalism.

The Third Republic

The Third Republic at first did nothing to change this state of affairs. In fact, the tariff law of 1881 gave the non-autonomous colonies an additional concession by providing that their tariffs were to be prepared by the Council of State rather than by simple ministerial decree.[135] The germs of a far-sweeping revision were present, however. In 1878 and 1882 extra-parliamentary *enquêtes* resulted in recommendations of a return to the "truly republican" policy of assimilation, which had been followed during the Revolution, and a law of 1884 brought Algeria within the metropolitan tariff system.[136] Full accomplishment of this reform, however, was left for the Méline Tariff.

In the early 1880's the French tariff and colonial systems were thus in a transitional state. The main structure was still that of the Second Empire, but important modifications had been made, and more were clearly foreshadowed. Thus the basic factors that were to culminate in the Méline Tariff were already evident. French agriculture already had elements of organization; it had begun to press strongly for protection; its curve of economic well-being had begun to level off, and in some respects, particularly with reference to viticulture, had begun to decline. The tariff system was no longer professedly liberal; the colonial system was moving in the direction of assimilation, called for by nationalist economic theory. While these factors and tendencies were all present, they had not been synthesized into the single complex trend that led to the Tariff of 1892. The depression of the 1880's, the organization of *syndicats agricoles* and nationalist economic theory were fused into this trend, and these will be considered in turn in the chapters that follow.

134 Girault, *Colonial Tariff Policy*, pp. 76-80.

135 Levasseur, *op. cit.*, vol. II, p. 494.

136 Girault, *op. cit.*, ch. ii, pp. 84 ff.

CHAPTER II

A DECADE OF DEPRESSION

THE years 1873-1896 have been called the era of the Great Depression. Secular trends and short run variations combined in a period of low prices, diminished business activity in many lines and widespread social unrest. They were in part the basis of a tendency toward political and economic nationalism which began to dominate the world scene in the late nineteenth century.[1] French agriculture, relatively resistant to change, withstood the early years of this decline. Its curve of economic well-being leveled off, but at first did not fall. In the 1880's, however, its fortunes dropped, in harmony with those of the economy as a whole. Stability and quiescence gave way to insistent, vocal and organized demand for aid and relief. In studying this development it will be well first to consider variations in the fundamental bases and institutions of French agriculture between 1882 and 1892. This task is facilitated by the agricultural *enquêtes* of those years.

Population

The agricultural population continued to decline, according to all indicators.[2] (Figures in thousands)

	Total	Urban	% of total	Rural	% of total
1881	37,672	13,097	34.8	24,576	65.2
1891	38,343	14,311	37.4	24,032	62.6

AGRICULTURAL POPULATION

	Active	Domestics	Families	Total	% of National total
1881-2	4,959	1,954	11,336	18,249	48.4
1891-2	4,831	1,832	10,773	17,436	45.4

1 See Jean Lescure, *Des crises générales et périodiques de surproduction*, 5th ed., 2 vols., Paris, 1938; Albert Aftalion, *Les crises périodiques de surproduction*, Paris, 1913.

2 Ministère de l'Agriculture, *Statistique agricole de la France: résultats généraux de l'enquête décennale de 1892*, Paris, 1897, p. 391; Bureau de la Statistique générale, *Statistique générale de la France: résultats statistiques du dénombrement de 1891*, Paris, 1894, p. 65.

The rural population continued to fall, absolutely and relatively, in the 1880's at about the same rate as before. The fall in agricultural population of over 800,000 is not in itself startling, but the percentage decline relative to the national population is noteworthy. It dropped from 53.1% in 1861 to 48.4% in 1881, 4.7 points in twenty years, and fell 3.0 points in the ten years following. The decline was greatest in the marginal elements of the agricultural population, among families and servants, who found more attractive opportunities and employment in the cities.

Division of the Land

Similarly, although with far less certainty, we may say that the active population fell mostly among the group least bound to the soil, the day laborers.[3]

LANDOWNING FARMERS (in thousands)

	Working only for selves 1	Working also for others as Tenants 2	Share-croppers 3	Day laborers 4	Total land-owners 5
A1882	2,151	500	147	727	3,525
B1892	2,199	476	123	589	3,387
B–A	48	—24	—24	—138	—138

NON-OWNING FARMERS (in thousands)

	Tenants 6	Share-croppers 7	Day laborers 8	Total 9	Tenants 2+6	Share-croppers 3+7	Day laborers 4+8	Total Farmers 5+9
A1882	468	194	753	1,416	968	342	1,481	4,941
B1892	586	221	621	1,428	1,062	344	1,210	4,815
B–A	118	37	—132	12	94	2	—271	—126

The most notable increase is in the class of non-owning tenant farmers, the significant fall is in the number of day laborers, whether or not landowners. The latter group was marginal in the agricultural economy, and would be both the readiest to leave and, in a land of small farms, the most easily dispensed with. But we should be careful not to read too much into the

3 *Enquête 1892*, pp. 354, 374.

other data. We cannot say with any certainty, for instance, that the fall in number of landowning tenants and sharecroppers corresponds directly with the rise in landowners farming only for themselves. With a stable cultivated area the fact that the total number of farmers dropped would seem to imply an increase in average land per farmer, but it should be noted that the number of farm operators, as distinct from laborers, actually rose, from 2,813 thousand to 3,006 thousand. The *enquêtes* give two entirely different estimates of the number of farm units (*exploitations*). According to the first, in 1882 there were 5,672 thousand *exploitations* covering 49,582 thousand hectares, averaging 8.74 hectares, and in 1892 there were 5,703 thousand units covering 49,378 thousand hectares, averaging 8.66 hectares.[4] There were more farms (*exploitations*) than farmers (*exploitants*), however, and it is therefore necessary to divide the areas by the number of farm operators (excluding day laborers and owners also farming as cash tenants and sharecroppers): in 1882 the average farmer worked 17.63 hectares, and 16.43 hectares in 1892.

The second estimate deals with types of tenure, and gives the number of times a given type is found. This too yields results greater than the number of farm operators, but is of interest as the first indication of the relative importance of types of tenure in terms of area.[5]

(In thousands)

	Owner-farmed			Crop-sharing			Cash Tenancies			General Average
	Units	Area	Av.	Units	Area	Av.	Units	Area	Av.	hec.
1882 . . .	4,325	19,380	4.5	348	4,539	13.0	750	8,593	11.9	11.68
1892 . . .	4,193	18,324	4.4	349	3,767	10.8	1,078	12,629	11.7	11.55

Dividing these areas by the number of owner-farmers, sharecroppers and cash tenants (including owners also farming in

4 *Ibid.*, p. 364; *Enquête 1882*, p. 278.

5 *Enquête 1882*, tables p. 177; *Enquête 1892*, tables p. 237. Sub-marginal pasture lands, forests, moors and uncultivated lands were excluded from these estimates.

these categories), we obtain the following results in hectares:

(In thousands)

	Owner-farmed	Crop-sharing	Tenancies
1882	9.00	13.56	9.24
1892	8.32	10.95	11.90

All our figures point to a small decline in the average land worked by the individual farm operator, to a gain in numbers and area for cash tenancy. There is one inconsistency: whereas the number of owner-operators rose, that of owner-operated units declined. This may be cleared up, however, by the following table, on areas of farms, which notes an increase in the number of very small workings.[6]

(In thousands)

	Very small Under 1 hect.		% Total Area	Small 1–10 hect.		% Total Area
	Number	Area		Number	Area	
1882......	2,168	1,084	2	2,635	11,366	24
1892......	2,235	1,327	3	2,618	11,245	23

	Medium 10–40 hect.		% Total Area	Large		% Total Area
	Number	Area		Total Number	Area	
1882......	727	14,846	30	142	22,296	45
1892......	711	14,313	29	139	22,493	46

The lower ratio between owner-farmers and owner-operated farms in 1892 indicates concentration of holdings, which is contradicted by the rise in owner-farmers and the correspondingly lower average area per owner-operated farm. But the rise in owner-farmers in all probability affected very small farms most, with too small a total area to influence the general tendency. With reservations as to the reliability of the available data, and bearing in mind the very small amplitude of all changes recorded, we may risk the conclusions that owner-operated farms grew in number and fell in size, that sharecropping lost and cash tenancy gained in both respects.

6 *Enquête 1892*, p. 363.

Although added information for the later period makes more detailed analysis possible, these trends were already evident in the data presented in the previous chapter, and the same may be said of population changes. Hence it is fair to say that there is no evidence of either causes or effects of depression in the material we have so far discussed, but rather of the long run relative decline of agriculture previously mentioned. It is worth noting, however, that the changes observed in population, tenure and size of farms, would all tend to restrict the incidence of depression. With the exceptions of truck gardening and grape growing, low acreage is indicative of an approach toward subsistence farming, which is less intimately related to the general market. The same is true of the decline in families and auxiliary labor. Further, unless farm rents were to remain stable, the marked rise in tenancy would place a larger share of the burden of economic dislocation on the shoulders of the landlords. Unforunately, the estimates of absentee ownership given by the *enquêtes* are quite worthless, for they result from the highly questionable assumption that the number of absentee landlords was roughly equal to the total of sharecroppers and cash tenants.[7]

Crops and Livestock

The general conclusion reached above, continuation of previously observed tendencies without notable acceleration, is applicable to the distribution of land among crops.[8]

Grain areas fell slightly, but the drop in production reflects a poor year. Average annual wheat production in the period 1876-1885 was 101.7 million hectoliters, and 107.1 million hectoliters in 1886-1895.[9] Beet acreage rose, but production fell, owing to a change in standards resulting from a law of 1884, which placed a premium on sugar-rich beets, rather than large beet production.[10] Previously noted increases in potato acreage and

7 *Enquête 1882*, p. 344.

8 *Enquêtes 1882, 1892*, tables.

9 *Enquête 1892*, p. 104.

10 *Ibid.*, p. 180.

AREAS IN THOUSANDS OF HECTARES

	Wheat	All Grains	Garden Crops	Potatoes	Sugar Beets	Other Ind. Crops	Vineyards
1882	7,191	15,090	774	1,338	240	275	2,197
1892	7,166	14,827	707	1,474	271	260	1,800

	Woods, Forests	Fallows	Orchards, Parks	Fodders, Pastures	Wastes, Marshes
1882	9,455	3,644	842	10,188	6,512
1892	9,522	3,368	935	10,705	6,471

PRODUCTION IN THOUSANDS

	Hectoliters			Quintals				
	Wheat	All Grains	Wine	Potatoes	Beets	Hemp, Flax	Uncultiv. Fodders	Annual Fodders
1882...	129,339	295,254	33,582	100,994	88,504	758	320,086	150,989
1892...	117,449	208,549	29,038	154,190	72,519	424	287,664	191,166

production, and declines in industrial crops, vineyards (owing to phylloxera), fallows and wastelands continued. Estimated uncultivated pasture crops declined, as a result of the poor harvest, but the further rise in all pasture lands and in annual cultivated forage crops gave evidence of continued growth in animal husbandry, substantiated by the data on dairy products comparable for the first time.[11] (See table p. 68).

Improvement and decline in all instances followed patterns evident in the years prior to 1882. It is correct to say that, internally, agriculture progressed on the whole (although the vineyards still suffered from phylloxera) and continued to undergo changes long under way. Significant advances were made in mechanization and improvement of farm equipment. From 1882 to 1892 multiple plows rose in number from 158 to 199 thousand, threshers from 211 to 234 thousand, seed drills from 29 to 47 thousand, mowers from 19 to 39 thousand, reapers from 16 to 23 thousand.[12] This increased use of farm machinery undoubtedly contributed to the fall in number of farm laborers, noted above.

11 *Enquêtes 1882, 1892,* tables.

12 *Enquête 1892,* p. 422.

(In thousands)

	Cattle	Sheep	Pigs	Horses	Goats
1882	12,997	23,809	7,147	2,838	1,851
1892	13,709	21,116	7,421	2,794	1,845

Production in Thousands of Kilograms

	Beef, Veal	Mutton	Pork	All Cheese and Butter	Milk hectol.
1882	685,006	149,137	386,996	189,547	68,206
1892	730,038	142,849	455,107	268,676	77,013

Average Weights in Kilograms

	Bulls, Oxen	Cows	Sheep
1882	465	321	35
1892	482	335	35

Foreign Trade

There was no fall in demand for the products of French agriculture. Estimated in terms of domestic production plus net imports, consumption rose in all major lines, although not to the full extent of the adverse balance in agricultural commodities. For this favorite argument of agrarian protectionists becomes somewhat less eloquent when wine is subtracted.[13] Wine

Special Commerce in Millions of Francs

	1	2	3	4	5	6	7	8
	Agri. Imp.	Agri. Exp.	(1)–(2)	Total Imp.	Total Exp.	(4)–(5)	Wine Imp.	Grain Imp.
1881	2041	784	1256	4863	3562	1301	363	520
1882	1956	776	1180	4822	3574	1248	315	502
1883	1912	746	1166	4804	3452	1352	377	375
1884	1771	737	1034	4344	3233	1111	344	360
1885	1722	726	996	4088	3088	1000	389	233
1886	1877	747	1130	4208	3249	959	518	262
1887	1628	706	922	4026	3247	779	444	289
1888	1765	758	1007	4107	3247	860	438	375
1889	1732	884	848	4317	3704	613	384	366
1890	1655	860	796	4437	3754	684	350	364
1891	1937	796	1141	4768	3570	1198	401	532

13 *Tableau décennal du commerce de la France*, 1877-1886, 1887-1896, vol. I. The items included are listed in Chapter I, note 57.

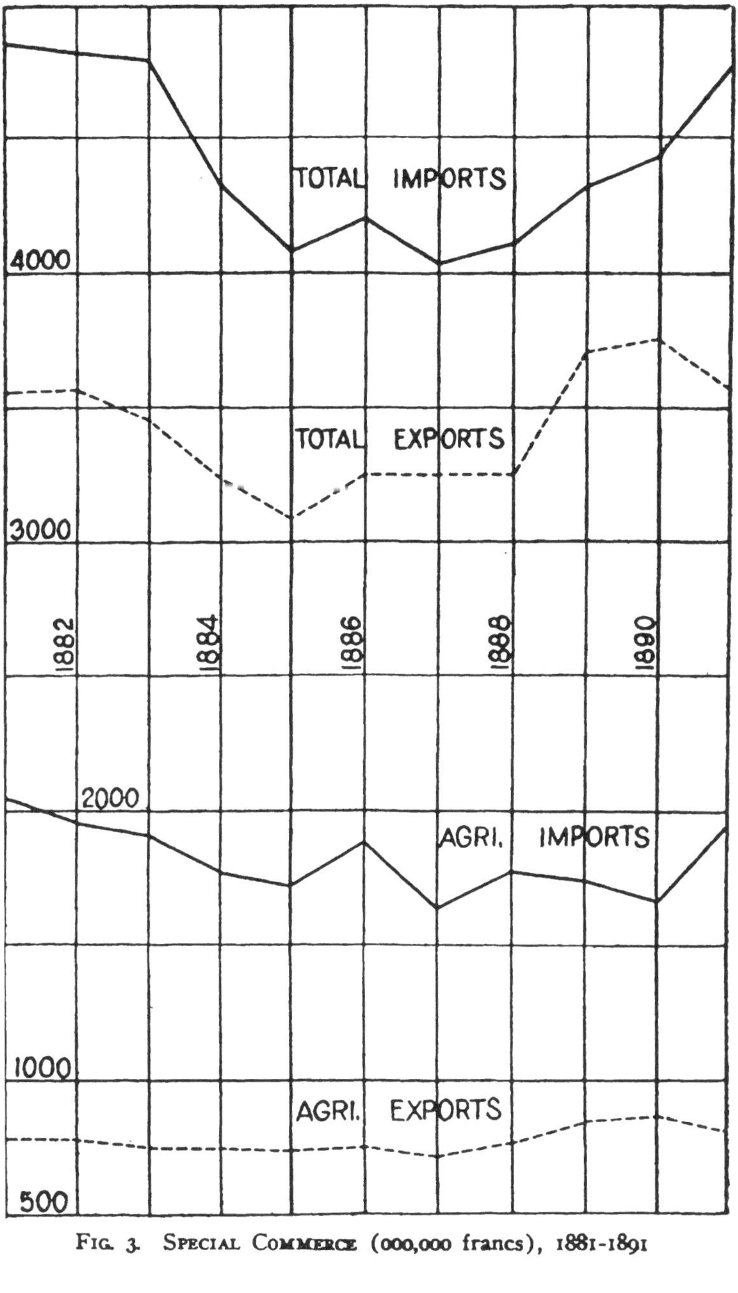

FIG. 3. SPECIAL COMMERCE (000,000 francs), 1881-1891

and grains together accounted, on the average, for forty-four per cent of all agricultural imports, and for seventeen per cent of total French imports.

The agricultural import surplus varied from eighty-six per cent of the total import surplus in 1883 to one hundred thirty-eight per cent in 1889, but this connotes no departure from previously observed conditions. With the exception of the vineyards, it cannot be said that the internal structure of French agriculture gave evidence of depression. Relative to urban, industrialized society, agriculture continued to fall back in the 1880's, but this seems to have been in pursuance of a broad fundamental change, not the result of an economic crisis. It is in the relationship of agriculture to the rest of the economy, in its contacts with an ever-widening market, that the evidence of depression is to be seen.

Prices, Land Values and Wages

Prices of agricultural commodities fell, more sharply than those of various products which farmers might consume. In the following table an index of agricultural prices (weighted average of relatives, based on market reports) is compared with an index of prices of "various products" (arithmetic average of relatives, based on price data of the *Commission des valeurs en douane*). While the latter cannot claim to represent accurately farm consumption, and is based on figures of only limited validity, the difference between the two series indicates, in a very rough way, the degree to which price changes adversely affected the farm population in the late 1880's.[14]

14 The agricultural list is composed of the following commodities, with their 1881 values (PQ) in parentheses: wheat (2,955), maize (120), barley (225), oats (854), beef (692), veal (241), mutton (231), pork (596), butter (251), cheese (158), potatoes (879), edible oil (28), wine (2,435), sugar (384), rape seed oil (17), hemp (36), flax (45). Prices for the following were drawn from the tables in Ministère du travail et de la prévoyance sociale: Statistique générale de la France, *Salaires et coût de l'existence à divers époques jusq'en 1910*, Paris, 1911: wheat (1883-91), beef, veal, mutton, pork, potatoes, butter, cheese, wine, sugar, rape seed oil, edible oil (see Ch. VII, note 55). Prices for the following were taken from the quotations

PRICE INDEXES, 1881 = 100

	1 Agricultural commodities	2 Various products	2–1
1881	100	100	0
1882	103	100	—3
1883	96	95	—1
1884	91	87	—4
1885	87	83	—4
1886	87	83	—4
1887	84	87	3
1888	85	94	9
1889	84	100	16
1890	86	101	15
1891	87	93	6
Average fall from base:			
1882–1886	7.2	10.4	
1887–1891	14.8	5.0	
1882–1891	11.0	7.7	

Bearing in mind the deficiencies of the second series, it appears that the position of agriculture deteriorated rapidly in the second half of the decade, and that the election year, 1889, and 1890 show the greatest gaps between the two lists.

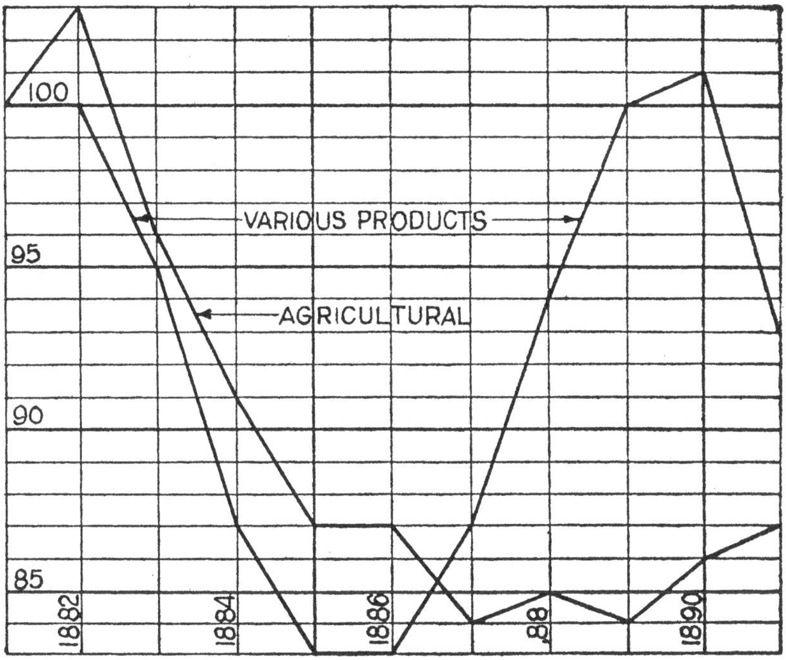

FIG. 4. PRICE INDEXES, 1881-1891. Base 1881 = 100

Land values fell sharply, and, from the evidence of the *enquêtes,* more rapidly than rents.[15] The fall was most marked in the case of tillable lands, and, surprisingly, least pronounced in that of vineyards. (Francs per hectare)

	Tillable Soil		Pasture Lands		Vineyards	
	Value	Rent	Value	Rent	Value	Rent
1882	2023	65	2692	96	2381	102
1892	1694	58	2358	88	2132	96
% fall	16	11	12	8	10	6

No convincing explanation can be given for this phenomenon, but, if the procedure of the *enquête agricole* was the same as that employed by the Ministry of Finances,[16] it may be suggested that on the one hand, the very best vineyards, producing luxury wines, were held continuously by wealthy families, and were unlikely to be sold or rented, and on the other hand, vineyards especially suffering from phylloxera would be unlikely to find buyers or tenants. In all instances rents declined more slowly than land values, but this must be taken with some reservation. The increase in tenancy between 1882 and 1892 largely took the form of oral agreements, which may not have entered fully into the reports of the *enquêtes.*[17] The prevalence of relatively long term leases, noted below, would tend to brake the fall in rents.

of the *Journal d'agriculture pratique*: wheat (1881-1882, adjusted to above in 1883), maize (Toulouse 1881-1887, adjusted to Paris price used in 1888-1891), barley and oats (Paris Wednesday closing price, adjusted in 1891 to fit index 1891-1909), hemp, flax (Bergues 1881-1882, 1885-1891; Picarde 1883, 1884 adjusted to former in 1885). Lack of consistency in quotations necessitated these adjustments.

The "various products" list is composed of the following: coffee, cocoa, cast iron, iron bars, copper, tin, lead, coal, oil, cotton, wool, sodium nitrate, building wood, cotton cloth. The prices were taken from the *Tableau décennal du commerce de la France,* 1887-1896, vol. I.

15 *Enquête 1892,* p. 412.

16 "Value" was estimated from records of sales, "revenue" (or rent) from records of leases. See C. Gimel, "De la nouvelle évaluation du revenu des propriétés non bâties," *Journal de la Société de statistique de Paris,* vol. XXV, 1884, pp. 299 ff.

17 *Enquête 1892,* p. 315.

Of course, the most direct way of observing the depression would be to compare farm income with farm costs. The *enquête* of 1892 notes, in precise numbers, the drop in total agricultural net income from 1,198 million francs in 1882 to 800 million francs in 1892. The net taxable income, or rental value, of all unbuilt property fell from 2,646 million francs in 1879 to 2,582 million francs in 1884.[18] Unfortunately, the data do not justify or afford the luxury of such precision. We have indicated the trend of farm income roughly by means of a price index intended to be representative of farm production. We have observed it to fall faster than an index of prices of " various products." Unfortunately, it is hardly possible to set up a representative index of farm costs. The data are inadequate for such items as rent (a cost to the tenant and income to the landlord), or wages; and, when the different economic positions of various classes of farmers are considered, it will be seen that no adequate system of weighting could be developed. We may, however, observe fluctuations in wages (to a very limited extent), taxes and the cost of fertilizer.

The *enquêtes agricoles* fail to present a clear picture of wage changes. On the one hand, the daily pay of day laborers (*journaliers*), who numbered 1,481 thousand in 1882 and 1,210 thousand in 1892, declined; on the other hand, the annual earnings of farm servants [*domestiques de ferme,* including workers (*laboureurs*), carters, shepherds and male and female servants, personal assistants and agents (*maître valet et commis*)], who numbered 1,954 thousand in 1882 and 1,832 thousand in 1892, actually rose.[19] (See table p. 74).

Weighting these changes by the number of persons in each category in 1892, we find that the average wage had fallen, for 1,672 thousand persons, about 7%, and had risen, for 1,470

18 *Ibid.*, pp. 440 ff.; Ministère des Finances, Direction des contributions directes, *Annuaire des contributions directes,* 1897, p. 58.

19 *Enquête 1892,* pp. 419 ff. See also, A. Souchon, *La crise de la main d'oeuvre agricole en France,* Paris, 1914, pp. 52 ff., 362 ff.; Pierre Régnier, *L'ouvrier agricole,* Paris, 1924, pp. 27 ff.; Daniel Zolla, *L'agriculture moderne,* Paris, 1913, p. 281.

PER-DIEM WAGES OF DAY LABORERS, FRANCS

WITH BOARD

	Summer			Winter		
	Men	Women	Children	Men	Women	Children
1882	1.98	1.14	.74	1.31	.79	.52
1892	1.85	1.08	.69	1.30	.79	.47
% fall	6	5	7	.7	0	11

WITHOUT BOARD

	Summer			Winter		
	Men	Women	Children	Men	Women	Children
1882	3.11	1.87	1.31	2.22	1.42	.94
1892	2.94	1.78	1.23	2.04	1.35	.97
% fall	5	5	6	8	5	—1

ANNUAL WAGES OF FARM SERVANTS, FRANCS

	Assist-ants	Work-ers Carters	Cowherds, Shep-herds	Cheese Work-ers	Male Servants Under 16	Male Servants Over 16	Female Serv-ants
1882 ...	465	324	289	431	140	295	235
1892 ...	493	360	317	489	151	304	202
% rise .	6	10	9	12	7	3	—12

thousand persons, about 7%. Thus, if we cannot say precisely how, and to what degree, wages changed between 1882 and 1892, we can at least state that they did not constitute a significantly declining cost to agricultural management.

Other Costs

The very nature of the French tax system made it unresponsive to economic fluctuations. The principal tax affecting French agriculture was on the " net revenue of unbuilt property." This was calculated by the *Direction des contributions directes* from the records of actual land leases, independently of its estimates of the gross value of the land (*valeur vénale*). The estimates on which taxes were based throughout this period were made between 1879 and 1881, and the base rate remained unchanged till 1890. Actual tax receipts, 1883-1891, were as follows, in millions of francs[20]

20 *Annuaire des contributions directes*, 1897, pp. 84-85.

1883	247	1886	251	1889	253
1884	248	1887	252	1890	257
1885	250	1888	252	1891	242

There were other taxes: that on "built property," affecting farm homes and other buildings; on openings (*portes et fenêtres*); extremely heavy legal fees on transfer of property.[21] The actual, as distinct from legal, tax rate obviously rose as property values declined, and receipts from the unbuilt property tax were highest in 1889 and 1890, years previously pointed to as the worst in the period for French agriculture.

Artificial fertilizer prices fell markedly, as the products came into wider use. The price of one hundred kilograms of sodium nitrate fell from an average of 37.50 francs in the period 1877 1880 to 31 36 in 1882-1885 and 24.21 in 1887-1890.[22] But consumption rose greatly. Imports of sodium nitrate rose (with prices falling) from an average of 22 million francs in the first period to 24.2 million francs in the second period and 36.4 million francs in the third period.[23] Increased use brought a rise in total expenditure despite the lower per-unit cost.

We obviously do not have sufficient information for a precise statement of agriculture's balance sheet. We do, however, have some indications that gross income fell more rapidly than costs. But our analysis of agriculture's depressed condition is far from complete. We are not yet in a position to say whether this was a depression, in the cyclical sense, or a secular trend: we have yet to indicate what products, regions and classes were principally affected by these changes.

Analysis and Conclusions

The rise of prices from 1850 to 1873 and their fall from 1873 to 1896 has been widely noted. Explanations of this phenomenon have been given two principal emphases. One points especially to the fall in gold production after the initial boom following

21 See Zolla, *Études d'économie rurale*, Paris, 1896, pp. 65-66; P. Ronce, *La crise agricole*, Paris, 1900, p. 99; Souchon, *La propriété paysanne*, Paris, 1899, pp. 126 ff.

22 Zolla, *La crise agricole dans ses rapports avec la baisse des prix et la question monétaire*, Paris, 1903, pp. 92-93.

23 *Tableau décennal du commerce de la France*, 1877-1886, 1887-1896, vol. I.

1848, and the widespread adoption of the gold standard in the 1870's, leading to monetary contraction and consequent fall of prices in the latter part of the nineteenth century.[24] The other emphasizes the general movement of economic activity. Lescure argues that prices rose in the 1850's and 1860's following the stimulation afforded by railroad building, and fell when this stimulus ceased to operate. He contends that directional changes in prices preceded monetary changes.[25] Whether or not gold shortage and demonetization of silver, or otherwise diminished stimulus to economic activity was operative in lowering world prices in general, special factors affected French agricultural prices.[26] If we break down the price index of French agricultural commodities, and observe some of its principal components, significant variations appear [27] (see table p. 77).

The decline in wine prices preceded the 1880's. Wine and sugar are special cases, the first being affected by phylloxera, the second by a subsidized overproduction.[28] The fall in wheat

24 Zolla tends to emphasize this hypothesis (*Études*, pp. 312 ff.), but also urges the importance of lower transportation costs and increased production (*Crise*, pp 144 ff.). Ronce denies the monetary explanation, and declares "there is no agricultural crisis. There is simply a modification of the economic situation of peoples; there is an increase in the world's productive capacities; and the abundance of products, far from being a passing phenomenon, must fatally rise ...". (*op. cit.*, p. 121, also pp. 78 ff.). Comte Joseph Imbart de la Tour, on the other hand, denies that new world production caused the fall in prices (*La crise agricole en France et à l'étranger*, Nevers, 1901, p. 63). See also, Adrien Moras, *La crise du blé*, Paris, 1902, p. 60; Noël Beaurieux, *Le prix du blé en France au XIXme siècle*, Paris, 1909, p. 68; Augé-Laribé, *Évolution*, pp. 15 ff.

25 Lescure, *Hausses et baisses des prix de longue durée*, Paris, 1933, pp. 27 ff., 44 ff.

26 See Zolla, *Études*, p. 251. The very controversial question of bimetallism would require an extended treatment. See Georges Rastel, *Les controverses doctrinales sur le bimétallisme au XIXe siècle*, Paris, 1935, and G. M. Boissevain, *The monetary question ...*, trans. by A. T. Warner, London and New York, 1891.

27 For a discussion of similar data see Walter T. Layton, *An introduction to the study of prices: with special reference to the history of the nineteenth century*, London, 1920, pp. 66 ff.

28 *Loc. cit.*; E. Boizard and H. Tardieu, *Histoire de la législation des sucres*, Paris, 1891.

prices reflects the great advance in transportation, indicated by the decline in freight rates.[29]

RATE PER BUSHEL OF WHEAT, NEW YORK TO LIVERPOOL, REDUCED TO RELATIVES

1866–1870	100	1881–1885	64
1871–1875	148	1886–1890	50
1876–1880	117		

In short, it was when contact with the world market increased, and with respect to those commodities most affected by the entry into the world market of new producing nations, that prices fell. This development made itself felt in France

Price relatives:	Wheat	Wine	Potatoes	Sugar
1881	100	100	100	100
1882	96	99	151	99
1883	85	98	118	95
1884	71	92	116	96
1885	73	90	93	94
1886	73	90	106	86
1887	79	86	91	85
1888	84	79	91	92
1889	79	78	89	93
1890	85	79	70	93
1891	92	75	76	94
Average fall from base:				
1882–86	19.8	6.2	—16.8	6.0
1887–91	16.2	20.6	16.6	8.6
1882–91	18.0	13.4	— .1	7.3

	Group averages			
	Maize, Barley, Oats	Flax, Hemp	Butter, Cheese	Beef, Veal, Mutton
1881	100	100	100	100
1882	106.3	107	97.5	108
1883	99	96	97	114.7
1884	98	92.5	93	108
1885	98	93.5	92.5	98.7
1886	88.7	90	93.5	93.3
1887	85	91.5	92.5	83.7
1888	91.3	87.5	92	91.7
1889	90	77	93	87.7
1890	94.3	71.5	93.5	96.7
1891	100	70.5	94.5	99
Average fall from base:				
1882–86	2	4.2	5.3	—4.5
1887–91	7.9	20.4	6.9	8.2
1882–91	4.9	12.3	6.1	1.9

29 U. S. Department of Commerce and Labor, Bureau of Statistics, *Transportation routes and systems of the world,* Washington, 1909, p. 20.

somewhat later than in England, and evidence of it is to be seen in the fact that French and English prices tended to move more closely together in the 1880's.[30] Thus depression affected principally wheat farmers, and, owing to a special case, vine growers. Correspondingly, cattle and dairy farmers suffered less.

If this analysis is correct, it should be supported by data relating to forced sales, land values and rents. There would seem to be little question in the first instance. In the following table, forced sales in twelve representative wheat departments, twelve wine departments, twelve cattle or dairy departments and forty-six of the remaining departments, are reduced to relatives.[31] (Base 1873-1879=100)

	Wheat	Wine	Cattle	46 Dept's
	100	100	100	100
1880	112	111	106	104
1881	123	108	117	109
1882	126	126	123	101
1883	134	152	137	108
1884	148	153	149	116
1885	170	169	133	124
1886	173	204	149	157
1887	194	242	179	182
1888	206	242	178	197
1889	214	228	205	200
1890	191	216	194	186
1891	159	197	149	164
Average 1880–1885	135.5	136.5	127.5	110.3
Average 1886–1891	189.5	221.5	175.7	181.0

Of course, these figures fail to destinguish between purely agricultural and rural, or even urban, property. But France is

30 Comparing Sauerbeck's foodstuffs index with that of the Bureau de la statistique générale (in each case base 1891-1900=100), we find that English numbers exceeded French numbers by an average of 11.5 points in 1857-1868, 8.1 points in 1869-1880, 2.6 points in 1881-1891; *Annuaire statistique*, 1911, p. 210*.

31 Source, Ministère de la Justice, *Comptes générales de l'administration de la justice civile et commerciale en France et en Algérie*, 1873-1891. Of course, it is extremely difficult to select departments as representative of a particular type of agriculture, owing to the lack of intensive specialization in most parts of France, and the widespread planting of wheat. It should be noted, therefore, that all of the departments listed below grew other crops than their specialty, and that many departments not listed were significant producers in the three categories compared. The criteria used were

and was a country of many small and moderate-sized cities, rather than a few great ones, and it is likely that no bias occurs. In the wheat and wine departments the number of sales rose rapidly in the early 1880's, and at an increased rate in the second half of the decade. The position of the cattle departments was somewhat better than that of the first two in 1880-1885, and best of all four in 1886-1891. In the forty-six departments, it was only in 1886 that the rate of increase of forced sales began to approach those of the first two groups, and it never quite equaled them. These data too point to the election year 1889 as the worst for agriculture.

With regard to land values we have the evidence of the *enquête* of the *Direction des contributions directes* in 1879, and its revision in 1884, and that of the *enquêtes* of 1882 and 1892. For the latter, which also contain data on rents, we have chosen the modal category, closely approaching the mean, third quality tillable lands.[32] The first series does not distinguish as to character of land.

Average value per hectare (Base 1879 = 100)

	Wheat	Wine	Cattle	46 Dept's
1884	92	93	98	101

Third quality tillable land (Base 1882 = 100)

	Value			Rent		
	Wheat	Cattle	46 Dept's	Wheat	Cattle	46 Dept's
1892	73	87	83	86	92	91

percentage of total and of tillable acreage devoted to wheat (or wine) and production; the cattle or dairy departments were selected on the basis of cattle per total and tillable acreage and milk, cheese and butter production. Seven departments were excluded because they fitted two classifications: Haute Garonne, Isère, Loire-Inférieure, Maine et Loire, Nord, Seine et Marne, Seine et Oise. The department of the Seine was also excluded. The wheat departments: Aisne, Eure, Eure et Loir, Gers, Lot et Garonne, Oise, Pas de Calais, Saône et Loire, Deux Sèvres, Somme, Tarn et Garonne, Yonne. The wine departments: Aude, Charente-Infèrieure, Dordogne, Gironde, Hérault, Indre et Loire, Lot, Puy de Dôme, Pyrénées Orientales, Rhône, Tarn, Var. The cattle departments: Ain, Calvados, Cantal, Côtes du Nord, Finistère, Jura, Loiret, Manche, Morbihan, Haute Savoie, Seine-Inférieure, Vendée.

32 *Enquêtes 1882, 1892*, tables; Ministère des Finances, *Bulletin de statistique et de législation comparée*, vol. XIII, 1883, I, pp. 576 ff., vol. XXIV, 1888, II, pp. 685 ff.

Again it appears that the wheat and wine departments suffered more than the rest of France, and that the position of the cattle departments, somewhat worse than that of the group of forty-six in the early part of the 1880's, improved markedly by the end of the decade.

The question still remains as to what sections of the agricultural population were most affected by the hard times. Clearly vine growers large and small would suffer to the extent that their particular vines were stricken with phylloxera. Small, owner operated vineyards predominated.[33] The case of wheat is much more complex. The French economist Zolla makes much of the point that a good proportion of this crop, and more of the other grain crops were consumed on the farm, for seed and food purposes.[34] Hence, he argues, the quantities so used do not enter into the market. This is not necessarily true with respect to consumption, especially of wheat, for the farmer might well market all his wheat and restrict his own cosnumption to the cheaper grains. To the extent that it is true, however, the larger the farm, the greater the proportion of grains sold. Thus price fluctuations would be most felt by large farms. As will be recalled, tenant farms had a higher average area than owner operated or crop-sharing farms. It may be assumed, therefore, that large owner operated and tenant farms suffered most from the falling wheat price. It is extremely difficult to say whether landlords or tenants were most affected. Rents fell more slowly than land values, according to our data. If the assumptions made above regarding these data are correct, however, it would not necessarily hold that the tenants always suffered from such a lag. The increase in tenancy in 1892 was explained as representing a large number of oral agreements, mostly in the northwestern departments, important wheat producers. In 1882 fifty-six per cent of the leases were for six years or more.[35] Thus in the case of recorded leases, whether or not the landlord would suffer a fall in rent would depend on the date of termination of the lease, but the average decline would be

33 *Enquête 1882*, p. 344. This is borne out by a comparison of lists of "small-holdings" departments and wine departments, *ibid.*, tables.

34 Zolla, *Le blé et les céréales*, Paris, 1909, p. 62; *Crise*, pp. 97-98.

35 *Enquête 1882*, p. 327.

slow because of the long duration of these contracts. In the case of verbal agreements, it is reasonable to suppose that they were not fully represented in the *enquête* summaries, and that they would be for shorter periods, would be more flexible, and decline more rapidly, at the landlord's expense. We have seen that these oral contracts occurred principally in wheat areas, and, indeed, that rents moved in somewhat closer harmony with land values in the leading wheat departments than in the rest of the country.

While the principal wheat and wine areas may have been the chief sufferers, the nation as a whole felt the decline. It must be remembered that grain crops, and wheat especially, predominated in France. Most French farms grew at least some of these products.[36] In only ten of the eighty-seven departments, including that of the Seine, did grain crops occupy less than half the tillable land in 1882, and only in Corsica did they fall below forty per cent.[37] Zolla points out the arithmetical truth that if costs decline at the same rate as receipts profits will fall at this rate. And costs fell more slowly than receipts.[38] In a farm he analyzed, where wheat yielded fifty-nine per cent of the receipts, a twenty-six per cent fall in its price (together with a sixteen per cent drop in the price of rye, which had accounted for about three per cent of receipts) led to a seventy-seven per cent fall in profits. But could fluctuations in grain prices seriously affect the fortunes of farms which did not specialize in these crops? The influence of the price of a given commodity would depend on the importance of that commodity to the particular farm. But wheat was not only widely produced, but, proportionately, even more widely marketed. Even where it was not the farm specialty, it was frequently a leading source of cash income. Nor was it easy to change to crops whose prices were more stable. Aside from the fact that wheat still yielded the highest return of all field crops,[39] the very nature of the land in-

36 See the comment of E. Lecouteux, JAP, series 6, vol. XLVII, 1891, I, p. 610.

37 *Enquête 1882*, pp. 8 ff.

38 Zolla, *Crise*, pp. 111 ff.

39 See *Enquête 1882*, p. 14, *Enquête 1892*, p. 16; Zolla, *op. cit.*, pp. 116 ff.

fluenced the choice of crops in some instances and dictated it in others. Further, the weight of tradition favored wheat, and the farmers, expecting good days to return, continued their accustomed ways. Augé-Laribé writes [40]

> The fall in prices did not affect all farmers equally. If we had a great many data for all regions and for all types of holdings, we would doubtless see that the agricultural crisis was not quite as disastrous as has been said. . . . But the fall of prices is incontestable, and it is evident that it did not occur without producing a loss in income for some, for others a real *malaise,* and ruin for a few.

We may therefore suggest that grape growers and wheat growing large proprietors, and to a lesser degree tenants, were the principal sufferers. The cattle raising areas, mainly in Normandy and Brittany (also Savoy and the department of Jura) were somewhat less affected at the opening of the decade and were in a somewhat better position than any other part of France at its close. Livestock duties enacted in 1885 and 1887 had apparently been effective.[41] It was not an agricultural depression or crisis in the cyclical sense. French agriculture had long profited from the very effective protection afforded by distance, poor means of transportation and lack of competitors. This situation changed rather suddenly, in the 1880's, and the appearance of a crisis was given to what was a long run basic development. Agricultural leaders saw the old physical wall crumble, as the increasing production of new lands could economically affect the markets of the old world. And they turned toward artificial, political methods of protection embodied in tariff walls.

As we have seen, the election year, 1889, and 1890 were the worst years of the decade for French agriculture. Therefore we shall not be surprised to find the northern wheat districts and southern wine areas returning deputies who were strongly protectionist, but we shall also find that the very core of agrarian protectionism lay in Normandy and Brittany.

40 Augé-Laribé, *Évolution,* p. 15.

41 See p. 152 below.

CHAPTER III

THE SYNDICATS AGRICOLES

AGRICULTURAL organizations prior to 1884 were characterized by two features which prevented their creating rural mass movements: they were either too limited in powers and functions or their membership was socially too restricted. As we have seen, national and provincial agricultural societies and *comices* fulfilled the functions of academies, distributing prizes and spreading technical information. *Syndical* organizations formed under the law of June 21, 1865 were limited to specific projects of rural improvement. The *Société des agriculteurs* drew its members from the highest stratum of the agricultural population. None of these organizations was capable of development into a popular agricultural pressure group, and none could be constituted till the legal bars to professional association had been lowered.[1] In 1880 a bill granting freedom of association and assembly was introduced, but only the latter provision was enacted.[2] In 1883 the Ferry cabinet, in carrying out the republican program, renewed the attempt to secure authorization for labor unions, and after modifications which exempted religious communities from the benefits of the law, the act of March 21, 1884 was passed.[3] It was designed only to enable industrial labor to organize. Agriculture had not even been considered when, at the second discussion of the bill in the Senate, M. Oudet, representing the department of Doubs, moved that article 2, reading

> the professional *syndicats* have as their exclusive object the study and defense of economic, industrial and commercial interests,

1 See p. 44 above.

2 Charles Seignobos, *L'évolution de la troisième république (1875-1914)*, vol. VIII of E. Lavisse, ed., *Histoire de la France contemporaire depuis la Révolution jusqu'à la paix de 1919*, Paris, 1921, p. 72.

3 *Ibid.*, p. 104.

be amended to include the words *et agricoles*. The reporter of the commission declared that no one had thought of excluding agriculture, and the amendment was adopted without further discussion.[4]

The method of organization provided by the law was extremely simple. A group of interested persons, French citizens in full possession of civil rights, could meet, draw up statutes and by-laws, elect officers and register with the mayor of the commune in which the *syndicat* was situated.[5] Only two limitations were placed on the *syndicats*: first, the word " exclusive " implied that the organizations were not to be political in character;[6] second, *unions* of *syndicats* were not to possess legal personality. That is, they were not authorized to own real estate or act at law, or buy or sell.[7]

In August 1884, Waldeck-Rousseau, the Minister of the Interior, circularized the prefects on the administration of the new law. After urging all officials to help the new associations and popularize them, he stated:

> Imbued with the idea that association of individuals according to their professional interests is less a weapon of combat than an instrument of material, moral and intellectual progress, [the legislature] granted the *syndicats* legal personality to enable them to bring their salutary activities to the highest degree of effectiveness.[8]

This grant of rights, long sought by industrial labor, was not premature in agriculture. In 1881 the *comice* of Villeneuve-

4 Comte de Rocquigny, *Les syndicats agricoles et leur oeuvre*, 2nd ed., Paris, 1906, pp. 9, 10. The text of the law is given in *Principales mesures* . . . , pp. 1, 2; SD, 1884, p. 451.

5 Rocquigny, *op. cit.*, pp. 21, 22.

6 Maurice Genin, *Les associations agricoles dans l'ancienne France et sous le régime de la loi du 21 mars 1884*, Lyon, 1893, p. 222.

7 Maurice Launay, *Étude sur les unions des syndicats agricoles*, Paris, 1911, p. 31.

8 *Annuaire des syndicats agricoles établi à l'aide de documents réunis par le Ministère de l'agriculture*, Paris, 1911, p. 6.

sur-Lot had formed an association for the common buying of fertilizer, and the next year the *comice* of Rouen followed this example. The first group to register under the new law was the *Syndicat des agriculteurs de Loir-et-Cher,* which had been formed in 1883 by the departmental professor of agriculture, M. Tanviray, for the collective purchase of chemical fertilizers.[9] An outside impetus was necessary, however, to bring the farmers to unite in these associations. At first the *Société des agriculteurs de France* took little notice of the *syndicats,* merely mentioning newly formed groups in its bulletin.[10] In 1884 there were only five *syndicats* and in 1885 there were only thirty-nine.[11] In the latter year, however, members of the *Société des agriculteurs* began to examine the possibilities of this new type of agricultural organization. M. Deusy, an influential member of the society, was asked to report on the law of 1884 and the *syndicats,* and he declared

> Gentlemen, you wonder as to the reason for the precarious state, the inferiority which so severely affect our agriculture? . . . Why are French and foreign industry protected among us while agriculture bears all the burdens of the pretended commercial liberty imposed upon it? . . . In short, why is it possible thus to violate all the principles of economic, fiscal and political equality? Because agriculture is not represented, because [agriculture] has until now been denied the right of association, which should always be free.[12]

9 Rocquigny, *op. cit.*, pp. 11-15; Augé-Laribé, *Évolution*, pp. 170-171; see Tisserand, *Rapport sur l'enseignement agricole en France publié par l'ordre de M. Viger, ministre de l'agriculture,* 2 vols., Paris, 1894, vol. I, p. 14.

10 BSAF, vol. XVI, 1884. The only mention of *syndicats* in 1884 was a brief reference to the founding of the *syndicat* of Villasavary, p. 581.

11 *Enquête, 1892,* tables, p. 436. The data on the agricultural *syndicats* are not altogether reliable. Some failed to register and some registered *syndicats* existed in name only. See Rocquigny, *op. cit.*, pp. 47-48. An *Annuaire des syndicats agricoles* published in 1889 (probably the predecessor of L. Hautefeuille, ed., *Annuaire des syndicats agricoles et de l'agriculture française,* published at Paris, 1890-1895) states that there were 834 *syndicats agricoles* at that time. This is undoubtedly exaggerated.

12 CRSAF, vol. XVII, 1885, p. 207.

Another member stated that the *syndicats* were the full and effective representation of agriculture. " The *Société des agriculteurs* should be the center of all the *syndicats*; having received the mandate of each of them her power for the defense of agricultural interests would be immense, her word would be heeded. . . ." [13]

The *Société des agriculteurs* appointed a committee headed by a jurist, M. Sénart, to study the question, and despite the objections of some who feared that organization of *syndicats* might lead to strikes among the rural population, adopted a report favorable to the promotion of *syndicats*. M. Deusy was delegated to draw up model statutes, and then was sent on a lecture tour to carry the word of the new organizations through the countryside. He went from village to village, urging the leading proprietors to form *syndicats*. At the same time other members of the society and heads of *comices* and provincial agricultural societies, most of which were connected with the *Société des agriculteurs*, joined the campaign.[14]

The growth of the *syndicats* was steady if not spectacular. From five in 1884 and thirty-nine in 1885, the number of these associations progressed as follows, according to the *enquête* of 1892: [15]

Year	*Syndicats*	Membership	Average Membership
1886	93	Not given	
1887	214	" "	
1888	461	" "	
1889	557	" "	
1890	648	234,234	361
1891	750	269,928	360
1892	863	313,800	364

If we assume that the average membership of the *syndicats* was about the same in 1886-1889 as in 1890-1892, we obtain the

13 *Ibid.*, p. 495.

14 *Ibid.*, pp. 213 ff., 498; vol. XIX, 1887, p. 21; BSAF, vol. XVII, 1885, pp. 381 ff., 437; vol. XVIII, 1886, pp. 46-47, 812; vol. XIX, 1887, pp. 275-276.

15 *Enquête, 1892*, tables, p. 436.

following estimates of total membership: 1886, 33,480; 1887, 77,040; 1888, 165,960; 1889, 200,520. These associations, therefore, comprised only a small percentage of France's active agricultural population, but, if well organized, they were a sufficiently numerous minority to be effective in pressure politics.

Many and varied were the operations in which these organizations engaged. In the early stages of their development cooperative purchase of fertilizer was the principal object. In some cases the *syndicat* merely acted as agent for its members, and bills were paid individually. In others purchases were grouped through the president of the *syndicat* and members were mutually responsible for payment. Uniform quality was insured by chemical analysis.[16] Their range of activity was soon extended, however, to include other products of interest to farmers, such as seeds, fodder, tools, etc. Indeed, it was not long before they showed signs of becoming cooperative general stores, and incurred the opposition of village merchants. This trend was not approved by the leaders of the movement, and it was checked by the adoption of one of two policies. First, cooperatives might be established alongside the *syndicats*, or the *syndicat*, being a legal person, might join an existing cooperative. Second, contracts might be concluded with local merchants whereby the members of the *syndicat* would receive reductions varying up to fifteen per cent of the list price of articles in return for their organization's promise to trade exclusively with the contracting merchant. While the *syndicats* were at first usually offices where orders were given and grouped, *syndical* stores, carrying stocks suited to the estimated needs of the members, became increasingly common. Collective purchases, frequently in carload units, brought great saving to the membership, and especially to the small peasants who had previously been the prey of numerous intermediaries.[17] Unfortunately there are few data as to the

16 BSAF, vol. XVII, 1885, p. 779.

17 Rocquigny, *op. cit.*, pp. 162-163, 170 ff., 270-273.

syndicats' annual business.[18] The comte de Rocquigny, leading authority on these associations, gives the following figures for the twenty-five leading *syndicats* in 1900. These organizations had a membership of 118,650: they handled transactions amounting to 22,857,000 francs, or an average of 192.6 francs per member. These figures are undoubtedly higher than the average for all *syndicats*. If we assume, however, that in the early years of the movement each member accounted for about 150 francs yearly, by applying our previous estimates of the total *syndical* membership, we arrive at the following suppositions as to the gross yearly business of all *syndicats*:

1886	5,000,000 francs	1890	35,000,000 francs
1887	11,500,000 francs	1891	40,500,000 francs
1888	25,000,000 francs	1892	47,000,000 francs
1889	30,000,000 francs		

While these figures are obviously rough estimates, they do indicate steady progress of the *syndicats*. M. de Rocquigny states that in 1900 yearly business amounted to about 200,000,000 francs.[19]

Collective buying was not the only task assumed by the *syndicats*. Many organizations engaged in collective sale of their members' products, though this activity was not uniformly effective. Difficulties in providing the amounts contracted for, variations in quality, and a tendency on the part of the peasants to unload their poorer products on the *syndicats* combined to limit the effectiveness of cooperative selling.[20] Nevertheless, some *syndicats* were extremely successful. Usually they operated through licensed commercial agents, but it was not uncommon to contract with a single buyer for the members' entire

18 Publication or collection of such data were not required by law. A recent effort of a member of the staff of the *Société des agriculteurs de France* to secure the information by circularizing the *syndicats* met with negligible response and was abandoned.

19 Rocquigny, *op. cit.*, pp. 171, 175.

20 Marquis de Marcillac, *Les syndicats agricoles: leur action économique et sociale*, Paris, 1913, pp. 105-106.

crop, as in the case of certain *syndicats* of olive growers. Early in their existence the *syndicats* attempted to enter into trade relations with government agencies. The first of such transactions took place in 1887 when the war ministry contracted for 500 quintals of wheat with the *Syndicat des agriculteurs de l'Indre*.[21] This promising market was partially closed in 1890, however, by a decree of the Council of State which ruled that the *syndicats,* being non-commercial organizations not subject to trade licenses (*patentes*), had no right to submit bids, although they could act through licensed agents. The result of this ruling was to limit transactions between *syndicats* and government agencies to direct purchases by the latter.[22] In many instances profitable dealings occurred between different *syndicats*, through direct communication and advertising in *syndical* publications.[23]

Efforts were made to create business relations with the urban consumer's cooperatives. At the 1893 congress of the Union of Consumer's Cooperative Societies, several men prominent in the agricultural *syndical* movement, including Le Trésor de la Rocque and Kergall of the *Société des agriculteurs,* joined with representatives of the cooperatives in an attempt to make the alliance possible. A joint committee was formed, but the effort did not succeed. Despite the occurrence of occasional local transactions, the commercial mechanism of the *syndicats* had not been developed sufficiently for the urban cooperatives to make a regular practice of buying from them.[24]

Another important activity of the *syndicats* was the purchase of agricultural machinery which would otherwise have been unavailable to small farmers. These *syndicats d'industrie agri-*

21 Rocquigny, *op. cit.*, pp. 180, 185.

22 Rocquigny, *La coopération de production dans l'agriculture: syndicats et sociétés coopératives agricoles* (Mission de l'Office du travail), Paris, 1896, pp. 192-193.

23 Rocquigny, *Syndicats*, pp. 181-182.

24 *Ibid.*, pp. 183-184; J. Gaumont, *Histoire générale de la coopération en France*, 2 vols., Paris, 1923-1924, vol. II, pp. 192-194.

cole, which did not appear until some years after the passage of the law of 1884, usually operated in the following fashion. The *syndicat,* either by membership subscription or outside loan, bought and owned the equipment and rented it to its members. While there were the inevitable difficulties arising out of the brevity of harvest seasons and several members' desire to use the machinery at the same time, this practice undeniably brought great benefits to the peasants.[25] In a similar fashion, livestock breeding was improved by *syndical* purchase of registered animals. The opening of Stud-books, Herd-books, etc., aided the progress of animal husbandry.[26]

Credit and insurance ranked high among the interests of ahe *syndicats.* In 1852 the *Crédit foncier* had been established, but, belying the implications of its name, it expanded farm credit very little. In the period 1852-1895 the *Crédit foncier* lent a total of 780,077,564 francs on *rural* properties, as against 3,065,753,-864 on urban properties.[27] Further, since these loans consisted of long-term mortgages, they were of little assistance to farmers who needed money to buy livestock, seeds, or equipment.[28] In 1860 a bank, *Le crédit agricole,* was created with the object of furnishing credit to agriculture and affiliated industries by discounting local agricultural paper.[29] Unfortunately, this institution turned toward more promising fields: in 1873-1876 it lent 168 million francs to the Khedive of Egypt, and in 1876 its career ended, the *Crédit foncier* taking over its accounts.[30]

25 Marcillac, *op. cit.*, pp. 111-113; Augé-Laribé, *Évolution*, pp. 209-210.

26 Rocquigny, *Coopération*, pp. 60-61, 65-67.

27 Henri Lamane, "La dette hypothécaire en France," *Journal de la Société de statistique de Paris*, vol. XXXVI, 1895, p. 217.

28 Antoine Lecomte, *Les associations agricoles professionnelles et mutuels*, Paris, 1907, p. 163.

29 Henry Sagnier, *Le crédit agricole en France: ses origines, son essor, son avenir*, Paris, 1911, p. 5.

30 Louis Dop, *Le crédit agricole: le crédit foncier de France dans le rôle de banque centrale*, Paris, 1901, pp. 226 ff.

It was clear that large banks would not make credit available to the peasants. In 1882 the government unsuccessfully attempted to secure the passage of a bill creating small mutual-credit banks, but it remained for the *syndicats* effectively to start the extension of farm credit. In 1885 the *syndicat* of the arrondissement of Poligny formed a mutual-credit society in accordance with a law of 1867 on non-profit corporations. Commencing with a capital of 10,000 francs, soon increased to 17,000, its loans rose from 5,000 francs in 1885 to 127,000 in 1890, at rates first of 5% and then 4%, with no losses occurring. Loans were for ninety-day periods, several times renewable. Other *syndicats* followed this lead with great success.[31] In 1889 a committee headed by Jules Méline, deputy of the Vosges and Minister of Agriculture in 1883-1885,[32] and including the marquis de Dampierre, president of the *Société des agriculteurs de France*, drew up recommendations for legislation introduced in the Chamber by Méline in 1890, and which resulted in the law of 1894.[33] About 1893 a new type of farm-credit organization came into being in France, modeled after the Raffeisen banks which had been so successful in Germany. They took the name of *caisses Durand*, after their most active proponent, a Lyonnais lawyer.[34] In these societies loan funds were provided from the interest received, after initial capital had been raised by subscription. They were extremely conservative in policy, and members were mutually responsible for repayment of loans.[35] Many *syndicats* created *caisses Durand*, and indeed, some were themselves organized following the formation of these farm loan banks, which joined to form the Union of Rural and Workers'

31 Sagnier, *op. cit.*, pp. 8, 11, 13.

32 The Ministry of Agriculture was separated from that of Commerce and established independently in 1881 (Seignobos, *op. cit.*, p. 85). On Méline see below, ch. VI, especially notes 8, 9.

33 Sagnier, *op. cit.*, pp. 17-19. See Chapter VII below.

34 Rocquigny, *Syndicats*, p. 301; *Encyclopaedia of the Social Sciences*, vol. I, p. 533; vol. XIII, p. 70.

35 Sagnier, *op. cit.*, p. 14.

Banks in 1893.[36] In general, however, it must be said that farm credit was in its early stages at the time of the passage of the Tariff of 1892.

As we have seen, agricultural insurance had long been known in France,[37] but in the 1880's it began to develop rapidly, usually taking one of two forms. On the one hand, a group of farmers, ordinarily already united in a *syndicat,* could form a mutual-insurance society: on the other, by making collective arrangements with an established commercial-insurance company, the *syndicat* could secure sizable reductions in premiums.[38] In a field where spread of risk is of the highest importance, the latter form of insurance has naturally had the greater success. The *syndicat* usually acted as representative of the insurance company, receiving a major portion of the first year's premiums and from 5% to 10% of succeeding premiums as its compensation. Part of this money was used to pay for administrative costs, and the rest was returned to policy-holding members of the *syndicat.* Risks of fire, workmen's accidents, loss of livestock and damage from hail were covered in this fashion, which the leaders of the *syndical* movement considered preferable to the small independent mutuals. The latter were usually restricted to coverage of loss of livestock.[39]

The *syndicats* were extremely active in popularizing new farming techniques, and in general in providing agricultural education. They published bulletins containing practical and market information of value to the farmers. Some *syndicats* employed "professors of agriculture," and established laboratories and experimental fields in which solutions to members' problems might be developed. These technical experts chemically analyzed fertilizers and pest destroyers and visited members' farms to

36 Rocquigny, *op. cit.*, p. 302.

37 Above, p. 41.

38 Albert Blanchoin, *L'assurance mutuelle agricole: éssai sur l'assurance corporative*, Paris, 1935, pp. 20 ff.

39 Rocquigny, *op. cit.*, pp. 322 note 1, 325-326.

give them advice. Lectures, and contests with distributions of medals and cash prizes for the best field or animal, helped to spur the peasants to improvement. Lessons in practical agriculture had been introduced into the elementary schools in 1879, and in connection with these courses *syndical* leaders in Brittany established examinations, upon successful completion of which certificates and diplomas were issued. Given the reluctance to change, and the traditional character of French farming, the educational activities of the *syndicats* undoubtedly helped the peasants to learn new ways and improve their techniques.[40]

In addition to these services, the *syndicats* frequently engaged in social work for the benefit of members of their families. The leader in this regard was the *syndicat* of Belleville-sur-Saône, which at first limited itself to mutual protection against the costs of illness, and arranged for the division of a sick member's work among his colleagues. Later it provided for aid to orphans and aged by meeting the cost of their upkeep in the homes of farmers who were members of the *syndicat*.[41] Other *syndicats* organized old-age pension societies, based on equal contributions by participants and the *syndicat* itself, and which enjoyed state subsidies under a law of 1856. Ordinarily, however, it was difficult for peasants to contribute amounts sufficient to create adequate pension funds.[42]

The jurisdiction of the *syndicats* varied greatly. Some were limited to communes, others to cantons, some were departmental in scope. The *syndicats* were strong and numerous in Brittany, Burgundy, Anjou, Gascony and Provence, weakest in central France and Champagne.[43] In addition to the regular associations more or less local in character, there were several

40 Marcillac, *op. cit.*, pp. 173-182; Rocquigny, *op. cit.*, ch. X; Tisserand, *op. cit.*, vol. I, pp. 11-76.

41 Rocquigny, *Les syndicats agricoles et le socialisme agraire*, Paris, 1893, pp. 314-316 (hereafter referred to as *Syndicats ... et le socialisme*).

42 Rocquigny, *Syndicats*, pp. 358-359.

43 *Ibid.*, pp. 52-53; Hautefeuille's *Annuaire* for 1890 shows a wider distribution and greater strength in Normandy than credited by Rocquigny.

specialized *syndicats* operating throughout France. The most important of these was the *Syndicat central des agriculteurs de France,* formed in 1886 by the *Société des agriculteurs* to bring the advantages of its laboratory facilities, collective purchase, and market bulletins to members of adhering *syndicats* and to individuals in regions where the development of *syndicats* was as yet inadequate. Presidents of *syndicats, comices,* and prominent landowners were circularized and urged to support the new organization.[44] The *syndicat central* prospered, and in the period 1886-1900 averaged over four and one-half million francs annual gross business.[45] By 1891 among the other general *syndicats* were the *syndicat pomologique de France,* founded to aid apple growers and cider producers, the *syndicat général des sériculteurs de France,* formed in the interest of silk-worm producers, the *syndicat des éleveurs de chevaux en France,* etc.[46]

One organization active throughout the country is of especial interest to this study: the *syndicat économique agricole,* founded in 1889 by M. Kergall, an energetic member of the *Société des agriculteurs.* This organization made no sales, no purchases, conducted no research, and did not attempt to improve farming techniques. It was purely and avowedly a propaganda agency, formed to mobilize the peasants grouped in the *syndicats,* and based on the belief that "great movements of opinion do not occur of themselves," and that "the action of even a small group of resolute men succeeds in creating them." The *syndicat économique agricole* published at Paris a weekly paper, *La Démocratie rurale,* and an annual *Almanach de la démocratie rurale,* a small brochure which brought Kergall's propaganda

44 That is to say of *syndicats* belonging to the *Union centrale,* discussed below. The *Syndicat central* was formed because unions had no right to engage in commercial activities, p. 84, above; BSAF, vol. XVIII, 1886, pp. 503-509.

45 Hautefeuille, *op. cit.*, p. 965; Rocquigny, *op. cit.*, p. 118.

46 Rocquigny, *op. cit.*, pp. 128-132.

down to a very simple level.[47] Assisted principally by two deputies, the republican Flourens and the royalist vicomte de Lorgeril, and by M. Deusy, Kergall toured the country and enthusiastically carried his arguments to the *syndicats* and the farmers who belonged to them.[48] It was this organization, as we shall see, which was the keystone of the political campaign which contributed greatly to the passage of the Méline Tariff.

It is evident that the activities of the *syndicats* reached into most phases of the farmers' lives, and tended to make of their members, bound by many social and economic ties, closely knit groups which might be expected to stand together politically. It is equally clear, however, that some of their endeavors were bound to create hostility. In 1887 a court at Evreux condemned a *syndicat* which had been created to repair damages caused to crops and property by man or game, on the ground that this closely limited objective violated the law of 1884, which called for the defense of occupational interests in a broader sense.[49] In the following year the chemical products association of Paris accused the *syndicats* of operating for the benefit of individuals, rather than for general purposes, basing its argument on the decision of the Evreux tribunal; of being commercial organizations and therefore subject to the *patente;* and lastly of being illegal coalitions attempting to force down the prices of fertilizers.[50] With the approval of the Finance Minister, the Minister of Commerce, Pierre Legrand, answered these protests in a letter to the president of the Chamber of Commerce of Paris. He rejected the first and third complaints, saying that the law of 1884 would indeed be empty if it did not permit a *syndicat* to buy for its members. As to the allegation that they were commercial organizations which should be required to have com-

47 DR, December 8, 1889. The *Almanach* contains proverbs, homely wisdom and extremely frank propaganda.

48 For example, DR, May 10, 1891, November 30, 1890; see Rocquigny's comments on Kergall and his organization, *op. cit.*, pp. 120 ff.

49 CRSAF, vol. XX, 1888, p. 61.

50 *Ibid.*, p. 57.

mercial licenses, he ruled that they could be so considered only if they took middlemen's profits, or if the benefits of their operations were extended to non-members. The legal position of the *syndicats* was thus assured for the time, although further difficulties arose later.[51]

The *syndical* structure would have been incomplete without the organization of unions of *syndicats*, provided for by the law of 1884. While the individual *syndicat* would necessarily be closer to the peasants, the union would be closer to the agarian leadership. In 1886, accordingly, the council of the *Société des agriculteurs de France* decided to patronize a union of *syndicats*, which would be formed under conditions subject to its approval. It sent out a call for a meeting of presidents and secretaries of *syndicats* to take place in March 1886 at its headquarters in Paris. This congress, presided over by M. Deusy, resolved to form a union on the following bases:

1. It would not engage in politics.
2. It would not assist, directly or indirectly, any financial combination.
3. It would study what could legally be done under the law of March 21, 1884.
4. It would be understood that nothing would be done without the approval and patronage of the *Société des agriculteurs de France*.[52]

The first president of the *Union des syndicats des agriculteurs de France* was Henri Le Trésor de la Rocque, vice-president of the *Société des agriculteurs*, and at its founding the union comprised 74 *syndicats*. The following year its membership rose to 234 *syndicats*, to 340 in 1890, and it had reached 412 by 1891.[53]

51 BSAF, vol. XX, 1888, pp. 509-511.

52 BSAF, vol. XVIII, 1886, pp. 199, 329, 343.

53 Adrien Toussaint, *L'union centrale des syndicats agricoles, ses idées directrices*, Paris, 1920, pp. 42, 46. The *Syndicat central* was the companion organization of this union. See note 44; Hautefeuille, *op. cit.*, gives the figure of 357 for 1890.

This union, the " keystone of all the [*syndical*] organizations," was " imbued with the spirit of the *Société des agriculteurs de France,* and is a direct offspring of this great association." [54]

The formation of this organization, which soon became known as the *Union centrale* . . ., was the first major step in the grouping of *syndicats*. In 1887 M. Deusy took part in the organization of the Union of *Syndicats* of the Pas-de-Calais.[55] The Union of the *Syndicats* of the Southeast was founded in 1888, with headquarters at Lyon. It covered ten departments, from Saône-et-Loire on the north to Ardèche and Drôme on the south. Other unions, extending over nearly the entire country, had been formed by 1894,[56] and according to official figures the number of unions progressed as follows: [57] 1886, 2; 1887, 7; 1888-1891, 9; 1892, 14. General, departmental, and regional unions have been cited. There were, in addition, unions based on the provinces of the *ancien régime,* such as the Union of Agricultural *syndicats* of Normandy, founded in 1892. For reasons which will appear below these and the regional unions were far stronger than those which followed departmental boundaries. These different types of unions were not mutually exclusive: a *syndicat* belonging to the Union of Pas-de-Calais might also join the Union of the North and the *Union centrale*.[58]

While the unions were of course forbidden to engage in commercial activities, they were extremely effective agencies of the

54 Rocquigny, *Syndicats . . . et le socialisme*, p. 90.

55 BSAF, vol. XIX, 1897, pp. 275-276.

56 Launay, *op. cit.*, pp. 48-49. As with the *syndicats* themselves, statistics of unions must be taken with reservation, because some existed only on paper and others did not furnish accurate information on the number of adhering *syndicats*. *Ibid.*, p. 58.

57 *Enquête 1892*, tables, p. 436. There is no information available as to the total membership of *syndicats* affiliated with unions. This membership undoubtedly bears a higher ratio to the total number of *syndicats* than does the number of affiliated unions, for the strongest *syndicats* were most apt to join unions.

58 Launay, *op. cit.*, p. 53. Some regional unions had sub-unions. The Union of the South-east, for example, had ten such divisions.

syndical movement. They conducted research, and collected market data which were made available to affiliated *syndicats*. Their meetings were forums on economic and other " non-political " questions of interest to agriculture, and their publications carried their leaders' opinions into the peasants' homes. The unions were very active in stimulating the *syndicats* to extend their services to the farmers, and to provide credit and insurance. " The Union of the South-east had become a veritable ministry: its different services responded to all the needs of a rural population voluntarily subject to its authority." Above all, by their programs and resolutions, by their active lobbying with public officials, the unions served to give voice to the point of view of a seemingly united peasantry.[59]

This point of view, which animated the agricultural *syndical* movement and represented it before the country, was a compound of the associationist doctrines of Social Catholicism on the one hand, and of nationalist economics on the other (the latter, which resulted from the fusion of doctrines of state intervention with modern nationalism, will be discussed in Chapter IV). Social Catholicism, according to the late Professor Moon, stemmed from a reaction against economic liberalism, which moved many Catholic thinkers in the half-century following 1815. While these men disagreed in many social and political particulars, they shared in common a rejection of the chrematistic ethics of the dominant economic school. They looked back to the medieval gilds as examples of Christian equity, and forward to a reorganization of society along lines dictated by principles of Christian charity. Before the Second Empire two trends were in evidence. One was a tendency to unite social reform with political democracy, the other to couple Catholic social philosophy with political reaction. The June days of 1848 and the succeeding revulsion against a political democracy tinged with social reformism " left a deep impress upon the body

59 Comte L. de Vogüé, with the collaboration of Marius Pelud, *Émile Duport, la leçon de ses oeuvres*, Lyon, 1909, p. 75; Rocquigny, *Syndicats ... et le socialisme*, p. 64.

of ideas which was to form the heritage of the Social Catholic movement under the Third Republic." The movement began to take form in the years following the disaster at Sedan.[60] From the Belgian Périn and the engineer-sociologist Le Play,[61] it had inherited an emphasis on a Catholic social order, an opposition to both individualism and socialism; and from thinkers such as Ozanam and Lacordaire, its desire for social reform, which gained in significance as Social Catholicism became a practical, active force.[62]

Shortly after the end of the Franco-Prussian War, two army officers, comte Albert de Mun and marquis René de La Tour du-Pin, founded the *Oeuvre des cercles catholiques d'ouvriers,* in an effort to create by free association resistance to socialism among the workers. De Mun and his associates "at first worshipped a purely aristocratic ideal,—'the devotion of the governing class to the poorer classes.'"[63] Later, as practical reforms came increasingly to the fore, de Mun was attacked as a socialist, which he denied, although as a member of the Chamber of Deputies he frequently sympathized with the Left rather than with the economic liberals of the Center and Right.[64]

60 Parker Thomas Moon, *The Labor Problem and the Social Catholic Movement in France: a Study in the History of Social Politics,* New York, 1921, pp. 27-28, 38, ch. II.

61 Le Play's principal works are *Les ouvriers européens,* Paris, 1855, and *La réforme sociale en France,* Paris, 1864. Périn was a prolific writer, and the following are among his more important works: *Les lois de la société chrétienne,* 2 vols., Paris, 1875; *Le socialisme chrétien,* Paris, 1879; *Premiers principes d'économie politique,* Paris, 1875.

62 Moon, *op. cit.*, p. 318.

63 *Ibid.*, pp. 82 ff. La-Tour-du-Pin's leading work is *Vers un ordre social chrétien: jalons de route 1882-1907,* 5th ed., Paris, 1928, a collection of articles; de Mun's major work is *Ma vocation sociale,* Paris, 1908.

64 Moon, *op. cit.*, p. 181. Among the reforms advocated by de Mun and his followers were: freedom of organization (he wished the law of 1884 so to be modified as to favor mixed unions having a gild character); shorter work days, child-labor limitation, social insurance, arbitration of labor disputes, etc. *Ibid.*, pp. 101 ff.

After noting de Mun's denial of the allegation of socialism (CD, 1891, p. 2491), de Rocquigny remarks (*Syndicats ... et le socialisme,* p. 76, note 1):

Up to 1883 de Mun and his followers gave allegiance to the comte de Chambord, Legitimist pretender to the throne of France. At the latter's death in that year they turned to the Orléanist candidate, the comte de Paris, but this association was brief. In February 1892 Pope Leo XIII, in a letter to the clergy and Catholic laity of France, urged acceptance of the Republic. De Mun and his followers in the *Oeuvre des cercles catholiques* and the publication *l'Association catholique,* accepted this *ralliement* and pledged their loyalty to the Third Republic. Not all Catholics took this step, for the monarchist tradition was still strong. But royalist or *rallié,* Catholic social thinkers shared the belief in an economy ruled by justice rather than by irresponsible freedom, and in varying degrees of state intervention in social matters.

Three significant points in French Social Catholic doctrine should be noted. First, there is the opposition to materialistic socialism, even though many specific reforms were advocated by both movements. Social Catholics opposed the notion of class war, and believed instead in union of classes. Second, it was felt that when the Revolution destroyed the gilds, it left nothing but the anarchy of economic liberalism in their place, wherefore Social Catholicism believed in the adaptation of the governing principles of the medieval gilds to the modern scene. From this was logically derived the concept of professional or functional representation. Although, according to Moon, Le Play and some of his followers did not sympathize with this notion, they did believe strongly in *patronage,* benevolent action of capitalists and great landowners toward the lower classes. But de Mun had advocated professional representation as early as 1882, and the Catholic political party, the *Action libérale populaire,* made it an integral part of its later program. It was felt that gild or-

" Nevertheless, without applying to M. de Mun an appellation against which he has good reason to protest, many intelligent men reproach him with holding the interests of labor too much above those of capital, although they are equally respectable, and of speaking to the workers . . . too often of their rights, too rarely of their duties." De Mun was more sympathetic to labor-reform measures than either La-Tour-du-Pin or the agrarian *syndical* leaders.

ganization would provide a basis for true representation, where the farmer would be represented as a farmer, the merchant as a merchant, not merely as citizens living in a certain area. Alongside of the Chamber and Senate, or possibly replacing the latter, would sit a " gild congress." Third, the followers of both Le Play and de Mun advocated the revival of some degree of local autonomy, of regionalism, to limit what they considered the despotism of an over-centralized government. This point too found expression in the later programs of the *Action libérale populaire*.[65]

In general the anti-individualistic philosophy of Social Catholicism was a firm support of both association to promote group interest and of an interventionist policy which ignored the dethroned laws of liberal economics. It called for corporatism *within* the state, rising from the voluntary union of individuals, rather than the *corporate state*, imposed from above.

While writers on Social Catholicism tend to ignore the agricultural phase of its activity, its influence was very strong in this regard.[66] As early as 1879 the Association of Saint Fiacre, grouping truck farmers in the Paris region, had been formed by Maurice Maignen, a lay brother of the congregation of Saint Vincent de Paul, who had first interested de Mun and La Tour-du-Pin in social action.[67] This organization was later transformed into a *syndicat*. Within a few weeks of the enactment of the law of 1884, the *Association catholique* declared that while the law had been designed as an implement of class war, in the hands of the *Oeuvre des cercles catholiques* it might become an instrument of social peace. The development of *syndicats* and farm-credit banks under the leadership of prominent landowners was urged, to provide agricultural representation,

65 Moon, *op. cit.*, pp. 60, 101, 156, 166 ff., 276, 358, 394.

66 This is true of Moon's volume which is, of course, specifically related to labor problems, and of Georges Weill, *Histoire du catholicisme liberal 1828-1908*, Paris, 1909.

67 *La corporation: journal de l'oeuvre des cercles catholiques d'ouvriers*, October 15, 1892; Moon, *op. cit.*, p. 82.

save the peasants from usury, and create peace between classes in the countryside. Geoffroy de Grandmaison, chronicler of *l'Association catholique,* declared that the trend toward association "in the agricultural world favors us more than anyone else. . . ." [68] The following year a congress of Catholics of Normandy resolved that the "creation of Christian agricultural *syndicats,* already begun in Calvados and Orne, be supported and imitated by the Catholics of the other departments of Normandy." [69]

This position was approved by the section on social studies of the *Oeuvre,* headed by La Tour du Pin, "the apostle of the resurrection of the corporative idea in France," and including such prominent members of the *Société des agriculteurs* as the comte de la Bouillerie, Delalande, Milcent and de Gailhard-Bancel, all of whom were extremely active in promoting *syndicats.*[70] In many instances it was the local *cercle catholique* that took the initiative in forming a *syndicat.*[71]

The Church supported this activity. Abbé Noël declared that the priest should be the initiator of *syndicats,* and stated that his Bishop had ordered each country curé to found a *syndicat* in his parish.[72] Cardinal Rampolla, the Papal Secretary of State, transmitted the apostolic benediction to Louis Durand, the chief organizer of farm-credit banks. When a friend remarked that one "could not found rural banks without Heaven and confession," Durand replied "confess and form rural banks." [73]

68 AC, vol. XVII, 1884, I, pp. 482-483; vol. XVIII, 1884, II, p. 112; vol. XXI, 1886, I, p. 115.

69 *Ibid.*, vol. XXI, 1886, I, pp. 117-118.

70 Samuel de Lestapis, *Notions élémentaires d'organisation professionnelle agricole*, Paris, 1922, p. 4 and note 1.

71 AC, vol. XXII, 1886, II, p. 101; vol. XXVI, 1888, II, p. 238.

72 Abbé L. Noël, *Le syndicat agricole mixte paroissial: par un curé de campagne*, Arras, 1895, pp. 4-5.

73 Louis Durand, *Les caisses rurales, leurs origines, leur avenir: conférence faite . . . au congrès de l'Union catholique de la Gironde en 1895*, Bordeaux, 1896, pp. 18, 21.

By 1892 there were seventy-eight *syndicats* affiliated with the *Oeuvre des cercles catholiques,* and all of these were members of the *Union centrale.*[74] They differed from the ordinary *syndicat* only in their confessional character and a somewhat greater emphasis on social work.[75] The influence of Social Catholicism was not limited to these *syndicats,* however. The names cited above are evidence of its weight in the *syndical* movement. The Union of the South-east was first headed by a prominent Catholic, Gabriel de Saint-Victor. Louis Delalande was president of the Union of Normandy, and became head of the *Union centrale* on the death of Le Trésor de la Rocque. The comte de la Bouillerie was first president of the Union of the West.[76]

An extremely interesting event occurred in 1889. In that year the *Union centrale* invited all *syndicats,* affiliated and unaffiliated, to a congress at Paris, to be presided over by the marquis de Dampierre, president of the *Société des agriculteurs.* One of the leaders of the union remarked that it would be an excellent occasion to draw up the *cahiers* of demands and griefs of agriculture: " What was done in 1789 for the general interests of the country must be done for agriculture in 1889 . . .".[77] At the same time the *Oeuvre des cercles catholiques* arranged assemblies in eighteen of the old provinces of France to commemorate the meetings which preceded the Revolution.[78] In June 1889 all the assemblies united at Paris. Albert de Mun had condemned the *inorganisation* of society, the chaos and lack of social order: the centenary assembly voted resolutions calling for professional representation and decentralization and held that in agriculture both aims might to a great extent be accomplished by *syndicats* and their provincial unions. Further

74 *Corporation,* June 4, 1892.

75 Rocquigny, *Syndicats,* p. 144.

76 AC, vol. XXVIII, 1889, II, p. 64; Rocquigny, *op. cit.,* pp. 82, 87, 96.

77 *Bulletin de l'Union des syndicats et du syndicat central des agriculteurs de France,* December 16, 1888.

78 AC, vol. XXVIII, 1889, II, p. 42.

resolutions supporting other phases of the *syndical* program were passed, as we shall see later.[79]

Related to Social Catholicism in leadership and ideas, the agricultural *syndicats* set themselves clearly in opposition to the tradition of the Revolution of 1789. "The French Revolution, in destroying the old corporations, which for so many centuries had offered the generations of the past a guardian shelter, put nothing in their place. . . ." [80] The result, the *syndical* leaders felt, was that labor and peasants were delivered over to unbridled competition, that social chaos and economic crises weakened family and national ties, that belief in a class struggle developed. They knew, however, that a simple return to the *ancien régime* was out of the question. The once-protecting gilds had, during the eighteenth century, degenerated into "closed corporations, rigid guardians of obsolete privileges." [81] A large gap or "twilight zone" existed between the authority of the state and individual liberty. Was this sphere to be governed by individualism, "that is to say, by incoherence and weakness? It is here where free association intervenes, indispensable to group and coordinate individual efforts, and not less indispensable to resist . . . the encroachments of the state in a sphere which does not belong to it." [82] The two elements necessary to society, wrote Kergall, of the *Syndicat économique,* are individual liberty and governmental authority: the individualist school approves only the first, the *étatistes* only the second. Free association reaches a correct, modern solution by conciliating the opposition between these two principles.[83] Free professional

79 *Ibid.*, pp. 80-81; H. de Gailhard-Bancel, *Quinze années d'action syndicale*, Paris, 1900, p. 142; below, pp. 163-164.

80 Toussaint, *op. cit.*, p. 8.

81 A. Courtin, *Les congrès nationaux des syndicats agricoles*, Paris, 1900, p. 7.

82 Kergall, *Rapport sur la doctrine sociale des syndicats agricoles françaises* (presented to the International Congress of Sociology, Genoa, 1899), Paris, n. d., p. 9.

83 Kergall, *Du rôle social des syndicats agricoles*, Paris, 1897, p. 3.

association, which draws its inspiration from the encyclical *Rerum novarum*,[84] enables the sons of those who inaugurated the nineteenth century as the century of the rights of man, to usher in the twentieth century as that of the duties of man.[85]

> Let us use this marvelous instrument, unite our efforts in a common love of the fatherland, and under the eye of God, march resolutely toward social progress through agricultural *syndicats*. The future is theirs: association will save France from revolution.[86]

Some form of professional representation had long been demanded by leading agrarians. As early as 1868, in its first year, the *Société des agriculteurs* asked that the agricultural chambers created by Napoleon III be given life. Year after year the society renewed its demands, expanding them to include a hierarchy of representative assemblies to be elected by genuine *agriculteurs* in communes, cantons, and departments, with a central chamber at Paris.[87] On several occasions bills were introduced providing for systems of agricultural representation, but were opposed by the *Société des agriculteurs* because the assemblies were to include government appointees and representatives of farm laborers and were to be consulted only when the government chose to do so.[88] Before these legislative proposals developed, however, the possibilities of the *syndicats* had become evident. In 1885 a member of the *Société des agriculteurs de France* remarked: "Yesterday we demanded official representation; today the question has changed in character; it is genuine legal representation that the law [of 1884] authorizes." [89] As long as the chambers of agriculture have only a paper existence, the *syndicats,* created by free association,

84 Gailhard-Bancel, *Petit manuel pratique* . . . , 8th ed., Paris, 1908, p. 14.

85 Kergall, quoted in Rocquigny, *Syndicats . . . et le socialisme*, p. 101.

86 Émile Duport, Saint-Victor's successor as president of the Union of the South-east, in Vogüé, *op. cit.*, p. 364.

87 See above, p. 42. Luçay and Sénart, *op. cit.*, pp. 166 ff.

88 CRSAF, vol. XXII, 1890, pp. 70-71; vol. XXIII, 1891, pp. 681-683.

89 *Ibid.*, vol. XVII, 1885, p. 216.

> are genuine representative assemblies, more interested in defending the rights of citizens and in serving the interests of the country than in smoothing the passions and holding in check the rancor of parties.[90]

Indeed, this was felt to be truer representation than ordinary election based on territorial districts: ". . . if everyone votes no one is really represented. Only freemasonry." [91] The genuine interests of the farmers are represented in the agricultural *syndicats* and their unions.

In seeking decentralization through the medium of these unofficial assemblies, unions of agricultural *syndicats,* the leaders of the movement did not place faith in the departmental divisions of France. They felt that departments did not synchronize with economic areas, and, above all, they could not appeal to any of the basic devotions existing among men, since they were arbitrary and artificial administrative units, with no roots in the past. The old provinces, however, were of a different order:

> The provinces. At this word memories of race, customs, language, literature, of glorious history and autonomous local assemblies waken *en masse* in our spirit. . . . Profound, indestructible sympathies remain attached to this word, which recalls to us our origins, and how our ancestors, little by little, without losing their own peculiar genius, contributed to the creation of national unity.[92]

Thus it was that unions based on the provinces, or on economic regions, were created, although, as we have seen, this was no bar to the coexistence of departmental unions.

Socialism was the *bête noire* of the agricultural *syndicats,* as of the Social Catholics. Striking at property, small as well as

90 Gailhard-Bancel, *Quinze années*, p. 137; Rocquigny, *Syndicats . . . et le socialisme*, p. 47.

91 Gailhard-Bancel, *Les syndicats agricoles et l'union des classes* (address to the general assembly of the National Catholic Congress), Valence, 1898, p. 14.

92 Rocquigny, *op. cit.*, p. 72.

large, calling upon an authoritarian state to suppress liberty, denying God and country, it was regarded as the herald of a collectivist barbarism far worse than any that had been before.[93] Socialism was held to be the result of the individualist chaos, and free association must hold the front line and keep alive in the country the true France, the traditions which have made her great.[94] Let us build *syndicats* and we shall see "the terrible wave break at the foot of the dike we shall have erected, for we build it through love of country and with the aid of God." [95]

Socialism had already made significant gains among the industrial workers, and the *syndical* leaders feared that it might soon invade the countryside.[96] At the Havre congress of 1880 the socialists attacked small holdings as uneconomic and necessarily leading to exploitation, and in any event bound to disappear because of concentration of land ownership. In 1892, at Marseille, however, the socialist position was modified. In a program designed to appeal to farm laborers and small owners, specific reforms, including social insurance, minimum wages, etc. were proposed, but collectivization of land was not demanded. In 1894 the congress of Nantes declared that small peasant holdings would not be expropriated when the socialist state came into being.[97] There were, however, more concrete reasons for the landowners' fear of socialism. In the fall of 1891

93 Gailhard-Bancel, *Manuel*, pp. 7 ff.

94 Toussaint, *op. cit.*, p. 8.

95 Letter of Émile Duport, in Gailhard-Bancel, *op. cit.*, p. 10.

96 Some leading works in socialist agrarian doctrine are: Émile Vandervelde, *L'exode rurale et le retour aux champs*, 2nd ed., Paris, 1910; Michel Augé-Laribé, *Le problème agraire du socialisme* (vol. VII of *Bibliothèque socialiste internationale*), Paris, 1907; Karl Kautsky, *Die Agrarfrage: eine uebersicht über die tendenzen der modernen Landwirtschaft und die Agrarpolitik der Sozialdemokratie*, Stuttgart, 1899, translated into French by Camille Polack as *La politique agraire du parti socialiste* (vol. VI of *Bibliothèque socialiste internationale*), Paris, 1903; Jean Jaurès, *Oeuvres de Jean Jaurès: textes rassemblées, présentés et annotés par Max Bonnafous*, 8 vols., Paris, 1931-1937, vol. III, pp. 168-188, vol. VI, pp. 275-286.

97 Léon Blum, *Les congrès ouvriers et socialistes français*, 2 vols., Paris, 1901, vol. II, pp. 62, 136; Augé-Laribé, *Grande ou petite*, pp. 182 ff.

woodsmen in the department of the Cher struck for higher wages and better conditions. In 1892 a similar strike occurred in the department of the Nièvre, and by June of the latter year there was a congress of *syndicats des bûcherons,* (lumbermen's unions) composed of 23 *syndicats* with 3,893 members.[98] The comte de Rocquigny pointed out that these were regions of large landholdings, where an agricultural proletariat had come into being and where home crafts to supplement earnings had lost their value in the face of rising industrialization. The leaders of the *syndicats* stated the preservation of peasant land ownership as one of the principal aims.[99]

Syndical opposition to socialism focused on the class struggle concept. The leaders of the movement emphasized the difference between their organizations and the urban labor unions. Theirs were " an instrument of progress and social peace," the others " an arm of war against the employers." [100] Both sought improvement of the situation of the lower classes, but the agricultural *syndicats* would achieve this through cooperation of all social and economic ranks, while the labor unions vainly hoped for betterment through a victorious class war.[101] The reason for this difference was, they held, that from the very first great landowners joined the peasants in organizing the *syndicats.* De Marcillac recognizes the existence of another factor, however, which we must consider basic:

> To tell the truth, the situation in agriculture is different than in industry. There is nothing which can properly be called a *patronat* as distinct from an agricultural proletariat.[102]

There was little chance, it was felt, of union between urban and agricultural *syndicats,* for a member of one of the latter organ-

98 R. Garmy, *Histoire du mouvement syndical en France des origines à 1914,* Paris, 1933, p. 162, L. H. Roblin, *Les bûcherons du Cher et de la Nièvre: leurs syndicats,* Paris, 1903.

99 Rocquigny, *Syndicats . . . et le socialisme,* pp. 122, 137.

100 *Ibid.,* p. 8.

101 Lestapis, *op. cit.,* pp. 6, 7.

102 Marcillac, *op. cit.,* p. 26.

izations, who probably owned some land, had the leading proprietors of the district as fellow members, and could feel no animosity toward them.[103] There is much insistence on this mixed character of the *syndicats*.[104] They were open to landowners great and small, to sharecroppers, tenant farmers and day laborers. They worked for the good of all, and not for gains at the expense of any particular group. In this lay the guarantee of social peace.

The promoters of the *syndicats* keenly felt the responsibilities of the upper classes. H. de Gailhard-Bancel, one of the movement's leading spirits, condemned capitalism and at the same time vigorously defended property rights and the *patronat*. In making this distinction he declared that capitalism was the exaggeration of these institutions, " the deformation, the abuse which despoils their sacred character in making them materialistic, which weakens their rights in suppressing their duties." [105] In carrying out their social obligations, the great landowners should take the lead in forming and directing *syndicats*. Anyone could organize a *syndicat*, but for certain men it was a duty: ". . . the great agriculturalists, the squires, the wealthy or comfortably situated landowners who have the leisure and education, and who, by reason of wealth or family, hold an important position in their district." [106] The leaders of the *syndicats* were in fact recruited, for the most part, from this class: former statesmen and officers, great landowners, the old nobility, " sometimes possessors of the greatest titles in the heraldry of France. . . ." Others were of more modest origin, but the great majority " had a patrimony sufficient to permit them to busy themselves with social works without worrying about daily bread." [107] The ideal was one of benevolent interest and leader-

103 Rocquigny, *op. cit.*, p. 23.

104 Courtin, *op. cit.*, pp. 13-19; Rocquigny, *Syndicats*, pp. 37-38.

105 Gailhard-Bancel, *Quinze années*, p. 163.

106 Gailhard-Bancel, *Manuel*, p. 18.

107 Toussaint, *op. cit.*, pp. 22-24. See also Rocquigny, *Syndicats . . . et le socialisme*, p. 26, and Abbé Noël, *op. cit.*, pp. 77-78.

ship of the lower classes, of *patronage,* the intervention of those well placed in behalf of the less fortunate. In this way corporative societies, based on common professional interest, could be created. The spirit, if not the form, of the medieval gilds might be revived and the class war averted. This attitude is well illustrated by the following tale:

> I shall never forget the words spoken to me by a young peasant one day, when from the top of his hill he pointed out to me the roof of my home, which shone in the sun across the plain: " We like to see your château, it's our star."
>
> Oh! . . . will not the union of classes be almost accomplished, the social question itself nearly solved, the day when of all the châteaux, of all the homes a little higher and more luxurious, the peasants of France will say: " It's our star." [108]

Naturally enough, such were not the only considerations in the great landowners' desire to lead the *syndicats.* When the *Société des agriculteurs* was debating the formation of the *Union centrale,* Louis Milcent, prominent both as Social Catholic and *syndical* chieftain, declared:

> there are some *syndicats* whose spirit is excellent, others whose spirit might be detestable. There are some headed by professors of agriculture, functionaries, and from which the proprietors are excluded. We do not wish to join them, we wish the proprietors to be at the head of the institution. In a word, there must be guarantees.[109]

Especially in view of the upper-class origin of the *syndical* leaders, and of the fact that many of them were associated with anti-republican parties, it was to be expected that the political rôle of the *syndicats* would receive careful consideration. The Third Republic was not yet wholly secure in this period. True, royalism had received a definite check in the defeat of President MacMahon, but royalist sentiment was still very much alive,

108 Gailhard-Bancel, *Union,* p. 14.

109 CRSAF, Vol. XVIII, 1886, p. 518.

and Boulanger, attempting to inherit the Imperial mantle, had not yet been forced to flee.[110] It was natural, under these circumstances, that "politics" would be identified with the question of régime, rather than with particular governmental policies. Hence the Abbé Noël could both advise that candidates for elective political office be asked to subscribe to definite programs in advance of election day, and at the same time write that

> To make even the most critical spirits understand that the *syndicat* has no political aims in so doing, [the *syndicat*] might demand the following political declaration of the candidate: I swear to respect in my votes, acts and words the constitution which now rules the French people.[111]

M. Deusy declared that politics were forever banned from the movement.[112] The marquis de Marcillac, who expressed the views of the *Société des agriculteurs de France,* stated that

> at the door of the *syndical* house each should abandon his political preferences and ambitions and remember only the interests of the profession, which, in agriculture above all, are so closely linked with those of the country. . . .
>
> The agricultural *syndicats* especially can rally to no banner, can have none other than one flag: that of France.[113]

Nevertheless, a model *syndical* program presented as among the aims of the society the consideration and suggestion of legislative and other reforms, and their support before the public powers.[114] As long as they demanded no changes in the French constitutional régime, the *syndicats* felt free to intervene in what we should call politics, the election of popular representatives. The *syndicat* of Calvados stated the principle that the *syndicats*

110 Seignobos, *op. cit.*, pp. 20 ff., 117 ff.; Alexander Zévaès, *Histoire de la troisième république*, Paris, 1938, ch. VI.

111 Abbé Noël, *op. cit.*, pp. 69-71.

112 BSAF, vol. XVIII, 1886, p. 1059.

113 Marcillac, *op. cit.*, p. 215.

114 Rocquigny, *op. cit.*, pp. 12-13.

"have the right and duty to support only those candidates who are resolved to protect agriculture." [115] We shall see later how this was put into practice.

The social rôle of the *syndicats* was summarized by their leaders under several broad headings. First, there was the struggle against socialism, in which they were felt to be highly successful. Second, in the words addressed to the 1890 assembly of the *Oeuvre des cercles catholiques* by the president of the *syndicat* of the Manche, the aim of his organization was "the rapprochement of all classes of society which constitute the agricultural population," through the formation of true professional gilds or corporations.[116] Third, the furtherance of agrarian aims through political activity which stayed clear of "*la politique*" —the constitutional question.

Of the slogans used by the *syndicats* none was more popular than that invented by M. Kergall, head of the *Syndicat économique agricole*: rural democracy. "Thus far democracy has signified demagogy among us. Henceforth we shall know a new democracy, a conservative democracy—rural democracy." [117] The Revolutionary Assembly, he declared, had decreed equality, which meant the transfer of power to the mass of the people.

> But this mass was not ready to take power. The bourgeoisie alone was. So that the Revolution, made for the people, benefited only the bourgeoisie. An aristocracy, that of money, took the seat of power from another aristocracy, the landed aristocracy.[118]

115 *Ibid.*, p. 50, note 1. Kergall stated: "Politics is the chaff; the social question is the grain; politics is yesterday; the social question is tomorrow ...." *Ibid.*, p. 100.

116 DR, June 1, 1890.

117 CRSAF, vol. XXII, 1890, p. 220. Kergall adds: "It [rural democracy] is ... a new social force with which demagogy will have to reckon, by which demagogy will be conquered, as the foreigner was five hundred years ago by a child of the soil, by that great figure of rural democracy, ... by Jeanne d'Arc, liberator of the land."

118 DR, December 1, 1889.

Now, however, the people, the rural democracy, were organizing in *syndicats,* and would demand a new spirit and attitude in attacking the basic problems of polity—not the empty and formal questions of politics. It was in this spirit, and in the desire to remove the *syndicats* from the controversy over constitutional issues that Émile Duport, of the Union of the South-east, wrote that a *syndicat*

> Is liberty in association,
> Is fraternity in profession,
> Is equality in the struggle,
> So that one may fearlessly place at the pinnacle of the edifice that very beautiful trinity: Liberty, Fraternity, Equality.[119]

The agricultural *syndicats,* therefore, stated as their aims: economically, to promote the well-being of their members by common purchase and sale, instruction, technical equipment, insurance, credit, etc.: socially, to create unity in the country, to oppose concepts of class war: politically, to agitate for specific enactments favorable to agriculture, to exert pressure on officials, candidates and deputies, but to be neutral in matters of party politics. It may safely be said that the ideas and leaders of Social Catholicism were extremely influential in creating the agricultural *syndical* movement and in shaping and directing its course.

Michel Augé-Laribé severely criticizes the *syndical* attitude as expressed above. Political reactionaries, he says, attempt to profit by raising the menace of socialism: " to defend their own holdings, the great landed proprietors strive to enlist the small farmers, to form ' the rural party, organized and capable of mobilization.' " [120] In denying the implication that the *syndicats*

119 Émile Duport, *Les engrais et les syndicats agricoles* (address to the Congress of Vintners of the Vienne, November 1888), Lyon, 1888, p. 6. He changes the usual order of Liberty, Equality, Fraternity.

120 Augé-Laribé, *Évolution*, p. 79. Augé-Laribé is a distinguished agricultural economist of left republican tendency. He was, as of 1939, with the International Institute of Agriculture at Rome.

are tools in the hands of enemies of the Republic, de Rocquigny points to *syndical* neutrality in this regard, and to the fact that prominent republican political leaders are intimately connected with the movement, frequently as heads of *syndicats*.[121] This was undoubtedly true, but it was equally clear that the *syndicats* were associated with conservative groups and parties, with both landowning " Conservatives " and bourgeois " Moderates." [122] We can agree with Augé-Laribé's conclusion that whether they " believe or call themselves . . . whites, pinks, reds or scarlets, the agriculturalists are equally conservative and traditionalist."

Continuing, he questions the non-confessional and non-political character of the *syndicats*: if principles of religion and politics cannot be brought under discussion in *syndical* meetings, it is because they " are above all discussion, for if one does not share them one has only to refrain from entering the association." [123] As to the contention that they are instruments of social peace rather than of class struggle, he wisely remarks that it would indeed be difficult to deny that they are at least implements of defensive war, and concludes that in agriculture as in industry there is a state of armed peace. Augé-Laribé states that the social rôle of the *syndicats* has taken preeminence over the economic activities for which they had originally been created. He points to the humble aim of the first registered *syndicat*, collective purchase of fertilizer, and how far the *syndicats* have strayed from this objective.[124]

These criticisms, from a republican point of view, serve to make clear the position of the *syndicats* in French life in the 1880's and 1890's. Fully expressive of some of the leading traits of the times, the opposition to both socialism and unbridled liberal economy, the attempt to find fresh ways to circumvent new

121 Rocquigny, *Syndicats . . . et le socialisme*, p. 51.

122 Augé-Laribé, *Grande ou petite*, p. 169. For the background of parties and politics in this period see Seignobos, *op. cit.*; Zévaès, *op. cit.*

123 Augé-Laribé, *Syndicats et coopératives agricoles*, Paris, 1926, pp. 22-23, 38.

124 Augé-Laribé, *Évolution*, pp. 173, 266; *Syndicats*, pp. 30-33.

economic problems, the curious distinction between politics and "*la politique*," the agricultural *syndicats* were ready to declare themselves to the nation as the true representatives of French agriculture. In the words of the comte de Rocquigny,

> In the absence of official representation of agriculture, this attempt at professional representation has genuine influence, especially since it is supported and guided by the *Société des agriculteurs de France*.[125]

Organization and doctrines of free association were the practical and theoretical response of agrarian leadership to the social and economic developments that threatened the institutions so long enshrined in France. But these weapons were not in themselves sufficient: in a world of national states the state could not be ignored. Thus *syndical* organization went hand-in-hand with protectionism, and free association with nationalist economic theory.

125 Rocquigny, *op. cit.*, p. 64.

CHAPTER IV

NATIONALIST ECONOMIC THEORY

THERE is a theoretical element in all economic legislation. Sometimes this element is stated explicitly, either in the law itself or in the course of debate. More often it is denied; the legislation then pretends to be completely practical, to divorce itself from all theoretical considerations. In either case, however, the theory exists, forming part of the intellectual *milieu* in which the legislation arises. The Méline Tariff was presented as a practical solution to pressing economic problems. The men who framed it, however, were influenced by the traditional elements of nationalist economic theory, and employed this approach as an apology for the Tariff of 1892, and it is therefore to our interest to consider this type of economic thought. In the late nineteenth century the outstanding French exponent of nationalist economic theory was Paul-Louis Cauwès, professor and Dean of the Faculty of Law of the University of Paris. He is generally recognized to have been the first teacher of note to introduce non-orthodox economic theory into the French university world.[1] Morini-Comby, in

1 See Charles Gide, *Revue d'économie politique*, vol. XXXI, 1917, p. 165, and the eulogy of Cauwès by his successor as Dean, Larnaude, pp. 165 ff. Paul-Louis Cauwès (1843-1917) taught at Nancy from 1867 to 1873, and then till his retirement in 1913 was a member of the Faculty of Law of the University of Paris, serving as Dean, and Vice-President of the University Council from 1910. His great work, *Cours d'économie politique, contenant avec l'exposé des principes l'analyse des questions de législation économique*, 3rd ed., 4 vols., Paris, 1893, first appeared in 1878 as *Précis du cours d'économie politique professé à la faculté de droit de Paris*. See the article by W. Oualid in the *Encyclopaedia of the Social Sciences*; Clough, *op. cit.*, pp. 220, 221, 305 ff.; Gaëtan Pirou, *Les doctrines économiques en France depuis 1870*, Paris, 1925, pp. 183 ff. Compare the above cited flattering eulogy with the notice in the liberal *Journal des économistes*, 6th series, vol. LIV, 1917, p. 285: "M. Cauwès preached national economics to suit the protectionist politics of M. Méline. He was the favorite of official circles which were annoyed with the classical economists who... refused to renounce their doctrine. M. Cauwès was perfectly suited to this task."

his *Mercantilisme et protectionnisme*, speaks of him as the most scientific and the most influential nationalist economist,[2] and for the purposes of this study Cauwès may be regarded as the culminating statement of nationalist economic theory. His influence on subsequent thinkers, such as Lucien Brocard, does not concern us here.[3] Our interest in him arises from the fact that he provided a systematic theoretical background for the Méline Tariff. Although there were many protectionist writers in France at the time,[4] he was the leading scholar among them, and he and Méline, the principal author of the Tariff of 1892, were fellow officers of the *Société d'économie politique nationale*.[5]

Cauwès declares that " List and Carey formulated the theory of protection of national industry: I merely adhered to it, with certain modifications . . . "[6] But Cauwès did not have to introduce the basic tenets of List and Carey to France. If, through them, he brought to France an economic system based in part on American experience and German ambition, they, in turn,

2 J. Morini-Comby, *Mercantilisme et protectionnisme: essai sur les doctrines interventionnistes en politique commerciale du XVe au XIXe siècle*, Paris, 1930, p. 87 note.

3 *Principes d'économie nationale et internationale*, 3 vols., Paris, 1929-1931.

4 For example, Jules Domergue, *L'évangile de M. de Bismarck*, Paris, 1884, *La réforme économique* (pref. by Jules Méline) Paris, 1890, *La comédie libre-echangiste*, Paris, 1891. Domergue was editor of *La réforme économique*. Also Edmond Théry, *Les progrès économiques de la France: bilan du régime douanier de 1892* (pref. by P.-L. Cauwès), Paris, 1909. Théry, editor of *L'économiste européen*, was a prolific writer, but the work cited constitutes his considered judgment on protection.

5 The *Société d'économie politique nationale* was founded at Paris, December 10, 1897. Méline was honorary president, Cauwès president, Jules Domergue general secretary. Unfortunately the records of the organization have not been preserved. The society disbanded during the War of 1914-1918. M. Georges Domergue, the editor's son, an officer of the *Association de l'industrie et de l'agriculture françaises* (founded in 1893 by Méline) made a gracious but unavailing effort to secure the records for the author. Cauwès declared that the society's motto would be: *Par la science, pour la patrie!* Cauwès, " L'économie politique nationale," *Revue d'économie politique*, vol. XII, 1898, pp. 97 ff.

6 Cauwès, *Cours*, vol. I, p. xiv.

had been influenced by, and had approved of, French interventionist policy, and especially, Colbert's administration.[7] Cauwès' intellectual inheritance includes the long tradition of French mercantilism, and its golden era under Colbert; continuing interventionism in the eighteenth century and the First Empire, the Restoration and the July Monarchy; the writings of such men as Forbonnais, Cantillon, Ganilh, Ferrier, Louis Say, Cournot and Dupont-White.[8]

7 Henry Charles Carey, *Principles of Social Science*, 3 vols., Philadelphia, 1858-1859, vol. III, p. 111. Friedrich List, *National System of Political Economy*, S. S. Lloyd, trans., London, 1885, pp. 57-58.

8 François Véron-Duverger de Forbonnais (1722-1800), *Principes économiques* (1754) "Collection des principaux économistes," Paris, 1847. Richard Cantillon (ca. 1685-1734), *Essai sur la nature du commerce en général* (1755), H. Higgs, ed., London, 1931. Charles Ganilh (1758-1836), *Des systèmes d'économie politique*, 2 vols., Paris, 1809; *Théorie d'économie politique*, 2 vols., Paris, 1815; *Dictionnaire analytique d'économie politique*, Paris, 1826. F. L. A. Ferrier (1777-1861), *Du gouvernement considéré dans ses rapports avec le commerce* (1804), 3rd ed., Paris, 1822; *De l'enquéte commerciale*, Paris, 1829. Louis Say (1774-1840), *Principales causes de la richesse ou de la misère des peuples et des particuliers*, Paris, 1818; *Considérations sur l'industrie et la législation sous le rapport de leur influence sur la richesse des états et examen critique des principaux ouvrages qui ont paru sur l'économie politique*, Paris, 1822; *Traité élémentaire de la richesse individuelle et la richesse publique et éclaircissements sur les principales questions de l'économie politique*, Paris, 1827; *Etudes sur la richesse des nations et réfutation des principales erreurs en économie politique*, Paris, 1836. Antoine Augustin Cournot (1801-1877), *Recherches sur les principes mathématiques de la théorie des richesses* (1838), ed. by G. Lutfalla, Paris, 1938; *Principes de la théorie des richesses*, Paris, 1863; *Revue sommaire des doctrines économiques*, Paris, 1877. Charles Brook Dupont-White (1807-1878), *Essai sur les rélations du travail avec le capital*, Paris, 1846; *L'individu et l'état*, Paris, 1857, *La centralisation*, Paris, 1860. In addition we might mention Gaspard-Thémistocle Lestiboudois (1797-1876), *Economie pratique des natione*, Paris, 1847, and the American Daniel Raymond (1786-1849), *Elements of Political Economy*, 2 vols., Baltimore, 1823. See, in addition to Morini-Comby, *op. cit.*, and Clough, *op. cit.*: Georges Dionnet, *Le néomercantilisme au XVIIIe siècle et au début du XIXe siècle*, Paris, 1901; James W. Angell, *The Theory of International Prices, History, Criticism and Restatement*, Harvard Economic Studies, Vol. XXVIII, Cambridge, 1926, chaps. VIII-XI; A. Dubois, *Précis de l'histoire des doctrines économiques*, vol. I, Paris, 1903; R. Maunier, "Les économistes protectionnistes en France de 1815 à 1848," *Revue internationale de sociologie*, vol. XIX, pp. 485 ff.

For all these writers (and many others, including Cauwès) the basic, underlying influence was the historical tradition of French mercantilism. Mercantilism was not, of course, the creation of any particular theorist or statesman. It is a name applied *a posteriori* to a series of economic policies practiced by many European states from the sixteenth to the eighteenth century. Antedating the rationalist current of the Enlightenment, mercantilism was not based on assumptions of all-embracing natural laws. It consisted in the adoption of specific practices to achieve desired ends. Mercantilism had arisen from the assumption, by the dynastic, national state, of powers previously exercised by local authorities. It was both the economic expression of the desire for national unity and power and an important means of achieving these ends. Given this heritage and this definition, by political authority, of the rôle of economic activity, the basic postulate of mercantilism was, necessarily, the justice and propriety of state intervention in economic affairs. Recognizing the nation as an economic entity, mercantilist writers and administrators held that it was the duty of government to stimulate and guide endeavors beneficial to the nation, and to discourage and prevent practices considered harmful.[9]

Differences among nations meant different standards of economic good. Mercantilist aims and policies therefore varied from country to country, and Professor C. W. Cole justly defines French mercantilism as

> that group of theories, policies and practises, arising from the traditions of the country and the conditions of the time, and upheld and applied by Jean-Baptiste Colbert during his years in office, 1661-83, in his effort to secure for the nation, and for the king who symbolized it, power, wealth and prosperity.[10]

9 For general studies of mercantilism see: Morini-Comby, *op. cit.*; J. W. Horrocks, *A Short History of Mercantilism*, London, 1925; Eli F. Heckscher, *Mercantilism*, 2 vols., London, 1935; René Gonnard, *Histoire des doctrines économiques: doctrines antérieures à Quesnay*, Paris, 1928; Dubois, *op. cit.*

10 C. W. Cole, *Colbert and a Century of French Mercantilism*, 2 vols., New York, 1939, vol. II, p. 558. See also, by the same author, *French Mer-*

We must remember that a general statement of Colbert's thought is really a deduction from the whole of his works and policies. He carried out no program elaborated prior to his accession to power, but rather inherited a tradition of intervention and control that stretched back into the Middle Ages, and, on the whole, proceeded from previously established precedents. His great achievement was to introduce order, harmony and effectiveness into the pattern of French mercantilism.

Colbert's aim was to make France rich and powerful. On both accounts he accepted a bullionist policy. It was not that he believed that precious metals could substitute for all other forms of wealth. In his day gold and silver were, more than ever before or since, the sinews of war, and the most liquid of assets, commodities for which the demand was unfailing. In a period in which credit facilities had not reached full development, the gathering and retention within a country of stocks of bullion seemed necessary for financial stability, the collection of taxes, the maintenance of economic activity, and national defense or aggrandizement. Another belief basic to the development of Colbert's policies was the view that the amount of wealth and trade in the world was more or less fixed, and that one nation could increase its share only at the expense of its rivals.

The first of these beliefs indicated the direction of French mercantilist policy, the second gave it its belligerent, aggressive character. In the absence of gold or silver mines in France or in the colonies, the nation could obtain bullion only through a favorable balance of trade. The expansion of national manufactures, and the export of their products, were positive means toward this end. Subsidies and regulations were employed to promote industries and insure quality. The rôle of protection

cantilist Doctrines before Colbert, New York, 1931; P. Boissonade, *Colbert, le triomphe de l'étatisme, la fondation de la suprématie industrielle de la France, la dictature de travail (1661-1683)*, Paris, 1932; P. Harsin, *Les doctrines monétaires et financières en France du XVIe au XVIIIe siècles*, Paris, 1928.

was to facilitate the functioning of this policy. Protective duties would prevent the foreigner from underselling home manufactures in France, and the consequent export of bullion. At the same time, the importation of raw or semi-finished materials would not be impeded, so that French industries would be adequately supplied.

The home market was not neglected. Colbert won at least partial success in improving internal communications and introducing a degree of system and order into tariffs, the law and commercial procedure: all tending to increase commerce within the nation. Nor was agriculture ignored, as has often been said, but it was less affected by Colbertian administration than commerce and industry. The rôle of agriculture was to make the nation self-sufficient with regard to foodstuffs, and to contribute to the stock of raw materials required by industry. Agriculture was less in need of stimulation and direction than the newer types of enterprise, but where, as in the case of horse-breeding, it seemed profitable to intervene, Colbert was quick to do so. Agriculture was thus an important, if unspectacular, combatant arm of seventeenth century French mercantilism.

Colbertian mercantilism had little fixed doctrine. What was constant was the concept of national welfare as the standard by which policies were to be judged. Short run individual interest frequently conflicted with long run national interest, and with its component, economic justice. Colbert therefore fostered the institution of gilds, collective entities more easily controlled than the individuals who composed them. Measures to prevent idleness on the one hand, and exploitation of workers and apprentices on the other hand, were included in this all-pervading complex of stimulation and regulation by a paternalistic state.

We have said that the belief that the world's wealth was more or less fixed gave Colbertian mercantilism its aggressive characteristics, and made supremacy rather than security among nations its goal. This does not imply that all the wars of Louis

XIV were waged for mercantilist ends. Colbert was too keen an observer to be unaware of the costs and risks of war, and only the Franco-Dutch struggle can be said to have fitted into his general program for the French state. The fighting character of mercantilism is, however, one point of differentiation from later French nationalist economic systems, which, as we shall see, emphasized security. Another extremely important distinction is that under the *ancien régime* economic considerations and interests were usually subordinated to political ends, whereas French economic policy following the Restoration, like British mercantilism after 1650, was the program of certain economic groups among the population. A third significant difference lay in the rôles assigned to bullionism and productivity. Mercantilism, combative and pragmatic, placed bullionism in the forefront, as the keystone of power economics, and the development of productive capacity in the background, as necessary to the accumulation of bullion, though also valuable in itself. The productivity concept became dominant in nationalist economics in the course of the nineteenth century. Lastly, it is worth noting that whereas a systematic doctrine of mercantilism can only be formulated *a posteriori*, and artificially, from scattered writings, policies and practices, nationalist economics became strikingly different in tone and character as it was given ever more formal theoretical expression.

This change was one aspect of the application of the rationalist scientific thought of the eighteenth century to the social studies. Mercantilism came under the attack of the Enlightenment, first in the thrusts of such men as Boisguilbert, Petty and Mandeville, then under the hammer blows of the Physiocrats, Hume and Adam Smith.[11] But the interventionist and nationalist stream continued to flow in the midst of the growing fervor for *laissez-faire* and natural law.

New ideas were developed, especially in the field of monetary and balance of trade theory, by such men as Law, Cantillon

11 See Dubois, *op. cit.*; C. Gide and C. Rist, *A History of Economic Doctrines from the Time of the Physiocrats to the Present Day*, R. Richards, trans., London, 1915; E. A. J. Johnson, *Predecessors of Adam Smith: The Growth of British Economic Thought*, New York, 1937.

and Forbonnais, perhaps the outstanding French mercantilist writer of the eighteenth century.[12] They worked free from the contradiction in mercantilist theory, the acceptance of the quantity theory on the one hand and advocacy of accumulation of bullion on the other.[13] Law turned from the doctrine of the favorable balance of trade, and held that an increase in the medium of exchange would produce prosperous business conditions.[14] Cantillon argued that a country should have net imports of products on which little labor has been expended, and net exports of products the greater proportion of whose value has been contributed by labor. For a time bullion will be imported, and may be accumulated and stored in the period preceding an adjustment of prices to a higher level and the consequent end of bullion imports. Thus he suggested a business cycle concept, and argued that if part of the accumulated bullion were retained, by wise intervention on the part of the state, each prosperity phase would reach a higher level than the one preceding.[15] Cantillon modified the crude bullionism of earlier mercantilism, but while he traveled a good part of the road which led Hume to liberalism, he turned, at the fork, to reconciliation with the traditional system. Similarly, but in a more closely reasoned and systematic fashion, Forbonnais steered between the extremes of bullionism and the absolute equation of money with all other goods. He did not believe the precious metals had any intrinsic superiority over other commodities, nor did he favor their accumulation, but he did argue that the transition from a smaller to a larger quantity in circulation had a stimulating effect on the economy, and that the consequent increased production prevented a rise in prices.[16]

12 Morini-Comby, *op. cit.*, pp. 80–81, denies that criticism of mercantilist practices by some of these writers should lead one to list them among early advocates of *laisses-faire*.

13 Angell, *op. cit.*, p. 211.

14 Dubois, *op. cit.*, p. 318.

15 Cantillon, *op. cit.*, pp. 181 ff.

16 Forbonnais, *op. cit.*, pp. 222 ff.

While Cantillon and Forbonnais protested against unnecessary and burdensome restrictions on business, they were questioning the execution of the policy of intervention, rather than the right of intervention itself. In short, they represent a more mature phase of mercantilist thought, reflecting the economic advances and institutional changes which had occurred between Colbert's day and theirs. They gave greater prominence than did seventeenth century mercantilists to the concept of productive capacity, but they followed their predecessors in accepting the right of the state to guide national economic development. They insisted on the distinction between national and private interest which was basic to the nationalist economics of the nineteenth century.[17]

The temporary triumph of rationalist political concepts in the Revolution did not produce a corresponding reaction in the field of economics. The Revolution most closely approached economic liberalism in sweeping away internal tariffs and in destroying the gild organization. But this was part of the process of transfer of control of public policy from the paternalistic state to private groups, a development that had risen in England from the Puritan Revolution over a century before. The French revolutionary state followed the nationalist policy of colonial assimilation, as we have seen. It employed protective tariffs, controlled prices, dispensed relief, and, as it developed from one phase of the Revolution to the next, became more powerful and more centralized. In the face of the liberal intellectual current, interventionism continued to exist. And under the First Empire it was carried to a higher degree of perfection.[18]

But the main current of economic thought ran strongly counter to the interventionist tradition. The English school gained predominance. In its hands and in those of its French

17 Discussed later in this chapter. They accept, with modifications, the mercantilist belief in qualitative differences among industries.

18 Clough, *op. cit.*, ch. II; Eli F. Heckscher, *The Continental System, An Economic Interpretation*, Oxford, 1922, intro.

followers, such as J. B. Say, economics grew into a formal study. All divergent theories were, to a greater or lesser degree, attacks upon it, and, perhaps unwillingly, followed its patterns and employed at least some of its terminology. Nationalist economics became one of a number of competing formal systems of theory. Because of its heterodoxy, however, this kind of doctrine at first found its proponents largely among pamphleteers and businessmen. Of the many who wrote in this vein some few achieved a prominence sufficient to cause their inclusion in histories of economic thought—the leading figures of a cadet line.[19]

Among them was F. L. A. Ferrier, Director-General of Customs under Napoleon from 1812 to 1815, whose principal work, first published in 1804, reached a third edition in 1822, conveniently marking the transition from Empire to Restoration and the continuity of economic thought at the time.[20] Ferrier felt the influence of English doctrine, but made no effort to compromise with it.[21] He condemned classical economics as thoroughly unrealistic, remarking that it disregarded national differences and that it was a speculative study that treated "men and peoples otherwise than God made them." [22] Ferrier hoped to achieve a practical analysis.

Starting with the nation as the unit in which economic activities take place, he held that a nation can be happy and prosperous only if it is independent, that independence rests upon power, and power upon wealth. Land is the first and basic source of wealth, agriculture and industry its creators. These the government must encourage, and maintain in balance with each other.[23] But he did not proceed, as one might have expected, to consider commodities exchangeable against specie of equal utility with precious metals. Because it can speed trans-

19 See Maunier, *op. cit.*

20 Ferrier, *Du gouvernement considéré dans ses rapports avec le commerce.*

21 Compare the tenor of his works with those of Ganilh, note 8 above.

22 Ferrier, *op. cit.*, pp. xix, xxvi, xxxvi.

23 *Ibid.*, pp. 3-10.

actions, be transferred more often in a given period of time, money in the form of precious metals was to be considered apart, as a good in itself.[24] Ferrier declared that the basic principles of his work were:

> 1. Bullion capital is the most precious of capitals, for it contributes to the creation and support of all the others.
> 2. A nation is always right in seeking to produce at home what it consumes.[25]

National policy, declared Ferrier, should therefore be directed toward increasing the national stock of specie, and toward self-sufficiency, and in deciding that policy he considered it necessary to distinguish between public and private interest. In domestic production and foreign and internal trade, he wrote, private interest may counter general welfare. It might pay a private capitalist to import cloth from England, but what harm this would do to French industry! [26] It was therefore the government's duty to balance, and, where necessary, override private interests.

Ferrier left no doubt as to the type of national policy he favored. He was an ardent admirer of Colbert, and in the main his proposals were the traditional tenets of French mercantilism.[27] It was the state's obligation to prescribe and enforce standards of quality so that French goods would always have the reputation of being best and uniform. Raw or semi-finished materials should be worked at home, and money should not be exported in exchange for goods other than raw materials. Otherwise specie would be drained from the country, and with the means of circulation gone, industry and trade would stifle.[28] " It is not the conquest of our neighbors' bullion that I desire," he wrote,

24 *Ibid.*, pp. 26, 108, 145.

25 *Ibid.*, p. 429.

26 *Ibid.*, pp. 301-308.

27 *Ibid.*, p. 503 note.

28 *Ibid.*, pp. 285 ff.

> I only ask that our own be conserved, and not in the least because of what it is worth, but because of the service it renders, as the mainspring of labor.[29]

This modified bullionism went hand in hand with a belief in a favorable balance of trade. Ferrier did not refute the Hume-Ricardo thesis that in the long run favorable or unfavorable balances cannot be maintained. He merely reiterated that a net export of specie was disadvantageous because, if continued for any length of time, it would make the nation dependent on rivals.

Hence Ferrier was a protectionist. The state, that good parent, must see to it that its children buy wisely, and build their resources. Tariffs should be only for protection, if possible, for revenue tariffs are barriers to trade! Ferrier ignored Adam Smith's argument that subsidies divert capital from its natural paths. He heartily approved this and other types of artificial stimulation, for the overriding consideration was the maintenance and expansion of the nation's productive capacity. "The protection which the government owes commerce in general reduces itself to a single point: the encouragement of production." [30] A balanced economy is essential, held Ferrier, and agriculture is aided by encouragements given to industry, because of greater demand for raw materials and for food for increased numbers of workers. Ferrier believed that domestic business was the basis and fundamental part of the national economy. The nation should strive

> to manufacture at home the greatest possible number of the things she consumes... the true domain [of foreign trade] is the exchange of products which cannot be made or grown with equal facility everywhere, because the soil or climate is unsuited, or for any other reason... [31]

29 *Ibid.*, p. 482; Dionnet, op. cit., pp. 117 ff.

30 Ferrier, *op. cit.*, p. 272.

31 *Ibid.*, pp. 268, 559.

If we maintain this kind of commerce we may hope for peace, he declared, any other "divides peoples more than it brings them together; it causes more wars than it prevents." [32]

Ferrier was defending the traditional system (in his own phrase "*l'administration commerciale*") against the attacks of the British economists and their followers. But in at least one important aspect he differed from Colbert. His was no longer an aggressive spirit, ready to overturn nations and battle steadily to raise France to the highest position among them. He hoped for and believed in national progress and increased greatness, but above all he wished to defend France's existing position, to prevent her from becoming, he said, a mere market for British goods.[33] His was not a "fighting doctrine," it was rather a doctrine of security. This note, the spirit of security, is a recurring one in French life and thought, and a source of both strength and weakness to modern France. While later nationalist thinkers advanced beyond him, while many of his tenets were modified, and others rejected outright, Ferrier typifies the underlying, conservative, almost instinctive interventionism and protectionism of numerous French statesmen and politicians of the late nineteenth and twentieth centuries. He is part of the long tradition of French nationalist economic policy, one expression of which is the subject of this study.

There were many others who wrote in a similar vein, but agreement on basic principles and attitudes more than outweighs differences in detail, and makes it unnecessary to do more than mention their names: Ganilh, Louis Say and Chaptal at the time of the Restoration; Lestiboudois and Mathieu de Dombasle during the July Monarchy. Ganilh, for example, differed from Ferrier in saying that foreign trade was more fruitful than domestic, since the latter merely maintained existing wealth without adding to it. Louis Say criticized both simple bullionism and the classical balance of trade doctrine, and argued that advantage in foreign trade must be measured by the

32 *Ibid.*, p. 561.

33 *Loc. cit.*

intrinsic utility of goods given and received. Lestiboudois was moved as much by the ordinary sentiments of nationalism as by economic considerations. But all three arrived at conclusions close to Ferrier's in all essentials, and with minor variations wrote in the spirit of the modified mercantilism which he expressed.[34] They were concerned with the place of the nation in the family of nations, and said little of the rôle of the state within the nation. Charles Brook Dupont-White, French despite his name, studied internal social problems, and concluded that it was the basic duty of the state to intervene, in the interest of justice, in the struggle between profits and salaries. This was his major concern, and it was in pursuing it that he accepted protectionism, although he opposed agricultural tariffs as creating a monopoly injurious to labor.[35] Augustin Cournot, who was among the first to develop a mathematical analysis of economics, reached a closely reasoned protectionist position for many particular cases, and advanced the productivity concept. His works, however, were in the realm of pure theory rather than mundane economic policy.[36] And if the anti-individualism of Dupont-White, and the brilliant, precise protectionist thinking of Augustin Cournot left the even course of French academic economists unruffled and undisturbed, they contributed something to the intellectual background of Paul Cauwès.[37]

From the empirical economics of Colbert, French interventionist and protectionist thought became more explicit and formal as economics developed into a discipline, and as writers sought to defend traditional practices (adapted to new political and social situations as mercantilism was an adaptation of medieval regulation to the needs of the dynastic state) against the predominant English school. Cauwès climaxed the development from dynastic mercantilism into the nationalist economics

34 Ganilh, *Théorie*, vol. II, p. 468; Louis Say, *Considérations sur l'industrie*, pp. 370 ff.; Lestiboudois, *Economie pratiquue*, pp. 40 ff.

35 Dupont-White, *Rélations du travail avec le capital*, pp. 190 ff., 235 ff.

36 This is especially true of his *Recherches*.

37 See Cauwès, *Cours*, vol. IV, p. 591; Brocard, *op. cit.*, vol. I, pp. 27 ff.

of the modern state, drawing on the living tradition of France as well as on the German List and the American Carey.

Like the latter, whom with rare frankness he calls his masters, Cauwès establishes his doctrine by means of an historical approach. But he is a better historian than either List or Carey. While the first book of List's major work was a series of sketches of the economic history of various nations. List did not study economic history in the hope of discovering some canon of interpretation. In the words of a recent French biographer and student of List, he is a poor historian who "looks upon the phenomena of history through the distorting lenses of doctrine."[38] Carey's works are replete with historical references, but he did not seek, in historical study, light on economic problems of the present. Carey drew examples from the past to support his theories or refute the beliefs of others.[39] To

38 Maurice Bouvier-Ajam, *Frédéric List, sa vie, son oeuvre, son influence*, Paris, 1938, p. 119. Friedrich List (1789-1846); his principal works in the field of economic thought are: *Outlines of American Political Economy*, Philadelphia, 1827, and the *National System of Political Economy*, first published at Stuttgart in 1841, translated by S. S. Lloyd, London, 1885. His collected works appear in *Schriften, Reden, Briefe*, ed. by E. von Beckerath *et al.*, 10 vols., Berlin, 1927-1935. Margaret E. Hirst, *Life of Friedrich List and Selections from his Writings*, New York, London, 1909, contains the *Outlines* and the *Introduction to the National System*, which does not appear in the English translation. See also Arthur Sommer, *Friedrich Lists System der politischen Okonomie*, Jena, 1927.

39 Henry Charles Carey (1793-1879); principal works: *Principles of Political Economy*, 3 vols., Philadelphia, 1837-1840; *The Past, the Present and the Future*, Philadelphia, 1848; *Harmony of Interests, Agricultural, Manufacturing and Commercial*, Philadelphia, 1850; *Principles of Social Science*, 3 vols., Philadelphia, 1858-1859; *The Unity of Law as Exhibited in the Relations of Physical, Social, Mental and Moral Science*, Philadelphia, 1872. On his early views see his *Principles of Political Economy*. See also, J. W. Jenks, *Henry C. Carey als Nationalökonom*, Jena, 1885; A. D. H. Kaplan, *Henry Charles Carey, a Study in American Economic Thought*, Baltimore, 1931, Johns Hopkins University Studies . . . series XLIX, no. 4; Ernest Teilhac, *Pioneers of American Economic Thought in the Nineteenth Century*, E. A. J. Johnson, trans., New York, 1936; C. H. Levermore, "Henry C. Carey and his Social System," *Political Science Quarterly*, vol. V, 1890, pp. 553 ff.; Teilhac, "H. C. Carey," *Revue d'histoire économique et sociale*, vol. XIII, 1925, pp. 418 ff.

Cauwès, however, history is not merely a source of supporting evidence for an *a priori* belief, nor is it a plastic to be shaped into a neat curve of evolutionary progression, as in the case of List's theory of evolutionary development.[40] According to Cauwès the method of economics is threefold: 1. direct observation and statistical analysis of contemporary phenomena, in the spirit of the comparative studies of the anthropologist; 2. historical analysis, with a view to understanding the order of social development, to determining what element of the present are relics of the past, to delineating the forces of certain traditions, so that theory may avoid running counter to them; 3. legislative experimentation. Cauwès denies that these methods lead merely to arid collections of facts. In the first place, all these studies involve a process of selection, which in itself carries meaning, and in the second place, speculation is not forbidden. Generalization is permissible, provided that it proceeds from, and is kept within the limits of observation.[41]

Economics, he declares, is not a science for its own sake. Its purpose is to enlighten men that they may better regulate economic life, its aim " individual well-being and collective prosperity through the means of an equitable division of services and riches."[42] Cauwès defines economics as the science of utility, which is the power of satisfying human needs.[43] Utility may be measured approximately, he writes, but there are as many ways of estimating it as there are theories of value. The value of a commodity to an individual may be considered in terms of its marginal utility, or in terms of its worth in exchange. The former is general, the latter applicable only to commerce. Both these definitions refer to individual wealth, that is, to utilities which have been appropriated by individuals.[44] To

40 List, *Introduction*, in Hirst, *op. cit.*, p. 303; Cauwès, *Cours*, vol. I, p. 83.

41 Cauwès, *op. cit.*, pp. 57 ff.; " Economie politique," pp. 99, 100.

42 Cauwès, *Cours*, vol. I, pp. 7, 64.

43 *Ibid.*, p. 260.

44 *Ibid.*, pp. 257-258.

this point Cauwès has made no sharp departure from either the form or content of orthodox economics. He accepts English theory in yet another significant aspect. It is an undeniable fact, he says,

> that the quantity of work available is measured by the available capital and revenue. A government can doubtless divert . . . labor by favoring one industry to the detriment of others, but, in principle, the sum total of labor cannot be increased indefinitely.[45]

It is Cauwès' social attitude that leads him to break sharply with economic liberalism. Unlike List, who was primarily inspired by a strong sense of German nationalism,[46] Cauwès is above all moved by his belief in justice as the criterion of economic good. Economics and ethics are closely related, he declares, and pure materialism, the *chrematistic ethic,* should find no place in economic thought. Carey had questioned

> the value of an analytical process that selects only the 'material parts' of man — those which are common to himself and the beast—and excludes those which are common to the angels and himself?[47]

Similarly, Cauwès writes that materialism " fixes attention on things considered as quantities, instead of on man."[48] Hence he turns to the nation, as the legal expression of the common good of men. But why merely the nation? Why not mankind? Because nations exist and struggle, the dream of perpetual peace remains a dream.[49]

In keeping with the tradition of French interventionist economics, Cauwès holds that individual and national wealth are

45 *Ibid.*, p. 162.

46 List, *National System*, pp. xl, 27-28; for his definition of a nation, *Outlines*, in Hirst, *op. cit.*, p. 162.

47 Carey, *Social Science*, vol. I, p. 31.

48 Cauwès, *Cours*, vol. I, pp. 8, 37.

49 *Ibid.*, pp. 134, 147.

different concepts. The former is measurable in terms of individual marginal utility or of exchange value. But scarcity is an element common to both standards. It is evident that the individual will attach greater value to a pair of shoes when shoes are scarce, and their exchange value too will be higher when they are not abundant. The nation, on the other hand, profits through plenty and loses through want.[50] In addition to the difference between national and individual interests, there are those between nations, and it is another error of the classical economists to ignore this fact.[51]

His belief in justice, rather than profits, as the criterion of social good brings Cauwès to question the worth of competition as the directing force of economic development. When the participants are unequal competition merely leads to enslavement, it stimulates only those who can enter the race with a good chance of success. Hence competition must be limited and regulated, either by law or by free association.[52] Since competition is adequate neither as a stimulant nor as a regulatory mechanism, another spark and another governor must be sought for the economic dynamo. Free association and government can fulfill these functions. Cauwès presents a broad picture of the state's rôle in economic life.

> 1. The state has functions relative to public order.... These are its essential attributes; 2. but the state is not a passive organ, ' it is its duty to be the active and intelligent promoter of public betterment.' The state is a lever for social progress, and from this concept derive the optional attributes of public authority; 3. the state is a national power; it personifies the solidarity of social forces. It is not a necessary evil, but an element indispensable to civilization; 4. between the state and the individual there is not antagonissm but cooperation: individual forces develop by virtue of the order created by the

50 *Ibid.*, p. 267.

51 *Ibid.*, pp. 24-25.

52 *Ibid.*, p. 119; vol. II, pp. 149-150.

> state, and their power of expansion is seconded by the impulse they receive from it [the state]; 5. this cooperation should be in harmony with the character and need of each country. Therefore the idea of an immutable type of faculties in either the extensive or restrictive sense must be abandoned.[53]

The state is an instrument that should be employed with discretion, with due regard to the particular character of a given situation. But what should be its aim in intervening in the economic sphere? The basic principle is "the harmonic and progressive development of national productive forces . . . ."

> A complex industrial régime is preferable to either an exclusively agricultural or manufacturing régime. . . . Normal nations (in the sense in which List employs this term), are complete organizations; their economic system resembles the physiology of the most perfect living beings; the various parts of which they are composed, agriculture, factories and commerce, are intimately related and subject to a law of internal growth; like the members of the same body, they languish or grow strong simultaneously.[54]

Cauwès' "law of the parallel development and the solidarity of the different branches of national industry" implies the necessity of a diversified economy.[55] He holds List to be wrong in affirming the superiority of the predominantly manufacturing nation. List, he says, was deluded by England's great prosperity. An economy such as hers is characterized by instability, and this is especially vicious because discontinuity is most dangerous in manufactures.

> Do not instability of credit, and frequency of industrial crises weigh much more heavily on the laboring classes in a country which is obliged to purchase abroad a part of its supplies of raw materials or foods?[56]

53 *Ibid.*, vol. I, pp. 187-188.

54 *Ibid.*, vol. II, pp. 477-478.

55 *Ibid.*, vol. I, pp. 138 ff.

56 *Ibid.*, vol. II, p. 491.

An entirely agricultural state is likewise weak: "exclusive agriculture is fatally stunted . . . ." The value of agricultural products rises when they are grown close to urban industrial centers.[57] Above all, however, "human productive forces are the foundation of all wealth . . . ." These are the technical knowledge, traditions in industry and agriculture, "the moral value of man, his conscientiousness in work, his energy," science and "the spirit of analysis."[58]

Since he believes that national policy should be directed toward the stimulation of the country's productive forces, Cauwès rejects mercantilist balance of trade doctrine designed to attract bullion. He does not go as far in the direction of orthodox economics as List, who wrote that the amount of the bullion stock was unimportant, any more than it was necessary for a wealthy man to keep gold bars in his safe. It was imperative, however, List believed, that a nation have specie at its command. He distinguished between "the mere *possession* of the precious metals and the power of *disposition* of the precious metals in international exchange."[59] He felt that the nation could achieve this end by developing its manufactures. Carey, on the other hand, declared that everyday experience had taught the farmer that he was prosperous when there was an adequate supply of money in rapid circulation, and that he suffered when money was scarce and circulated slowly.

> Money being to society what food is to the body—the cause of motion—rapidity of circulation is as much required in the one as in the other, and the greater it is, the more perfect will be the power of association, and the more certain the progress.[60]

Carey considered banknotes very useful, and especially because, as stimulants to circulation, they tended to attract specie. If

57 *Ibid.*, pp. 489-490; vol. I, p. 449.

58 *Ibid.*, vol. I, p. 430.

59 List, *National System*, pp. 227-229.

60 Carey, *Social Science*, vol. II, pp. 339, 362; Kaplan, *op. cit.*, pp. 79-81.

Carey seems to have approached John Law's monetary theory, Cauwès approaches that of Forbonnais, without achieving the latter's precision and clarity. The precious metals, Cauwès declares, are more than a mere interpreter of exchange value, more than simply one commodity exchangeable with other commodities. When a nation has an adequate supply of specie, the consequent rapid circulation stimulates production, he states, but beyond this money should not be considered a productive force. Hence its accumulation should not be the aim of national policy, but national policy should prevent its dissipation.[61]

Productivity theory led Carey to emphasize the development of the home market (involving less waste in transportation), and List to urge a domestic monopoly of internal trade for security, and expansion of finished goods exports and raw material imports for national advancement. Cauwès asserts the primacy of domestic commerce. Industries directed toward the conquest of foreign markets must expand, but they find it difficult to contract. Hence there is a closer relation between consumption and production in industries which aim primarily to supply the internal demand, and greater stability is consequent.[62] Cauwès further accepts, in large part, Carey's doctrine of waste in transportation and of the necessity for the development of local centers.[63]

In sum, Cauwès' normal, advanced nation is one with adequate, varied resources, a high level of intellectual attainment, with one principal and many secondary economic centers (a description of France), with well developed, diversified productive forces, with an active and intelligent administration. This is the end of national policy, to which protective tariffs are one of the most important means. Free trade does, it is true, extend international division of labor, but in so doing " sacrifices the

61 Cauwès, *Cours*, vol. I, pp. 322-323, 395; vol. II, pp. 168, 519 ff.

62 *Ibid.*, vol. II, p. 496; Carey, *op. cit.*, vol. I, p. 404, vol. II, pp. 74, 411, 424; List, *Outlines*, in Hirst, *op. cit.*, p. 229.

63 Cauwès, *Cours*, vol. I, pp. 137, 648; vol. II, pp. 500, 704; Carey, *op. cit.*, vol. I, p. 433.

division of labor in each state," by leading to excessive specialization.[64] Protection should be employed by new nations, otherwise they will never be able to develop industrially. It should be part of the process of acclimatization of new industries in old nations. Tariffs should be instituted to protect domestic producers against low-cost foreign competition, especially when the differential arises from taxation or cheap labor. The well rounded nation must be independent, and to this end requires military power and industry adequate for defense. The maintenance of industries for this purpose is another legitimate ground for protective duties.[65] For this reason, and because it is as much an industrial member of the economy as any other, agriculture is entitled to protection when it needs it, declares Cauwès. Here he disagrees sharply with List and joins Carey. List agreed completely with the English school that agricultural duties would merely divert capital from its natural course. Farm production might be stimulated, he wrote, but there would be no real gain in productive capacity. Less suitable crops would be grown, and choice of types of agricultural production is inherently governed by the nature of climate and soil. List concluded that agriculture might best be helped by stimulating industry, for growing industries provided expanding markets and higher prices for agricultural commodities.[66] Carey, on the other hand, approved highly of French agricultural policies: protection, monopoly of the home market, increased production to meet a rising domestic demand. They protected the small landholdings which, he felt, should form the broad base of society, for they developed association and decentralization.[67]

With Cauwès protection has become an instrument to be applied with reference to the whole complex of a national economy.

64 Cauwès, *Cours*, vol. I, p. 146.

65 *Ibid.*, vol. II, pp. 478 ff.

66 List, *National System*, pp. 161-163, 173-174; Hirst, *op. cit.*, pp. 105, 311-315; Bouvier-Ajam, *op. cit.*, p. 183.

67 Carey, *Social Science*, vol. II, pp. 91, 102, 112 ff.

> The measures of protection taken in favor of an industry should not be considered solely from the point of view of the interests of that industry, it is necessary further to observe the intermediary action which they are capable of exerting on other industries.... The general tariff should not alter the normal equilibrium among the various national industries because basically there is a solidarity among the interests of these industries....
>
> The extremely delicate ... duty of the legislator is to establish in the tariff laws a combination of duties carefully arranged so that each industry obtains the measure of protection necessary to enable it to contest with similar foreign industries. And this proper measure is capable of determination: it should be set according to the respective costs of production in France and the countries which are engaged in industrial rivalry with us....[86]
>
> It is not a matter of dispensing to all industries [agriculture is included in Cauwès' use of this word] a uniform dose of protection which would be inadequate for some, useless and even harmful for others. The equality in question signifies the right of each industry to protection, if it is necessary and in the measure necessary; it signifies, for example, that there should be no *a priori* distinction between agriculture and industry ... but that no branch of national endeavor [*travail national*] should be sacrificed to unequal competition.[69]

Here is a well rounded theory of protection. But what of the many objections raised against tariffs? These fall under the following heads: increased cost to the consumer, diversion of capital from natural, prosperous industries to unsuited, weak industries, stifling of initiative, interference with international trade and relations. How does Cauwès attempt to answer these objections? If prices do rise because of the imposition of protective duties, he says, it may be counted a national loss only if immediate private benefit and long run national interest are held to be identical, and this is not so. Further, the continuity of

68 Cauwès does not say whether this is to be fixed according to the average or most efficient units at home or abroad.

69 Cauwès, *Cours*, vol. II, pp. 553-558.

low foreign prices cannot be guaranteed in the absence of domestic production. The increased price is considered a loss to the consumer, but Cauwès declares he is also a producer, and if the benefits accruing to him from protection outweigh the costs, he is a net gainer. Lastly, Cauwès argues that unless demand is assumed to remain constant following the institution of a tariff, the foreign producer must absorb at least part of the tax.[70] The most significant answer to this particular objection arises from the general theory of protection, however: the competitive growth of domestic industry behind the tariff wall prevents an undue rise in prices.

The second attack on protection with which Cauwès deals is based on the fact that tariff barriers divert the course of capital into artificial, hence less profitable, channels. The underlying assumption here is, of course, that there is no qualitative difference between industries, that the sole measure of the worth of an industry is the rate of return it yields. But Cauwès believes, as we have seen, that there are certain types of production which are necessary to the general welfare of a nation, in providing diversity, and to its independence, in supplying military materials. He concludes that there is a difference between "the toy industry and the merchant marine, or between oil-cloths and agriculture."[71] Cauwès argues that it pays to protect production vital to national interest, and here again it is the distinction between private benefit calculated in terms of profit, and national benefit calculated in terms of productive forces that leads him to differ with the classical school.

Another anti-protectionist argument states that tariffs, by preventing competition, arrest technical progress and place a premium on inefficiency. But Cauwès answers that "rational protection" gives domestic producers no guarantee of profits.

> But import duties should only give industries which would be crushed by the free trade régime the possibility of maintaining

70 *Ibid.*, pp. 504-512.

71 *Ibid.*, p. 485: "Economie politique," p. 104. There would seem to be a contradiction between List's assertion of qualitative differences among industries and his views on the protection of agriculture.

> competition: this is not a right to profits for any business, even if poorly directed. Competition among the national producers, and between them and the foreign producers remains, but, with regard to the latter, in general conditions of equality.[72]

We must recall that Cauwès believes competition a stimulant only when it is between equals, a deterrent to progress when one side is too weak.

Lastly, we may consider the thesis that protection disrupts international relations and trade. Cauwès answers simply that industrial rivalry and international competition have not brought peace but war, and he flatly denies that protection lessens international commerce.

> A régime of rational protection . . . should not have the effect of diminishing the share of international commerce. Owing to the progressive development of the economic forces of the different nations, this commerce might in the future have an even greater expansion than it would have had under the régime of absolute liberty, given the relative superiorities of the period in which this régime would be applied. The protective system is therefore not the enemy of international commerce: it modifies rather than restrains its conditions.[73]

Cauwès does not attempt to reconcile the apparent contradiction between his rejection of the principle of comparative advantage and his belief in the possibility of greater trade among nations whose economies are likewise based on rejection of this concept. He declares that the internal market becomes the " principal center of a varied economic activity; only the excess production flows abroad and procures in exchange what national industry can in no way give, or could produce only at a great cost and less well." [74] Under such conditions, interna-

72 Cauwès, *Cours*, vol. II, p. 514.

73 *Ibid.*, p. 495. Morini-Comby (*op. cit.*, p. 165) states that Cauwès disapproved of trade treaties, and gives as evidence a quotation from the *Cours*, vol. II, p. 545. In reality this is a quotation by Cauwès of a statement by Jules Roche (see Ch. V, below).

74 Cauwès, *Cours*, vol. II, pp. 492-493.

tional trade must certainly be more restricted than under even relatively free trade.

Cauwès nevertheless remains far from the position of modern autarky. While with much less assurance than List, he looks forward to a day of international peace and free trade.

> The protection of national industries . . . is not most often perpetual; it is a transitional régime suited to the advancement of industrial education; it is a tutelage which should naturally cease at the age of full economic development; then, for industries whose development is completed, the barriers may be lowered. The system of rational protection does not . . . lead to the building of a Chinese wall at the frontiers to maintain national production in absolute isolation. . . . Freedom of commerce is in a sense the end toward which all nations which are clearly at the same point of industrial power should tend. To place rival industries face to face is to make them feel the spur of combat, to stimulate them by competition. An adult industry kept in a hothouse would atrophy, confident in possession of the internal market, unaware of the progress accomplished without.[75]

May it be remarked, however, that industries are the only infants which rarely admit that they have reached adult estate?

Thus far we have seen Cauwès as an advanced protectionist, as a theorist who has synthesized nationalist economics as it had developed to his day. The full measure of his advance beyond preceding thinkers, and evidence of the development of French nationalist economics, may be found in his attitude toward economic activities behind the tariff wall.[76] Ganilh, Louis Say and List all seemed content to let competition regulate domestic affairs. Carey's attitude toward internal intervention was not too clear: on the one hand he condemned competition in the strongest terms, on the other hand he opposed the strict industrial regulations of the highly centralized

75 *Ibid.*, p. 482; "Economie politique," p. 101.

76 In this respect Cauwès occupies a middle ground in the transition from mid-nineteenth-century liberal nationalism to its modern integral form.

Colbertian government.[77] Carey looked to protection from without and to association within to provide a balanced economy. Dupont-White believed the state must intervene in the interests of justice, and Cournot in the interest of sound and economic policy. Ferrier may properly be termed a neo-mercantilist, who favored an attentuated form of Colbertian regulation. Cauwès takes up this thread, but weaves with it a doctrine of free association, close to that of Social Catholicism, much more explicit than Carey's. He declares that individualism errs in seeing only one activating force in social life.

> In reality there are two, private and public. If the omnipotence of the state is a dangerous error, the same is true of absolute individualism. Individualism, nevertheless, contains a part of the truth: for things within its sphere, private initiative excels in discerning the attainable end and the appropriate means. ... It is most fortunate for a society that individual forces, full of ardor and energy, arise under the stimulus of need. It is for this reason that, when industry has reached a sufficient degree of development, free cooperation is the economic régime most favorable to social progress.[78]

Cauwès distinguishes between perfect and imperfect associations. The former are those in which members act in common for common ends, the latter in which members act together for their individual interests. Within these categories there are two types, which do not necessarily exclude each other. These are associations favoring private interests ("ordinary trade"), and those devoted to general interests, mutual aid and betterment, rather than simply profits. It is the imperfect association for general interests, exemplified by the *syndicats professionnels* (the *syndicats agricoles* included) with which Cauwès is most concerned.[79] Under the modern industrial system these organizations have a great rôle to play, and above all in France,

77 Carey, *op. cit.*, vol. II, p. 67, vol. III, p. 440.

78 Cauwès, *Cours*, vol. I, pp. 175-176.

79 *Ibid.*, pp. 119 ff.

> for the abolition of the old gilds did not only break the shackles of labor, but at the same stroke broke professional bonds. Thenceforth nothing united those who earned their livings at the same craft; the only relations existing are those which give rise to contracts of labor between separate individuals, often hostile to one another: on one side the employer, on the other the worker. Cannot association rebuild the natural bonds, mass the interests of capital and labor for collective defense, revive fine industrial traditions? [80]

Thus Cauwès has extended the framework of nationalist economic thought: social justice has been added to national strength as a criterion of economic good, free association takes its place besides state intervention as a means of reaching the goal of a just, independent and prosperous national society.

As with any nationalist economist, recognition of the nation as an economic entity is the primary basis of Cauwès' theories, yet it is true that

> It is less because of doctrinal considerations than practical necessity that Paul Cauwès emphasizes the importance of national economic studies, since nations are the only permanent cadres of human activities.[81]

Cauwès' point of departure is not late-nineteenth-century emotional nationalism, and it is therefore not surprising that his doctrine is defensive in character and makes no appeal for national supremacy. Like Ferrier, he seems to have realized that France would never again strive for hegemony in Europe, that maintenance of her position in the world, in a word, security, was now her aim. He assembled the many parts of nationalist economic theory and presented them in a system more fully rounded than that of any preceding thinker. Further, he applied the thought patterns which led him to protection, to internal affairs. Both Henri Sée and Bouvier-Ajam consider him to be a follower of *Kathedersozialismus*, but the relation is super-

80 *Ibid.*, p. 121; "Economie politique," p. 105.

81 Bouvier-Ajam, *op. cit.*, p. 294.

ficial, and essentially one of contemporaneity.[82] Lucien Brocard, his most prominent disciple, declares that Cauwès "held persistently to the tradition of the French mercantilists, ceaselessly opposed his *realistic* method to the *historical* method of the Germans." [83]

Cauwès was an eclectic. Classical and neo-classical concepts are joined to the main structure of List and Carey, the method and approach of the historian to deductive theory, and traditional French mercantilism is never far in the background. Cauwès went farther than List, says Brocard, along the road leading to the "meeting of national economics and political economy." [84] Beyond this, however, his belief in association, the adaptation of the gild to modern conditions, is clearly an approach to the economics of Social Catholicism—to the corporative system within the state, rather than to the corporate state. In conclusion we may quote Cauwès' most general statement of his position:

> political economy not only has an object, the search for laws which preside over social activity, but it has an aim; individual well-being and collective prosperity. It is important to clarify this notion: laws of utility unrelated to a known environment are poorly conceived; they must be as exactly appropriate as possible to each society, to each type of civilization; they should be generalized and extended only with prudence. . . . The truth lies in an eclectic doctrine which takes into account national customs, economic conditions and the propensity to progress. Thoroughly aware of the benefits of the established social order, this doctrine does not freely welcome plans for radical innovation, but it also remains distant from the economists enrolled under the banner of *laissez-faire*.[85]

82 *Ibid.*, pp. 295-296; Sée, *Wirtschaftsgeschichte*, vol. II, p. 504.

83 Brocard, *Principes*, vol. I, p. 330. Perhaps Brocard means that French historical method is realistic and German fanciful, for Cauwès certainly writes in an historical frame.

84 *Ibid.*, p. 49.

85 Cauwès, *Cours*, vol. I, pp. 33-34, 52-53.

The character and scope of nationalist economic theory thus underwent a great change during the nineteenth century. At the beginning of this pediod it was a theory to be distinguished from mercantilism, one which emphasized the development of a well-rounded, secure economy instead of an assault on foreign markets to obtain monetary wealth. The transition from mercantilism to nationalist economics was part of the change from dynastic to representative government. Mercantilism was the economic doctrine of a royal, authoritarian state, nationalist economics the doctrine of economic groups within a state ruled by an elected legislature. At the end of the nineteenth century it was to be distinguished, on the one hand, from autarky, for it denied absolute national self-sufficiency as the economic good; and on the other hand from simple protectionism, the demand for specific tariffs with little regard for overall national welfare or security. From a group of doctrines presented in opposition to the dominant, rationalist English school, nationalist economics evolved into an eclectic system which employed the methods of both the classicists and their historical critics to arrive at what its exponents termed realistic conclusions of practical significance to the legislator. It may be argued that the well known economic nationalism of List has been artificially extended to create a system which includes concepts which do not properly belong, particularly association and agricultural protection. But it must be remembered that List wrote for the relatively backward Germanies of the 1840's, and might well have written differently in a different land at a different time. And, in any event, it is here suggested that Cauwès represents a refinement and advance of nationalist economics far beyond List.

The principal differences between nationalist economics and orthodox theory are, first, that the former recognizes the nation as an economic unit, while the latter deals with abstract individual terms, and, second, that nationalist economic doctrine creates standards of internal justice and well-being, while classical and neo-classical economics are unquestionably materialistic (even in psychology). Commencing with the nation as an economic entity, nationalist economic theory distinguishes between short run individual and long run national advantage. The latter is not to be measured in terms of profit and loss, but rather in terms of the development of diverse productive facilities which insure national security and the growth of a rich, advanced culture. Protection is a powerful implement in achieving these ends, for under its guardianship infant industries can grow to robust adulthood, and essential activities without which national security is impossible, such as agriculture and the merchant marine, can withstand the attacks of even more fortunate foreign rivals. While the domestic market is all important, in that it provides stability and economy of transportation, foreign trade should not be excluded. Not only is it advisable for the national state to export, but it should import such commodities as it cannot produce, and permit a degree of competition from abroad sufficient to prevent decadence. Nationalist economics thus does not envisage complete exclusion of foreign products, and indeed looks forward to a very distant future of international free trade, in the somewhat naïve belief that there will be a greater exchange of goods among nations which limit international division of labor instead of giving it free rein. Within the nation, competition and individual initiative are in large part relied upon to keep prices down and stimulate technological improvement. But French nationalist economic theory, combining traditional *étatisme* with late-nineteenth-century doctrines of association, makes the state and private cooperation active forces for the regulation and advancement of the domestic economy in the interest of prosperity and justice.

It was this type of nationalist economic thought that provided the intellectual background for the Méline Tariff, for it harmonized especially well with the needs of the agrarian protectionists. The way in which they used this theory, together with the campaign for and the enactment of the Tariff of 1892 form the subject of the following chapters.

CHAPTER V

THE CAMPAIGN FOR PROTECTION

MOST French industrialists had always been protectionist, but it was the agricultural depression of the 1880's and the attendant organization of the *syndicats agricoles* which made French agriculture articulate in its demands. It was a time in which nationalist economic thought was in great favor. It was part of the strong current running toward integral nationalism. It was a rationalization for solving problems raised by secular trends in agriculture and industry and by the Great Depression. These doctrines therefore provided an apology for the agrarian leaders, and an intellectual meeting ground (to supplement one of expediency) between them and the industrialists. As in the period of the Restoration, an alliance between industry and agriculture won the day for protection.

The *Société des agriculteurs,* that " club of great landowners " which we have seen as the prime mover in *syndical* organization, also directed agriculture's protectionist campaign. It had attempted to secure the non-renewal of the commercial treaties and the enactment of high agricultural duties in 1881; but the tariff law of that year keenly disappointed it.[1]

> This double-faced tariff, free trade where agriculture is concerned, protectionist with regard to industry, has this result for the farmers, it delivers them over to foreign competition on the national market. . . .[2]

While the leaders of the *Société des agriculteurs* were practical politicians, they sought to justify their position by theoretical statements of nationalist economics. The productivity concept was one they frequently advanced:

1 See above, pp. 53 ff.

2 CRSAF, vol. XIV, 1882, p. 161.

> The aim we pursue is the defense of national production compromised by foreign competition. . . .[3]
> Some seek the country's prosperity in the national endeavor [*travail national*], others see only the ocean, that is to say, commerce with foreign nations.[4]

It was above all the doctrine of cheap goods that drew their attacks. They bitterly resented the name given them by French free traders — *les marquis du pain cher*[5] — and argued that low prices were no standard of economic welfare.

> They [the free traders] dream of low prices, without seeing that they are too often the consequence of misery; they do not understand that they offer to the foreigner the production they refuse their fellow citizens. . . . Ah! Free trade is a fine term, but it is the sacrifice of the weak to the strong, of a brother to his enemy.[6]
> . . . it is not the low price of agricultural products which can create the well being of the consumers; only the activity of labor, the development of agriculture and the prosperity of industry, which assure the laboring population of good wages and those who cultivate the soil of a legitimate remuneration, can bring prosperity and fortune to our country.[7]

To the agrarian leaders the chief instruments for economic progress were association and technical education at home and protection at the frontiers: "*Tout par la douane et la science, voilà notre formule.*"[8] Customs duties were to be compensatory in character, to eliminate differentials between foreign and do-

3 BSAF, vol. XXIII, 1891, p. 389.

4 CRSAF, vol. XVII, 1885, p. 735.

5 *Ibid.*, vol. XX, 1888, p. 170: CD, 1891, p. 715, allusion by Edouard Lockroy.

6 CRSAF, vol. XVIII, 1886, p. 110.

7 *Ibid.*, vol. XVIII, 1886, p. 123, Senator Pouyer-Quertier.

8 JAP, ser. 6, vol. XLV, 1890, I, p. 164. "All through customs and science, that is our formula."

mestic costs and taxes.[9] Further, each branch of national industry must be adequately protected. The protests of 1881 are recalled, and agriculture insists that it receive as much protection as industry. The aim should be

> to harmonize agricultural and industrial tariffs so as to fill by customs duties the differential between the prices of the French market and those at which foreign products can be sent to our ports, in such a fashion as to limit the profits of middlemen without materially increasing the prices of commodities. . . . [and] the elimination of tariff inequalities which have delivered agriculture over to foreign competition while industry obtained protection against this competition.[10]

While the position of the *Société des agriculteurs* was thus in general harmony with nationalist economics, in some respects it went beyond the theories we have discussed. Trade treaties, approved by List and objectively considered by Cauwès, were strongly condemned. Lecouteux, editor of the *Journal d'agriculture pratique,* declared:

> There is not a single agricultural association in France which does not firmly demand that all treaties of commerce be denounced at their expiration in 1892 and not be renewed.[11]

They differed even more sharply from the theorists with regard to specie and balance-of-trade doctrine, and adopted a crude bullionist position. M. Deusy, one of the leading oranizers of

9 CRSAF, vol. XVIII, 1886, p. 154: BSAF, vol. XXIII, 1891, p. 389. A favorite argument of the agrarian leaders was that increased customs revenues could be applied to the reduction of domestic taxes which burdened agriculture. See CRSAF, vol. XVIII, 1886, p. 154; *ibid.*, vol. XXIV, 1892, p. 591; BSAF, vol. XX, 1888, p. 147; de Luçay and Sénart, *op. cit.*, p. 65. This view involves the obvious contradiction that effective protective tariffs will yield little or no revenue unless imports are necessitated by deficiencies of home production. But the agrarian protectionists also insisted that domestic production would rise sufficiently behind the tariff to obviate the possibility of such deficiencies.

10 CRSAF, vol. XXI, 1889, pp. 181-182; see also JAP, ser. 6, vol. XLV, 1890, I, p. 693.

11 JAP, ser. 6, vol. XLV, 1890, I, p. 376.

syndicats agricoles, stated that reconquest of the domestic market was the first step in the application of the great economic law according to which

> one should strive to keep bullion in the country, and, indeed, attract money from abroad. The more a country exports, the richer it is, for exportation draws specie to it. The more a country imports, the poorer it is, for imports draw out bullion which never reappears.[12]

It is not surprising to find a somewhat "unscientific" attitude prevalent among these great landowners, for they were arguing their own special interest. They did not hesitate to assert the superiority of agriculture over industry and commerce. A vestige of Physiocratic doctrine appears in the declaration of M. Welche, head of the *Syndicat central,*[13] that agriculture "is the only truly creative industry, it feeds the country, its savings give life to industry and commerce. . . ."[14] Unchecked by restraints of academic writing, the leaders of the *Société des agriculteurs* appealed for protection on the grounds of pure emotional nationalism. M. Kergall, head of the *Syndicat économique agricole,* proclaimed:

> France, nothing but France! The cause is wonderful enough to inspire all hearts; the field is wide enough for good men of all parties to lend a hand, and the door which leads to it is big enough for all Frenchmen to pass through heads high.[15]

The theoretical views of the agrarian leaders cannot be dignified into a system. They were the rationalization of what they considered beneficial to themselves, hence to France. Nevertheless, nationalist economic theory is implicit in their beliefs, vulgarized though it be, and they occasionally referred to theorists

12 BSAF, vol. XIX, 1887, p. 817.

13 See above, p. 94.

14 BSAF, vol. XXI, 1889, p. 176.

15 DR, July 13, 1890.

by name, as when the marquis de Dampierre invoked the authority of "the greatest of American economists, Carey." [16] This relationship is emphasized by the position of Social Catholics, who played so prominent a rôle in the organization of *syndicats agricoles*. They shared the foregoing views on protection, attacked *laissez-faire* and trade treaties, demanded compensatory duties and equality in protection between agriculture and industry.[17] La Tour du Pin, whom we have seen as one of the foremost leaders of French Social Catholicism, declared:

> A state which is not master of its customs duties is not master of the development of its industries, and hence abandons its duty of assuring the well being of the people, a duty which is, nevertheless, its historic mission. . . .
> These considerations apply above all to agriculture, whose prosperity is the essential condition of national life. . . .[18]

The adherence of Social Catholics to protectionism and the close interrelationship between protectionism and the *syndical* movement shows that we are not dealing merely with the traditional protectionism that might be expected of very conservative Frenchmen. The emphasis on productivity and the balanced state is, as we have seen, the result of the development of nationalist economic thought in the nineteenth century. The insistence of nationalist theory on a diversified economy made it attractive to agrarian leaders who were well aware of the trend toward industrial ascendancy. Thus they adopted it, molding it toward their own ends. Their attitude is well summarized by M. Lecouteux:

> . . . . military France must be protectionist, for she needs much money to create an army, to build fortifications, to perfect her equipment, to nourish the country by the country, to have an

16 CRSAF, vol. XX, 1888, p. 20.

17 AC, vol. XXVII, 1889, I, pp. 434, 489, 758; 1889, II, p. 758. *Corporation*, Feb. 14, 1891.

18 AC, vol. XXII, 1886, II, p. 148: see, by La Tour du Pin, *Vers un ordre social chrétien: jalons de route 1882-1907*, 5th ed., Paris, 1929.

export surplus, to pay for the products she draws from aboard, and, in a word, that her national endeavor [*travail national*] be productive. . . . this will be the best means of serving the interests of the consumers, for, in order to consume, the masses of the population must first work.[19]

Our purpose is to record the translation of this attitude into political fact. The Méline Tariff was the culmination of a series of protectionist measures passed in the decade of the 1880's. The Law of 1881 had excluded grain and livestock from the treaties of commerce that were to be negotiated, and the protectionists devoted their efforts to the exploitation of this exception in the years preceding the election of 1889.

The first step occurred in 1885.[20] Duties on oxen were raised from 15 to 25 francs a head, on cows from 8 to 12, calves from 1.50 to 4, pigs from 3 to 6, sheep from 2 to 3 francs. Rye, barley and oats, on the free list since 1861, were taxed at 1.50 francs per 100 kilograms. The duty on wheat was raised from 0.60 to 3 francs per 100 kilograms, and that on wheat flour from 1.20 to 6 francs.[21] In 1887 duties on oxen were carried to 38 francs, on cows to 20 francs, on calves to 8 francs, and sheep to 5 francs. In the same year the duty on oats was raised to 3 francs, that on wheat to 5 francs (subject to reduction to 3 francs by ministerial decree in case of a shortage), that on wheat flour to 8 francs. Duties on cereal products such as spaghetti (*pâtes d'Italie*), which had been raised from 1.20 francs to 5.50 francs per 100 kilograms in 1885, were further increased to 8 francs in 1887.[22]

19 JAP, ser. 6, vol. XLVI, 1890, II, p. 511.

20 In 1884 the duty on raw sugar was raised from 3 to 7 francs per 100 kilograms, and the internal sugar tax was placed on beets rather than raw sugar. Since the official yield of refined sugar from a given weight of beets was set lower than could actually be obtained, a subsidy to French refiners was, in effect, instituted. See Levasseur, *op. cit.*, II, p. 565; Charles-Roux, *op. cit.* On earlier sugar legislation see above, p. 57.

21 *Principales mesures*, pp. 95 ff. Ashley, *op. cit.*, pp. 330 ff.

22 Arnauné, *op. cit.*, pp. 306-307. *Principales mesures, loc. cit.*

The *Société des agriculteurs* played an important rôle in the adoption of these increases. In November 1884 it sponsored a congress of delegates of provincial agricultural societies and *comices*.[23] It presented a draft tariff to this meeting, proposing that the wheat duty be raised to 5 francs per 100 kilograms, other grains to 3 francs, all flours to 9 francs. The duty on oxen was to be carried to 60 francs a head, on cows to 40 francs, on sheep to 7 francs and on hogs to 15 francs.[24] The *Société* realized, however, that they would be forced to accept less, especially since the government was divided on the question of protection and Méline, the Minister of Agriculture, felt that 3 francs on wheat was the best he could secure.[25] It was therefore decided to support the latter figure to " defend, with the government, the principle of a duty on wheat, etc.; [and] set forth the inadequacy of those proposed. . . ."[26]

The agricultural duties of 1885 were therefore only a compromise, and they had no sooner been enacted than the *Société des agriculteurs* began to press for further increases, raising the level of its demands higher than it had been before. In 1886 numerous *comices, syndicats* and agricultural societies voiced their demand for a higher duty on wheat.[27] Pouyer-Quertier, a leading protectionist senator and member of the *Société,* condemned the half measures taken in 1885 and rejected the notion that these duties should be given time to prove their worth or inadequacy. Instead, he proclaimed, the time had come to give agriculture real satisfaction, to give it the means for survival.[28] M. Léon Maurice, a member both of the *Société* and the Tariff

23 Luçay and Sénart: *op. cit.*, pp. xv, xvi.

24 CRSAF, vol. XVII, 1885, p. 150.

25 BSAF, vol. XVII, 1885, p. 325, statement of the president, the marquis de Dampierre. The cabinet was headed by Jules Ferry.

26 *Ibid.*, p. 31.

27 *Ibid.*, vol. XVIII, 1886, pp. 44-46, 180, 246 ff.; AC, vol. XXII, 1886, II, p. 747.

28 CRSAF, vol. XVIII, 1886, p. 115.

Commission of the Chamber of Deputies, urged the former to restate its demands and make them heard in the halls of the legislature, and his advice was speedily followed.[29] A plea for a duty of 7 francs per 100 kilograms of wheat was brought before the assembly of the *Société*, and this rate was justified as meeting the difference between domestic and foreign costs of production.[30] A bill calling for an increase to 5 francs had been introduced in the Chamber, and one of its authors, the Deputy Baucarne-Leroux, hastened to explain to the *Société* that this figure had been chosen only because it might more easily secure a majority than the 7-franc impost. He was answered with the statement that the *Société* was not a legislative body, and could therefore propose the duty it felt was actually necessary. This was done, and by a large majority the members of the *Société* pronounced themselves in favor of the higher figure.[31] Other proposals of duties were maintained. The *Société* asked that the rate on flour be raised from 6 to 9 francs per 100 kilograms, that on oats, rye and barley from 1.50 to 3 francs, on oxen from 25 to 60 francs a head, on cows from 12 to 40 francs, on calves from 4 to 15 francs, on sheep from 3 to 7 francs.[32]

Two parliamentary groups, one of the Right, headed by M. Barouille, the other Republican, led by Méline, had been formed in the Chamber to promote agricultural interests, and the *Société* instructed its legislative section to enter into relations with them.[33] Late in 1886 a delegation of the *Société* was received by the President of the Republic, the Premier and the Minister of Agriculture, all of whom declared themselves in sympathy with the *Société's* position.[34] And for the second time in 1886, representatives of about three hundred *comices, syndicats* and

29 *Ibid.*, p. 161.

30 *Ibid.*, p. 154.

31 *Ibid.*, pp. 159-160.

32 *Ibid.*, p. 269.

33 BSAF, vol. XVIII, 1886, p. 100.

34 *Ibid.*, vol. XIX, 1887, pp. 20-22; CRSAF, vol. XIX, 1887, pp. 31, 184.

provincial societies were convoked at Paris to enhance the *Société's* claim to speak for the farmers.[35] The campaign was only partially successful for, as we have seen, while the tariffs voted in 1887 represented an increase over those of 1885, they failed to satisfy the *Société's* demand for high protection. The struggle therefore continued.

It was marked by an alliance between the *Société des agriculteurs* and the *Association de l'industrie française*, by skilful pressure techniques and by a surprising lack of public debate on economic matters in the elections of 1889. Since 1886 French politics had been dominated by the figure of General Boulanger, and his black horse, Tunis.[36] Supported by diverse and conflicting groups of the right as well as left, Boulanger was elected to the Chamber from district after district. Unable to translate his bold words into political deeds when at the height of his popularity and success, he fled to Belgium on All Fools' Day, 1889, just when it seemed that the government might bring him to trial before the Senate sitting as High Court. The elections of September 1889 were thus really decided in April, for the Republicans won a clear victory. But the election had been fought over the issue of revision of the Constitution in a reactionary sense. Boulanger had been discredited, but he had never been more than a convenient hanger for many different colored coats. General Boulanger was defeated in April, Boulangism in September. Thus it was that the question of the tariff received little attention during the electoral campaign, although protection was victorious.[37] When the election was over, and the new

35 CRSAF, vol. XXI, 1889, p. 42.

36 On General Boulanger, see: A. Zévaès, *Au temps du Boulangisme*, 6th ed., Paris, 1930; Adrien Dansette, *Du boulangisme à la révolution dreyfusienne: le boulangisme 1886-1890*, Paris, 1938.

37 The Paris press of the period yielded only rare, minor notices regarding the question of protection. Bajkić (*op. cit.*, p. 27) remarks: "Of course, questions of commercial policy were brought before the voters, but always in last place, and were not in the least decisive for the results of the elections." Meredith (*op. cit.*, p. 19) is wrong in saying that "the elections of 1889... were fought on the tariff issue and resulted in the complete victory of the

Chamber prepared to meet, economic liberals discovered that they had lost a battle of whose existence they had hardly been aware. Gustave de Molinari, prominent liberal publicist, wrote in October 1889, that "The legislative elections which have just renewed the Chamber of Deputies have had an exclusively political character." [38] Two years later another author wrote in the liberal *Journal des économistes*:

> The last elections unfortunately took place under conditions such that it was not possible to bring the question of free trade before the voters. The partisans of economic isolation for France therefore benefited from the diversion caused by political struggles and, it must be said, from the indifference of the majority to the general interest. . . .[39]

While this may be an accurate generalization, it was no mere accident that protectionism rather than free trade profited by "political diversions." The *Société des agriculteurs* undertook another, more energetic campaign in cooperation with the *Association de l'industrie française,* and supported the decisive work of the *Syndicat économique agricole* in securing the deputies' support for protection before they were elected, and organizing them to enact it before the Chamber began to consider the tariff bill.

In 1888 the *Société des agriculteurs* appointed a committee to conduct an inquiry among the members of the *Société,* the *syndicats,* provincial societies and *comices* with a view to preparing a tariff schedule for consideration of its general assembly early

protectionists." The judgment of René Henry (*Revue politique et parlementaire,* vol. XIII, 1897, p. 17) fits the evidence more closely: "In 1889, a time when pure politics was at its height, it was nevertheless necessary for a candidate, no matter to what party he belonged, to be protectionist or free trader according to regions, otherwise his chances for success were nil." Méline's principal campaign speech was devoted almost entirely to the political question, and contained only an incidental reference to tariffs (*Le Temps,* Sept. 12, 1889).

38 JEC, 1889, p. 155.

39 *Ibid.*, 1891, p. 3.

in 1889.[40] This committee circulated a questionnaire among the various organizations, including requests for information as to what products met with foreign competition, costs of production, prices, duties desired and methods proposed. One hundred forty replies were received from fifty-nine departments, and while specific suggestions varied greatly, only three groups (ironically including the *Syndicat* of Remiremont, Méline's native town) favored the maintenance of the existing law. In general, the replies urged greatly increased tariffs and the abolition of trade treaties on the one hand, and reduction of land taxes on the other.[41] M. Lavollée, reporting for the committee, presented a list of duties as representative of the wishes of the majority. No request was made for an increase in the 5-franc duty on wheat, but it was proposed that the tax on wheat flour be raised from 8 to 10 francs, on oats from 3 to 5 francs, on cheeses from duties varying between 3 and 8 francs to one of 25 francs per 100 kilograms. It was asked that the duty on oxen be raised to 60 francs per head, on cows to 40 francs, on sheep to 10 francs.[42]

These replies furnished the basis for recommendations to the *Société* by its tariff committee, likewise reporting through M. Lavollée. The committee proposed three basic principles: one, that no treaties be negotiated, since they could be concluded only with small countries;[43] two, that agriculture receive the same protection, in ad valorem terms, as industry; three, that the general tariff be revised. What should be the basis for this revision, however? It would be ridiculous to apply duties equal to those of foreign nations. Russia has high tariffs on cloths and wines, and admits grain free. Would it not be preposterous to tax Russian cloth and wines and admit her grain free? Nor can the principle of compensatory duties be successfully em-

40 CRSAF, vol. XX, 1888, p. 53.

41 *Ibid.*, vol. XXI, 1889, pp. 71 ff.

42 *Ibid.*, vol. XXI, 1889, pp. 75-77.

43 A reference to the German situation rising from Art. 11 of the Treaty of Frankfurt: see Allix, *op. cit.*, vol. I, p. 56.

ployed, for it is all but impossible to decide on a standard of comparison abroad. Therefore, the report concludes, a general tariff equally applicable to all is needed. It should neither be prohibitive nor calculated to raise the cost of living, for harming the urban consumer would result in injury to agriculture, just as the reverse is true now.

> In fact, an increase in duties can be salutary and lasting only if moderate. . . . [We wish] by means of customs duties to reverse on foreign exporters a part of the enormous fiscal charges which today burden the French producer, but on the express condition that the sums derived from duties on agricultural products be devoted exclusively to the reduction of taxes which weigh on the rural population.[44]

The *Société des agriculteurs* accepted the report of the tariff committee with little debate and little change, and overwhelmingly approved the following resolution:

> Whereas the treaties of 1881-1882, concluded with lesser states, yield us inadequate advantages from the standpoint of exports while, owing to the most-favored-nation clause, they profit the great powers who have given us no tariff concessions in exchange,
>
> Whereas, in the present condition of Europe . . . there seems to be . . . no opportunity to conclude commercial treaties acceptable to national industry and agriculture,
>
> Whereas, at the expiration of the treaties of 1881-1882 the present general tariff . . . would assure French industry very appreciable protection but would leave agriculture without defence, at least for most of its products,
>
> Whereas, it is in conformity with justice, reason and patriotism to maintain complete equality of treatment between agriculture and industry,
>
> Whereas, it is essential not to give to the tariff to be established on agricultural products a prohibitive character and not to . . . create dearness dangerous to public nourishment and national industry, but only to compensate by means of taxes

44 CRSAF, vol. XXI, 1889, pp. 81-82.

> imposed on foreign goods imported into France a part of the excess charges with which equivalent French goods are burdened,
>
> The *Société* accepts the general tariff presented by its committee . . .
>
> And, in addition, adopts the following resolutions:
>
> 1. That the commercial treaties now in vigor . . . be denounced and not be renewed at their expiration;
>
> 2. That it be possible to double the duties of the general tariff to be established on the products of countries which, in general, impose on French products, whether raw or manufactured, duties exceeding twenty per cent, or which prohibit them.[45]

In all essentials the *Société des agriculteurs* had merely reiterated its position of long standing. The plea for moderation was dictated by obvious political prudence. The modification of the concept of compensatory duties from the usual basis of cost differentials to tax differentials was an added point of attraction to the agricultural population. The degree of moderation of the duties proposed by the *Société* will be considered in connection with the government tariff bill introduced in the Chamber on October 20, 1890. In the meantime let us note the remark of M. Maurice Boucherie, president of the *Société's* section on cattle, who considered the demands excessive:

> the tariff committee has given in to the desires of the *syndicats*. These societies, being still young, have not had time to study and fathom the question. . . . They have been carried away by a praiseworthy but dangerous sentiment, in the sense that it offers our implacable adversaries, the free traders, weapons against our just claims. Let us be moderate, and we shall have no reason to complain.[46]

The *Société des agriculteurs* had taken its position. It was now necessary to secure the support of industrial interests and to organize a campaign among the farm population. We have

45 Luçay and Sénart, *op. cit.*, p. 58.

46 CRSAF, vol. XXI, 1889, p. 336.

seen that an alliance between agriculture and industry had been formed prior to the elaboration of the Tariff of 1881, but that it failed to hold.[47] This *entente* was renewed prior to the preparation of the Méline Tariff. While Levasseur remarks that it was sealed in 1891,[48] it would be more correct to say that it was formed in 1888 and 1889, and in 1891 weathered the storms attendant upon its actual application to the process of writing the tariff law.

At its general assembly in 1888, the *Société* was addressed by one of its leading members, M. Marc de Haut:

> What adversaries does agriculture meet in this question of tariffs? She has not only to struggle against the partisans of free trade, the theorists whom she cannot in any event hope to convince. Opposed to her interests are those of industry.
>
> For a long time it was believed that there was necessarily a contradiction between the interests of these two branches of national activity; hence their old rivalry and the opposition for long years evidenced by industry every time agriculture sought to assert her rights. But for some time the struggle has been less keen; this prejudice has been shaken off and there is even a certain harmony between the needs of agriculture and those of industry; agriculturalists and industrialists seem to recognize this in the face of a crisis that affects them both. Besides these interests, between which there could be agreement, there are, it is true, those of commerce, which are considerable, and which it is impossible to harmonize with the others. It is this which makes the problem difficult, which complicates its solution. But it must be confessed that main consideration should be given the producers, agriculture and industry, and the needs of commerce should enter into account only secondarily.[49]

The reply of the industrialists was given at the banquet of the *Société des agriculteurs,* when M. Aclocque, head of the *Asso-*

47 See above, p. 54.

48 Levasseur, *op. cit.*, vol. II, p. 578.

49 CRSAF, vol. XX, 1888, pp. 43-44.

ciation de l'industrie française, and for years a member of the *Société,* declared:

> In magnificent terms M. Marc de Haut has told us that . . . in the future agriculture would march hand in hand with industry. I long hesitated, gentlemen, to accept the honor of directing the deliberations of our national industry, because this program . . . a program which was my own, a program which I have ceaselessly defended, was accepted by only a small number of adherents; but this minority is transformed today; it has not only become a majority, I can say it with joy, it has become unanimity. . . .
>
> I drink to the accord of agriculture and industry, to work and to peace.[50]

Marc de Haut returned the toast for agriculture:

> You have resolved, and industry has likewise resolved, to prepare between now and the expiration date in 1892 a bill for a new general tariff; we shall work at it together, and we shall harness ourselves together on this difficult task. . . .
>
> I therefore drink with you to the fertile union of agriculture and industry, to their fraternal equality, to the permanence of this happy accord and through it to the end of the unfortunate crisis which destroys us.[51]

Acting as the *Société's* envoy to the industrialists, de Haut attended the 1888 banquet of the *Association de l'industrie,* at which Méline was present, and delivered a warm plea for union. He closed by saying,

> As for the task of defending our common interests, we shall entrust it to M. Méline, and I drink, in closing, to the man who personifies, in France, the union and solidarity of industry and agriculture . . . to M. Méline!

Méline tactfully declined to answer him directly, but went on to declare that de Haut

50 *Ibid.*, pp. 223-224.

51 *Ibid.*, p. 226.

> has brought me, this evening, one of the greatest satisfactions of my life, in associating with my name the interests of French agriculture and industry. I have done everything to unite them, because I believe them inseparable, and as long as I live I shall have but one thought, to serve them as a connecting link.[52]

Thus the alliance between these powerful organizations was arranged in 1888. The *Société des agriculteurs* named a publicity committee to cooperate with a similar body of the *Association de l'industrie.*[53] The latter's press organ, *Le Travail national,* applied balm to lingering wounds by reprinting a resolution of the *Association's* executive committee, passed in 1880, expressing regret at agriculture's failure to win protection at that time.[54] Many difficulties were to arise, and it was not until 1889 and 1890 that agreement was reached on the essential question of protection of raw materials, but in the meantime there was an electoral campaign to be prepared and won.

The first step was the organization of the agrarian front, and to this end the *Société* gathered delegates of comices, provincial societies and *syndicats* in a preliminary meeting on February 18, 1889. They discussed and approved a series of protectionist resolutions and others calling for varied reforms in agriculture's favor.[55] Then in June 1889 a Congress of *syndicats agricoles,* called by the *Union centrale,* was opened by the marquis de Dampierre, president of the *Société,* who summoned the new organizations to stand in the van of agriculture's campaign for protection.[56] The following program was adopted by the Congress:

52 TN, vol. VI, 1888, p. 181.

53 BSAF, vol. XX, 1888, pp. 418-419.

54 TN, vol. VI, 1888, p. 180.

55 BSAF, vol. XXI, 1889, pp. 183 ff., 400 ff., 441 ff.

56 *Ibid.*, p. 596.

Agricultural Program

Discussed and voted in the meetings of the 20th, 21st and 22nd of June 1889 of the Congress of the *syndicats des agriculteurs de France* and approved by the general assembly of the *Société des agriculteurs de France.*

I. Protection of agriculture against foreign competition—Suppression of the régime of commercial treaties—Denunciation of commercial treaties expiring in 1892—Revision of the general tariff—A duty averaging fifteen per cent to be imposed on all foreign agricultural products similar to French products—Maintenance of the duty on wheat—A duty of ten francs per hectoliter on foreign wines—A duty to be established on raisins equivalent to the duty on foreign wines.

II. Reduction of the fiscal charges which burden the farmers. . . .

III. Railroad freight rates—Reductions in rates on fertilizer, agricultural machines, tools and products. . . .

IV. Miscellaneous measures—Loyal execution of the Law of March 21, 1884 on *syndicats agricoles* — Facilities to be given the *syndicats* for the creation of cooperative societies, insurance, pension and mutual-aid funds, etc.—Maintenance of the sugar legislation. . . .[57]

The Catholic *syndicats* were urged by their parent body, the *Oeuvre des cercles catholiques,* to take an active part in this Congress. While they realized that it would deal exclusively with economic matters, the Catholic leaders hoped that their moral and social approach might be expressed, and proposed that the Catholic *syndicats* agree beforehand on measures to be presented at the Congress.[58] They were later able to pride themselves on the fact that their *syndicats* had been "among the most outspoken" on the tariff question.[59] At the end of June 1889, the centenary assembly called together by Social Catholics to commemorate the last meeting of the old Estates adopted

57 TN, vol. VI, 1889, p. 418.

58 AC, vol. XXVII, 1889, I, p. 758.

59 *Corporation*, Feb. 14, 1891.

resolutions regarding agriculture very similar to those moved by the Congress. Indeed, they were sponsored by prominent members of the *Société des agriculteurs,* leaders in the *syndical* movement, Saint-Victor, Milcent and the comte de la Bouillerie. They called for professional representation for agriculture and extension of the *syndical* movement and its activities, compensatory duties, the end of treaties of commerce or the exclusion of agricultural products therefrom, reduction of railway rates.[60]

The program of the agrarian campaign had been elaborated, but it will be remembered that the *syndicats* and, indeed, the *Société des agriculteurs,* had proclaimed complete neutrality on and abstention from political matters. Their intervention in the elections of 1889 rested, therefore, on the distinction discussed above between political activity for economic and social ends and "*la politique,*" the constitutional question.[61] An early step in the campaign was to declare that no questions of "*politique*" were involved. Statements to this effect had indeed been made prior to 1889. In 1887 M. Deusy, an early leader in the *syndical* movement, declared in an address at Tours:

> Yesterday it was an axiom that every republican must be a free trader; tomorrow it will be a truth that one cannot be a republican, a democrat, a friend of the worker, a patriot, without at the same time being a protectionist.[62]

The *syndicats* were told that "the future depends, in large part, on our union, our energy and the perseverance of our efforts."[63] After disclaiming any political intentions, Welche, a prominent member of the *Société des agriculteurs,* stated:

60 *Ibid.*, Aug. 31, 1889; AC, vol. XXVII, 1889, I, p. 489; vol. XXVIII, 1889, II, pp. 80-81. See above, ch. III.

61 See above, pp. 111 ff.

62 BSAF, vol. XIX, 1887, p. 821.

63 *Ibid.*, p. 428.

> Under a government of opinion, the law should belong to the majority, they say; very well, you are in the majority. . . . Band together in your *syndicats,* study your needs, formulate your demands, draw up your *cahiers* of claims as your fathers did one hundred years ago, and on election day, entrust their defense to devoted men who understand and support your interests.[64]

M. Aclocque too disclaimed any political intentions, and declared that the united protectionist forces should concern themselves with the economic rather than the political opinions of candidates.[65] On September 5, 1889, he addressed a letter to the members of the *Association de l'industrie française,* asking them

> to obtain, either by personal intervention with the candidates, or with the Committees which endorse them, or by interpellations in public meetings, the promise that the candidates, if elected, will energetically defend the national endeavor [*travail national*]; that is to say, will pronounce themselves in all economic matters for the solution which would most favor French production and French workers. . . . We speak of agriculturalists and industrialists, because we are convinced that a close solidarity unites them, and because we are in perfect community of ideas with the *Société des agriculteurs de France.* Thus we urgently request you, in your different regions, to unite with the agriculturalists in the *démarches* we ask you to make, in order to give them especial forcefulness.[66]

The agrarian leaders went to the country, addressing public meetings, inspiring *syndicats* and provincial societies to greater efforts, organizing petitions and delegations.[67] Kergall, head of the *Syndicat économique agricole,* was extremely active, speaking in the name of his own organization and of the *Société des agriculteurs.* He tried to instill in the peasants a sense of their own electoral power: they need only organize to command. He

64 *Ibid.*, vol. XX, 1888, pp. 176-177.
65 TN, vol. VI, 1889, p. 157.
66 *Ibid.*, p. 425.
67 CRSAF, BSAF, vol. XXI, 1889, *passim.*

was careful to dissociate protectionism from anti-republican politics:

> We desire liberty of exchange full and complete. We ask only that it be complemented with equality in exchange. We are at the same time free traders and equal traders.
>
> Liberty and equality are two inseparable terms, and of their union only can be born the third term of the republican formula, fraternity.[68]

Speechmaking was too mild a practice for this ardent propagandist, however, and he resorted to more direct means. The following letter was sent to the *syndicats agricoles,* in the summer of 1889, over the signatures of Kergall and his fellow officers of the *Syndicat économique*:

> We have the honor to send to you the program of agricultural demands. These " *cahiers* " of French agriculture for the centenary of 1789 were drawn up by the Congress of *Syndicats agricoles,* . . . and were then ratified by the general assembly of the *Société des agriculteurs de France.*
>
> The Congress and the *Société* have done their task. Ours begins. . . . To pass from theory to practice there must be action, that is to say an appeal to the moral and legal force which assures the triumph of just ideas.
>
> At the present time a powerful, if not infallible method is available to us, besides the ordinary ways of influencing opinion.
>
> HAVE THE CANDIDATES SIGN THE PROGRAM OF AGRICULTURAL DEMANDS, WHICH, IF PUT INTO PRACTICE WOULD CUT SHORT THE AGRICULTURAL CRISIS.
>
> The rural voters exceed five million; this is a majority of the electoral body. If they wish, their defenders will be the majority of the Chamber, and they will wish it if we make them understand their interests. . . .
>
> [Followed by agricultural program, p. 163 above.][69]

68 DR, Nov. 30, 1890; JEC, 1890, p. 90.

69 TN, vol. VI, 1889, pp. 417-418.

Kergall's advice was followed, and candidates for the Chamber soon began to receive letters which declared:

> Sir: The undersigned agriculturalists and industrialists, justly preoccupied with the grave economic questions which the new Chamber will have to solve, consider it necessary to ask the candidates who present themselves to undertake to defend, if they are elected, the interests of agriculture and industry, and to vote measures best suited to maintain and develop French production. . . .
>
> Each of the undersigned expects to reserve his political preferences, but all have decided to support only those candidates who declare themselves resolved to uphold, under all circumstances, the national endeavor [*travail national*].
>
> The undersigned will make known the replies which are sent them, and they are beseeching all agriculturalists and industrialists to do as they do.[70]

The *Syndicat économique agricole* followed a like procedure. Letters were sent to the candidates enclosing the agricultural program and requesting their written adherence thereto. In Kergall's words,

> after a first moment of surprise—our representatives weren't accustomed to having their hands forced in this way—five hundred candidates replied, sending the *Syndicat économique agricole* their signatures at the bottom of the agricultural program. . . . A great number of the very ones who, scandalized by the great liberty taken by Rural Democracy, had refused to send their signatures, saw themselves obliged, before the attitude of their constituents, to make analogous commitments. All over France . . . the list of those who had accepted the agricultural program and of those who had refused was made known to the voters. Some *syndicats* . . . even posted this list.[71]

70 *Ibid.*, p. 427.

71 DR, Aug. 20, 1890. It has been impossible to confirm Kergall's figure as to the number of replies, no relics of the *Syndicat économique* being avail-

These forceful pressure tactics proved successful. Their effectiveness was greatly heightened by the fact that the issue of constitutional reform was the only really live one of the campaign.[72] Although the taint of reaction lingered on the banner of agrarian protection, even the most ardent republican might well hesitate to alienate the rural voters when, after all, the very existence of the Republic seemed to be at stake. The Republic triumphed in the elections of September 22 and October 6, 1889, held on the basis of single-member districts with provision for run-off elections. The groups which had united under the banner of Boulanger won only two hundred ten seats in the new Chamber, the Republicans three hundred sixty-six. There were forty-four Boulangists proper, sixteen of whom were returned by the Department of the Seine. The majority was composed of forty left-center deputies, two hundred sixteen moderates and one hundred radicals. The main source of anti-Republican strength was western France, in the old provinces of Brittany, Normandy, Anjou, and in Poitou and Gascony.[73]

If, as Kergall claims, some five hundred candidates promised him their support, most of these, as we shall see, must have belonged to the defeated reactionary forces. Nevertheless, a protectionist victory had been won, and Kergall did not wait for the opening of the tariff debate to begin the process of reaping its fruits. The method employed to secure the support of candi-

able. Many liberals felt obliged to trim their sails in the protectionist storm. See the remarks of Jules Siegfried (TN, vol. VI, 1889, p. 426). Léon Say, a confirmed liberal, signed the agricultural program.

72 A speaker at a meeting of the liberal *Société d'économie politique*, regretting that the *syndicats* had departed from their legitimate social and economic rôle to become centers of protectionist agitation, remarked that: "the same platform, that of the agricultural program, served parties seemingly most opposed [to each other]. It was no longer a matter of calling oneself republican or conservative, but it was above all necessary to be a defender of agriculture and a protectionist." JEC, ser. 5, vol. I, 1890, p. 89.

73 *Année politique*, vol. XVI, 1889, pp. 197-198. See André Siegfried, *Tableau politique de la France de l'ouest sous la troisième république*, Paris, 1913.

dates was surpassed in audacity only by the way in which the elected deputies were reminded of their pledge and organized to carry it out. On November 19, 1889, Kergall sent the following letter to the members of the Chamber who had acceded to his demand for signed commitments:

> Mr. Deputy,
> An important group of your colleagues who adhered to the agricultural program of the Congress of 1889, as you graciously did, have thought it would be useful to get together. In order to remove all political connotations from this meeting, this group, in which all opinions are represented, but which knows only one in agricultural matters, has graciously given the *Syndicat économique agricole,* previously charged with transmitting the common program and receiving adhesions, the great honor of entrusting it with the first convocation. It is by virtue of this that we ask you to attend the *private* meeting which will take place next Thursday, at the Hotel Continental. . . . The great number of acceptances we have received permits us to say there will be no absentee but politics.[74]

Kergall opened the meeting with an appeal for unity and perseverance, and was named member of the Provisional Committee of the Agricultural Group of the Chamber, although he was not a deputy. He considered this merely a token of appreciation for which he was duly grateful, and resigned before the next meeting.[75]

Both the comte de Rocquigny, member of the *Société des agriculteurs de France* and historian of the *syndicats,* and Elie Coulet, in his *Mouvement syndical,* state that about three hundred deputies attended this meeting.[76] While it is impossible conclusively to confirm or deny this figure it does seem to be exaggerated. *La Démocratie rurale* for November 15, 1891 con-

74 DR, Dec. 15, 1889.

75 *Loc. cit.*

76 Rocquigny, *Syndicats . . . et le socialisme,* p. 97; Coulet, *op. cit.,* p. 162.

tains a list of those deputies who signed the agricultural program and/or two other proposals. This list numbers two hundred twenty-one, and we may be permitted to conclude that the attendance at the Hotel Continental was certainly no greater, and in all probability lower than this number.[77]

Over two-thirds of the names appearing on this list were those of members of the Right. The Hotel Continental meeting therefore elected as head of the Agricultural Group the Rightist Deputy Admiral Dompierre d'Hornoy.[78] On November 25th, four days after this gathering, a Republican Agricultural Group met and unanimously named Méline president. This organization comprised one hundred twenty deputies.[79]

It was apparent that the two groups must unite if agricultural protection was to triumph. The Right took the initiative, and named a committee headed by Dompierre d'Hornoy to consult with Méline.[80] The result was that the more numerous Rightists fused into the smaller Republican group. On December 5th Méline was acclaimed as president of the unified Agricultural Group. De Juigné, former head of the Agricultural Group of the Right, and Develle, Republican ex-Minister of Agriculture, were named vice-presidents.[81] De Cassagnac, the Rightist deputy who moved Méline's election, declared that:

> The Right will courageously place itself at the head of this sacred task [of assistance to agriculture], on which depends the existence of the fatherland, and it proves, in joining with the Republican group, that every time national interest calls,

77 DR, Nov. 15, 1891. A list of deputies, by department and party, is given in *l'Année politique*, vol. XVI, 1889, pp. 346 ff. Against this reasoning is the fact that the comte de Rocquigny may well have had first-hand knowledge of the meeting. Unfortunately, it has been impossible to find a simple list of signatories of the agricultural program.

78 DR, Dec. 8, 1889.

79 TN, vol. VI, 1889, p. 563.

80 *Le Temps*, Nov. 27, 1889: TN, *loc cit.*

81 TN, vol. VI, 1889, p. 570.

> it can forget the spirit of party, to obey only the spirit of duty.[82]

Kergall was rather chagrined at the partial effacement of the Right, whose members had predominated at his meeting at the Hotel Continental, but—"Very well! the deputies of the Right have accepted everything, sacrificed all to a union indispensable to French agriculture." [83]

The reasons for this self-sacrifice are not hard to find. The Right, it is true, were originally the more numerous. Nevertheless it was they who entered into the Republican group, under Méline's leadership. But the unified Agricultural Group, as finally constituted, numbered three hundred and one deputies, of whom one hundred seventy-five were Republicans.[84] Only one hundred twenty were present at the first meeting of the Republican Agricultural Group; the rest entered after the unification. Had the situation been reversed, however, had Rightist leadership been maintained, the cry of anti-republicanism would have been raised against the agrarian protectionists, and the political issues of the campaign injected into the tariff question with results fatal to their cause. Méline's excellent standing with the industrialists, whose support was essential, was another factor in determining the outcome. On both these counts, therefore, it was logical that the Right, which formed the backbone of agricultural protectionism, should yield the foreground to the Republicans.[85]

While the Parliament met in special session on November 12, 1889, it was only in the Fall of 1890 that the tariff was introduced, and only in the Spring of 1891 that it came to the floor

82 DR, Dec. 8, 1889.

83 *Ibid.*, Dec. 15, 1889.

84 *Ibid.*, Jan. 19, 1890, contains a list of the unified Agricultural Group.

85 A group of "*Le Travail National*" was founded in the Chamber to represent industry, under Richard Waddington and Dautresme, Republican deputies of Seine-Inférieure. The *Association de l'industrie* expressed the hope that they would cooperate closely with the Agricultural Group. TN, vol. VI, 1889, pp. 559, 569.

of the Chamber of Deputies. In the intervening time, however, the groundwork, both legislative and political, had been laid. On January 20, 1890, Méline demanded the election of a Tariff Commission of fifty-five. This move was interpreted by some as an attack on the cabinet which was headed by the liberal Tirard.[86] The latter did not oppose the measure strongly, and on January 28th the Commission was named. It consisted of fifty Republicans and five Rightists; thirty-nine were protectionists, eight moderate protectionists and eight were considered free traders.[87] The composition of this body was clear evidence of the strength of the protectionist current, and therefore of parliamentary storms in store for the government. It was the Senate, however, that actually overthrew the cabinet.

On March 13, 1890 the Franco-Turkish commercial treaty of 1861 expired. The government had reached an accord with Turkey providing for reciprocal most-favored-nation treatment under treaties dating back to 1802 and 1838. This arrangement had escaped censure in the Chamber, but on the date of expiration of the pact, the Senate, against the wishes of the cabinet, voted an *ordre du jour* inviting " the government to negotiate with Turkey a *modus vivendi* destined to terminate with the commercial treaties now existing." Tirard and his Foreign Minister, Spuller, felt themselves personally involved in this defeat, and led their cabinet in resigning.[88]

They were succeeded on March 17th by a cabinet headed by Senator Freycinet, which was to remain in office throughout the period of elaboration of the tariff law. As Ministers of Commerce and Agriculture, he chose, to replace Tirard and Faye, who leaned toward economic liberalism, Jules Roche and Develle, both members of the unified Agricultural Group, the latter being a vice-president.[89]

86 *Année politique*, vol. XVII, 1890, p. 7.

87 *Loc. cit.*; CDP, 1891, p. 2; JEC, ser. 5, vol. 5, 1891, p. 6.

88 SD, 1890, p. 563. The vote on the *ordre du jour* was 153 to 95. See Arnauné, *op. cit.*, pp. 314-315; *Année politique*, vol. XVII, 1890, pp. 64-65.

89 See Émile Simond, *Histoire de la troisième république de 1887 à 1894: présidence de M. Carnot*, Paris, 1913, p. 107.

The ministerial declaration of the new government clearly indicated the changed attitude of the executive toward protection:

> The country has stated its wish to revise the bases of its tariff system. It awaits, not without impatience, the expiration of the treaties of commerce which still bind us to various nations, and it expects that from January 1, 1892, it will be wholly master of the arrangement of its tariffs. After a thoughtful study, it requires of them more effective protection for agriculture and the national endeavor [*travail national*]. The government unreservedly adheres to this thought. It will take measures so that, on the appointed day, nothing will hinder the liberty of the Parliament, even with respect to the friendly nation whose commercial relations with France were recently the subject of the deliberations of the Senate.[90]

In order to prepare its tariff bill, the government commenced an *enquête* among such organizations as Chambers of Commerce, *chambres consultatives* and trade associations, and sought the advice of the Superior Council of Industry and Commerce and the Superior Council of Agriculture.[91] Ninety-six of one hundred seven Chambers of Commerce requested the denunciation of the commercial treaties, and only thirty-five proposed that new ones be negotiated. Forty-five of fifty *chambres consultatives* took the same position, and only ten suggested new pacts: many departmental Councils General, meeting in April, 1890, joined in condemning the trade treaties.[92] It is worth noting, however, that among the Chambers of Commerce

90 CD, 1890, p. 563.

91 Levasseur, *op. cit.*, vol. II, pp. 365 ff.; A. J. Wolfe, *Commercial organisations in France: with a summary of governmental activities in promoting commerce*, U. S. Department of Commerce, Bureau of Foreign and Domestic Commerce, Special Agents, No. 98, Washington, 1918; see above, p. 42. The Superior Councils were appointed by the Ministers of Commerce and Agriculture, and therefore reflected the ministerial viewpoint, which, in this case, tended to be more moderate than that of the *Société des agriculteurs.*

92 BSAF, vol. XXII, 1890, pp. 319 ff., 531-532; Augier and Marvaud, *op. cit.*, p. 21.

recommending the negotiation of new accords were those of the great centers, Paris, Lyon, Marseille, Bordeaux.[93]

It is not surprising that the *syndicats agricoles* should have taken advantage of this opportunity to express their protectionist views, and the *Société des agriculteurs* again let its voice be heard. Its president, the marquis de Dampierre, sent a circular letter to the members of Parliament, and the Ministers of Agriculture, Foreign Affairs and Commerce, recalling the *Société's enquête,* and enclosing its tariff proposals for their renewed consideration.[94]

The Superior Council of Commerce and Industry recommended the denunciation of the existing trade treaties, but suggested that conventions of shorter duration, to expire simultaneously, be concluded on the basis of a double tariff. This system, comprising a general tariff applicable to all nations, and a lower, minimum tariff applicable to those states with which France had commercial accords, had previously been suggested by Waddington during the elaboration of the Tariff of 1881.[95] The advantages of this scheme were said to be, first, that it made France master of her tariffs, in that the rates of both schedules could be changed at will by Parliament, and, second, that it avoided the reprisals a single high tariff might invite. It was more flexible than the conventional system, more stable than the single tariff subject to continual legislative revision.

The Superior Council of Agriculture completed its work late in July 1890. Its tariff committee was headed by Lecouteux, one of the founders of the *Société des agriculteurs* and editor of the *Journal d'agriculture pratique,* who was more moderate in his protectionism than the leaders of the *Société.* He conceived the Council's duty and purpose to be to create " a tariff which aids the recovery of agriculture, without, on the other hand,

93 *Année politique,* vol. XVII, 1890, p. 132.

94 BSAF, vol. XXII, 1890, pp. 481 ff.

95 *Année politique, loc. cit.*; Clough, *op. cit.,* p. 225.

COMPARISON OF DUTIES ON SEV

	Old Law		Proposals of *Soc. des Agriculteurs*	Propos of Supe Council Agricult
	General	Conventional		
Horses	30 [a]	——	40 [a]	30 [a]
Hogs	6 [a]	——	10 [b] 10 [a]	6 [b]
Oxen	38 [a]	——	60 [a] 10 [b]	8 [b]
Cows	20 [a]	——	40 [a] 10 [b]	6 [b]
Sheep	5 [a]	——	8 [a]	6 [a]
Poultry	20 [b]	5 [b]	25 [b]	10 [b]
Fresh Beef	12 [b]	3 [b]	25 [b]	16 [b]
Pork, Bacon etc.	12 [b]	3 [b]	12 [b]	12 [b]
Salt Beef, etc.	8.50 [b]	4.50 [b]	20 [b]	20 [b]
Salt Pork	8.50 [b]	4.50 [b]	20 [b]	15 [b]
Soft Cheese	6 [b]	3 [b]	25 [b]	6 [b]
Hard Cheese	8 [b]	4 [b]	25 [b]	12 [b]
Combed or Carded Wool	25 [b]	25 [b]	50 [b]	30 [b]
Raw Slk	——	——	5 [b]	(tax o cocoon
Wheat, Grain	5 [b]	——	5 [b]	5 [b]
Wheat, over 10% Flour	8 [b]	——	8 [b]	8 [b]
Barley	1.50 [b]	——	3 [b]	2 [b]
Barley Flour	——	——	6 [b]	3.50 [b]
Rye, Corn	3 [b]	——	3 [b]	3 [b]
Rye, Corn Flour	5 [b]	——	6 [b]	5 [b]
Oleaginous Seeds	——	——	4 [b]	1.25 [b]
Carded Hemp	——	——	15 [b]	——
Wine	4.50 to 15° h.l. [c]; over 15° alcohol tax on volume above 51°; 4.50 on rest	2 h.l. [c] to 15°; over 15° alcohol tax on volume above 51°, 2 on rest	12 to 14.9° h.l. [c]; over 14.9° alcohol tax on volume above 14.9°, 12 on rest	.70 per ° h.l. to 12 over 12° per ° per h.l.

[a] per head. [b] per 100 kilograms. [c] per hectoliter.

RICULTURAL PRODUCTS (in francs)[97]

Government Bill		Chamber Tariff Commission		Méline Tariff	
eneral	Minimum	General	Minimum	General	Minimum
30 [a]	—	30 [a]	—	30 [a]	—
6 [b]	—	8 [b]	—	8 [b]	—
10 [b]	—	10 [b] *	—	10 [b]	—
20 [b]	—	10 [b]	—	10 [b]	—
5.50 [b]	—	15.50 [b]	—	15.50 [b]	—
20 [b]	15 [b]	20 [b]	—	20 [b]	—
20 [b]	—	25 [b]	—	25 [b]	—
10 [b]	—	12 [b]	—	12 [b]	—
22 [b]	—	30 [b]	27 [b]	30 [b]	27 [b]
12 [b]	—	20 [b]	15 [b]	25 [b]	—
6 [b]	3 [b]	25 [b]	15 [b]	25 [b]	15 [b]
12 [b]	8 [b]	30 [b]	20 [b]	25 [b]	15 [b]
2.50 [b]	25 [b]	32.50 [b]	25 [b]	32.50 [b]	25 [b]
—	—	—	—	—	—
5 [b]	—	5 [b]	—	5 [b]	—
8 [b]	—	8 [b]	—	8 [b] **	—
2 [b]	—	3 [b]	—	3 [b]	—
.50 [b]	—	5 [b]	—	5 [b]	—
3 [b]	—	3 [b]	—	3 [b]	—
5 [b]	—	5 [b]	—	5 [b]	—
–1.50 [b]	.75–1.50 [b]	1–4 [b]	.75–3 [b]	—	—
—	—	15.60 [b]	12 [b]	15 [b]	10 [b]
er ° per o 12°; 12° alcohol n each ° 12	.50 per ° per h.l. to 12°; over 12° .50 + alcohol tax on each ° above 12	1.20 per ° per h.l. to 10.90°; from 11° 1.20 + alcohol tax on each ° above 11	.70 per ° per per h.l. to 10.90°; from 11° .70 + alcohol tax on each ° above 11	1.20 per ° per h.l. to 10.90°; from 11° 1.20 + alcohol tax on each ° above 11	.70 per ° per h.l. to 10.90°; from 11° .70 + alcohol tax on each ° above 11

inimum of 50 fr. ** rising to 12 on 40% flour and above.

too radically and too abruptly changing the habits of protection acquired by industry over long years."[96] The rates proposed by the Council (see table, p. 174A) were therefore on the whole higher than those of the existing law, but lower than those demanded by the *Société des agriculteurs.*[97] A significant change was the conversion of livestock duties from a head to a weight basis. Lecouteux justified the increase in these rates on the ground that industry always asked for protection to improve its equipment: agriculture was entitled to similar aid, and since its principal equipment was the soil, constantly depleted by grain crops, it was necessary to grant protection to manure-producing livestock.[98]

The Council declined to vote on processed foods, including such products as spaghetti and jams, as falling more properly within the jurisdiction of the Superior Council of Commerce and Industry.[99] But it entered into conflict with the latter in a matter that revealed a basic divergence between industry and agriculture. It demanded a duty on raw silk, and, in proposing a five per cent *ad valorem* tax on cocoons, recommended that this be raised to twelve per cent if raw silk were kept on the free list. Similarly, it called for a surtax on sheep if wool were to be admitted free. The Superior Council of Commerce and Industry, on the contrary, insisted on complete freedom for silk and wool.[100] The difficult, and persistent, problem of raw-material protection thus appeared at the very beginning of the process of writing the tariff law.

The *Société des agriculteurs* was dissatisfied with the work of the Superior Council of Agriculture. While this body and its

96 JAP, ser. 6, vol. XLVI, 1890, II, pp. 77, 115.

97 The degree of increase should be measured against the conventional rather than the general tariff, for the most-favored-nation clause had made the latter on the whole inoperative. The figures in the table are drawn from CDP, 1891, pp. 14 ff.; JO, Jan. 12, 1892; CRSAF, vol. XXI, 1889, pp. 82 ff.; DR, Aug. 31, 1890; JAP, ser. 6, vol. XLVI, 1890, II, pp. 75 ff., 110 ff.

98 JAP, ser. 6, vol. XLVI, 1890, II, p. 78.

99 BSAF, vol. XXII, 1890, p. 628.

100 JAP, ser. 6, vol. XLVI, 1890, II, p. 110.

counterpart in Commerce and Industry were deliberating, a delegation of the *Société* visited Roche and Develle to urge upon them the moderation of the *Société's* proposals and to proclaim the falseness of the concept of raw materials. Roche replied evasively: with respect to purely agricultural products he would conform to the recommendations of the Minister of Agriculture, as for products converted by industry, he had to make reservations, but would pay great attention to the attitude of the *Société*. Develle promised protection for agriculture, but warned of the difficulties inherent in the problem of raw materials.[101] Despite this rather cautious reply, the *Société*, in disapproving the rates of the Superior Council of Agriculture, continued to hope that Develle would revise its schedules in their favor.[102] The *Société* also attacked the double tariff. Granting a minimum tariff by conventions was merely a subterfuge for trade treaties, it argued, and proposed instead that the general tariff be the minimum, to be raised whenever it was necessary to retaliate.[103] The marquis de Dampierre wrote to the members of the Senate and Chamber Tariff Commissions, comparing the schedules of the *Société des agriculteurs* and the Superior Council of Agriculture, vigorously attacking the latter and condemning the double tariff.[104] Recalling the tactics employed during the electoral campaign, Le Trésor de la Rocque, head of the *Union centrale*, sent a circular letter to the presidents of member *syndicats*, indicating the difference between these two sets of rates. He concluded:

> This differential appears extremely regrettable to our *Union*, and as one likely to prepare, on the part of the government, a solution which would be decidedly unfavorable to us. I thought you could take advantage of the Parliamentary recess, and of the sessions of the Councils General, to stimulate reso-

101 BSAF, vol. XXII, 1890, pp. 545 ff.

102 *Ibid.*, pp. 573, 627 ff.

103 *Ibid.*, p. 550.

104 *Ibid.*, p. 729.

lutions and *démarches* for the adoption of our proposals. The *syndicats agricoles* . . . will have every chance for success if they intervene without delay with the senators, deputies and councillors general of their departments who undertook, at the time of their election, to support the demands of agriculture. . . . [105]

Lecouteux warned against exaggerated demands on the part of the *Société des agriculteurs.* He declared that he had had too much responsibility in its creation to wish to see it tread dangerous ground. At the same time he used the intransigeance of the *Société* to support the position of the Superior Council of Agriculture. In a letter to Develle he pointed out that the increases recommended by the Council were absolutely necessary. They had the merit, he declared, of being more moderate than the proposals of some overzealous friends of agriculture, and hence would not encourage excessive "compensatory" increases in industrial duties.[106]

Although the general principle of protectionism was accepted, the difficulty always present in tariff making had arisen. There was no agreement as to what constituted "just and adequate" protection, and the decision as to particular rates was in the hands of Parliament.

105 DR, Aug. 31, 1890. The attention given the *Société des agriculteurs* may raise a question as to the activities of the *Société nationale d'encouragement à l'agriculture* (see above, p. 43). This organization favored agricultural protection, but did not, however, conduct any public campaign. Its leaders were Republican senators and deputies, and its membership was largely among officeholders. While its president, Senator Jules Guichard, congratulated the *Société nationale* following the passage of the Méliné Tariff, a *résumé* of the organization's activities since its founding included little besides holding competitions, granting prizes, etc. Its protectionist activities were probably confined to the Parliament, and in view of the constitution of the Agricultural Groups, were in all likelihood not undertaken as a body. See: JAP, ser. 6, vol. XLV, 1890, I, p. 267; vol. XLVII, 1891, I, p. 193; vol. XLVIII, 1891, II, p. 578; vol. XLIX, 1892, I, p. 275; *Bulletin Agricole*, Jan. 11, 1891.

106 Jap, ser. 6, vol. XLVI, 1890, II, pp. 256 ff.

CHAPTER VI

THE PASSAGE OF THE MELINE TARIFF

THE preliminary work of preparation had been completed by the end of the summer of 1890, and on October 20th Roche and Develle introduced the bill in the Chamber of Deputies. The *exposé des motifs* recognized that an overwhelming majority demanded a reorientation of policy, because " economic conditions have changed to such an extent that our tariff system no longer corresponds to their present state." The increase and spread of technical knowledge had destroyed the old monopolies of national tradition. New lands with low taxes, improved means of transport were factors in the new economic world. Even before the régime of 1881 had been instituted, the doom of free trade had been evident. Germany, in 1879, led a procession of nations toward protectionism, and France had no choice but to follow. Commercial treaties, defended as stable, and as being favorable to France's export industries, had been attacked as binding and anachronistic. With regard to both trade relations with other lands and the duties themselves, however, the government did not wish to race from one extreme to the other. Hence it urged its duties, as moderate, and the double tariff, as a fair compromise.[1]

The rates proposed by the government on agricultural products (see table, p. 174A) were generally higher than those suggested by the Superior Council of Agriculture, but lower than those demanded by the *Société des agriculteurs*. The latter was pleased with most duties on livestock and meats, which illustrated " the usefulness of the intervention of our *Société* and the solicitude of the Minister of Agriculture for agricultural interests." [2] It raised three objections, however. In another letter to

1 CDP, 1890, II (Sess. extra.), pp. 1 ff.

2 BSAF, vol. XXII, 1890, p. 982; CRSAF, vol. XXIII, 1891, p. 82.

the Tariff Commissions of the Senate and Chamber, the marquis de Dampierre declared that the minimum tariff maintained

> under another name, with all its disadvantages and almost none of its advantages, the régime of commercial treaties, whose abandonment the great majority of the country energetically demanded.[3]

With respect to raw materials, wool, skins and silk, the government draft would tend to

> keep agriculture in the difficult, unequal and unjust situation against which she has protested for over ten years. This situation could become even more burdensome in that the new general tariff in preparation increases, to a notable degree, and at nearly all points, the already significant protection covering most industrial products.[4]

Lastly, the *Société* argued that agriculture received much less protection than industry. They claimed that whereas duties on manufactured articles averaged between twenty-five and thirty per cent, agricultural rates did not exceed fifteen per cent, and the raw materials failed to receive even this modest protection.[5] Lecouteux, on the other hand, felt that with a few changes the government bill would achieve a proper balance among the various branches of national production, and he regarded its general schedule as a maximum which should not receive upward revision in Parliament.[6]

In this he was doomed to disappointment. The Tariff Commission of the Chamber had an overwhelming majority of protectionists, as we have seen. In considering the proposals set before it, the Commission, "pressed for time," conducted no *enquête,* but studied the data gathered in the period of preparation. In addition, it relied upon the researches of the various

3 BSAF, vol. XXII, 1890, p. 1061.

4 *Ibid.*, p. 1024.

5 Luçay and Sénart, *op. cit.*, p. xvi.

6 JAP, ser. 6, vol. XLVI, 1890, II, p. 878.

rapporteurs of the different sections of the bill. These men were selected on the basis of their competence in the fields in question, but, as Levasseur remarks, "they, by this very act, were personally interested in protection."[7]

The Commission started its work on October 28th; its conclusions were presented to the Chamber on March 3, 1891, by Jules Méline, its president and *rapporteur général*.[8] Méline

7 CDP, 1891, p. 2, *Rapport général* of Méline, Annex No. 1257; Levasseur, *op. cit.*, vol. II, p. 579.

An interesting sidelight on the proceedings of the Commission is given by this exchange in the Chamber (CD, 1890, p. 935):

"M. Georges Graux: When has the North ever broken its engagements?

"M. Edouard Lockroy: My God... I will remind you of what happened at the meeting before last of the Tariff Commission. Our colleague, M. Turrel, ...addressing the president of the Commission, said to him: 'But if you uphold the Tunisian Tariff you do harm to our wines, and in that case we won't vote your duty on corn...." (*Ah, ah! at the Left*).

"M. Turrel: Certainly: and I have nothing to take back of what I said. We are supporters of the solidarity of all agricultural interests, and of equal protection for all. (*Very good! and applause at various benches in the Center and Right*)....

"M. Méline: You try in vain to disunite us, you won't succeed, and we will prove it to you by our vote! (*Applause at the same benches*)....

"M. Bouge: Is this the way they make laws? It's an unspeakable bargain (*Exclamations at Center*)."

8 Méline was born at Remiremont, Vosges, in 1838. He studied and practiced law at Paris. During the siege of Paris in the Franco-Prussian War he was deputy-mayor of the First Arrondissement of the capital, but resigned during the Commune. In 1872 he was elected to the National Assembly from the department of the Vosges, which steadily returned him thereafter. His first executive position was that of undersecretary of state in the Ministry of Justice in the Jules Simon cabinet of 1876. In 1883 he was appointed Minister of Agriculture by his friend Jules Ferry. In the meantime he won increasing prominence in the Chamber. He was *rapporteur* on the Tariff of 1881, and in 1888 was elected president of the Chamber as a Moderate over the Radical Clemenceau (the vote was tied, but Méline won on seniority). Méline had been offered the Presidency of the Council of Ministers in February 1889, but had not succeeded in forming a cabinet. He finally became premier in 1896, and for two years held this post and the Ministry of Agriculture. The Méline government was characterized by a policy of conciliation toward the *ralliés*, and by the passage of a number of social reforms and the proposal of others. (See Moon, *op. cit.*, pp. 203 ff.) The cabinet fell on July 14, 1898 as a result of its position in the Dreyfus Case, which was epitomized by Méline's famous remark: "*Il n'y a pas d'affaire Dreyfus.*"

commenced by denying that the majority of the Commission was protectionist as such.

> It does not make an absolute principle of tariff protection, a sort of dogma, as has so long been made of free trade: in protection as in free trade it sees only processes of international regulation of exchange, good or bad, according to times, places, the economic and financial condition of different peoples. In its eyes, the best for a nation is that which assures it the greatest amount of work, since the more work there is, the more capital, and as a result more wages for the working masses. It is not surprising that England is a free trade country, and pushes all nations along the road of free trade; her very interest directs it thus.[9]

In the Chamber, and later in the Senate, he defended the protectionist position and initiated programs of agricultural aid such as the laws of 1894 and 1898 on mutual insurance. In 1915, at the age of seventy-eight, he returned to the Ministry of Agriculture in the Cabinet of Sacred Union. He died, aged eighty-seven, in 1925, and three years later a monument was erected to his memory in his native town of Remiremont. (See Gabriel Hanotaux, "Jules Méline," *Revue des deux mondes*, 7th series, vol. XXXI, 1926, pp. 440 ff.; Georges Lachapelle, *Le ministère Méline*, Paris, 1928; address by M. Cournault, president of the *Société des agriculteurs, Bulletin de l'Union des syndicats agricoles Vosgiens*, June 1938.

9 CDP, 1891, p. 2. Méline's economic and social philosophy was set forth in two books (*Le retour à la terre et la surproduction industrielle*, Paris, 1905, appearing as *The return to the land*, pref. and trans. Justin McCarthy, New York, 1907; *Le salut par la terre*, 2nd ed., Paris, 1920). Its keynote was that agriculture, less spectacular perhaps, was in the long run a more secure and wise field for investment and endeavor. Industrial capacity of the world had been over-developed, given the need and desire of nations for independence, hence protection. A return to the land was the most promising solution to the problem of the resulting industrial unemployment. Excessive intermediary costs, the scarcity of farm labor (partly resulting from the glamour of the cities) and credit difficulties were obstacles to this solution. Wise governmental aid and intervention might surmount these, he felt, especially in the three countries which had maintained a degree of balance between industry and agriculture—Russia, the United States and France. For the latter, a return to the land through small ownership is the way of escape from the dangers of economic crises, socialism and depopulation.

If the régime of 1860, merely modified by that of 1881, declared Méline, did not cause as much disaster as might have been expected, this was because France was relatively prosperous at that time. This system may well have aided a few export industries, but it sacrificed the basic ones—and agriculture. Since then the situation has changed completely. At that time each nation produced just about enough food for its own needs. Now the lands of Europe try to export, and there are the young countries,

> favored by nature and by their financial situation with exceptional advantages, a virgin soil almost without [monetary] value, for some, unbelievably cheap labor, the absence of military expenses and insignificant fiscal charges. In 1860 these peoples still slept. . . . America was still so far! As for India and Australia, who for an instant could have thought of them? One hardly thought of Russia.
>
> But suddenly there came the development of means of transportation and communication, the rapid decrease in freight costs, in a few years placing these great markets at our door. . . .

In addition, French producers had to face the severe financial burden resulting from the disaster of 1870. And other nations, including Germany and the United States, had adopted high tariffs. If France failed to take measures to defend herself, she would inevitably become the dumping ground of all Europe. All this, declared Méline, created "the imperious necessity of the revision of our customs duties in the direction of a just compensation between French and foreign production."

Méline dismissed the question of cheap goods on several grounds. Much like Carey, he identified trade with speculation, and felt that the object of national policy should be to diminish middlemen's profits, and secure lower prices through the expansion of national production.[10]

10 See also Bajkić, *op. cit.*, p. 445.

> The development of production, stimulating the natural play of internal competition, will ceaselessly tend to lower the prices of goods, and to keep them at a reasonable level. The great error of the free-trade school is to seek low prices through the invasion of foreign products, instead of in the increase and progress of national production: this kind of cheapness not only has the great disadvantage of ruining the producer, it is very often more apparent than real. The intermediary who is the master of prices awards himself all the profits. . . .

Adopting the productivity thesis of nationalist economics, Méline went on to praise the relative security of the national system, its avoidance of crises of overproduction and of dislocations of foreign origin.[11] He recognized the interdependence of the various branches of production, and the justice of their claim to equal treatment by the state. But, he declared,

> if the rule of justice and equality was easy to lay down, it must be recognized that it was not so easy to apply. Agriculture and industry are not separated by an insurmountable wall; there are meeting points between them where their interests seem to conflict, without one's being able to blend them and serve them at the same time.
>
> With the best will in the world, it is impossible, in these particular instances, to give them equal shares, and of sheer necessity one must choose and give preference to the dominant interest.

The Commission, he continued, has not been guided by the old, false doctrine of raw materials, and the proof of this is that it recommended duties on oleaginous seeds.[12] If it has not granted similar protection to wool, skins and silk, it is because this would tend to diminish rather than increase national production, and harm industries " which are the honor of France."

11 See Méline's address to the workers of Granges, Vosges, TN, vol. VIII, 1891, p. 525.

12 See also JAP, ser. 6, vol. XLV, 1890, I, p. 621.

Besides, indirect protection has been given to wool and skins by the increased rates on livestock and meat. Thus Méline felt justified in saying that the Commission had "applied the same principles to agriculture and industry, and that it had kept an equal balance among all French workers." While it was true that agricultural duties were on the whole lower than industrial ones, he argued, industry had to pay duties on most raw and semi-finished materials, and the more steps involved in processing, the higher the tariff should be. In any event, if industry were inadequately protected it would be unable to buy the products of agriculture.

To this point, Méline's position was closer to that of the nationalist economists than that of the *Société des agriculteurs.* He returned to the less academic, more traditional point of view with respect to balance of trade, in what Morini-Comby calls the weak point of his *rapport.*[13] After indicating the extent of France's adverse commodity balance, he declared:

> I well know that it will be objected that the general trade balance lies not only in the customs figures, and that it is composed of many other factors, such as French investments abroad, the money spent by foreigners in France, the profits of our exports, etc. We freely agree: but it will be granted that the movement of international commerce, as it appears in the customs tables, is, in any event, one of the very important factors in the general trade balance. . . .
>
> It is clear that we should be richer if our exports had been considerable and our imports less substantial: it is equally evident that if the balance is stated from the standpoint of the sum of French labor, one is forced to agree that that which the foreigner gave us through the increase of his purchases has in no way compensated for that which he has taken from us through [the increase] of his sales.

Having set forth and defended the work of the Commission, Méline turned to the question of the double tariff. He declared

13 Morini-Comby, *op. cit.*, p. 151.

that it was superior to both the conventional and single-tariff systems, being more flexible than the first, more stable than the second. Méline strangely disagreed with both the government and the majority of the Commission with respect to the exclusion of agricultural products from the minimum schedule. He conceded that it was advisable to exclude grain, for if the minimum were too low it would fail to protect, if the maximum were raised prices would soar. But to exclude livestock would make the minimum tariff less attractive to other nations, increase the difficulty of negotiations, and pave the way for a drive for a single tariff for all agricultural commodities, which, because of retaliation, might ruin their export trade. Nevertheless, he understood the fears of agriculture, based on past experience, and bowed to the will of the majority.[14]

Méline concluded by insisting on the moderation of the Commission's draft. Its rates, he said, will seem insufficient to those who have "dreamed of a régime of inflexible logic, applying symmetrically the same quantum of protection to all foreign products without distinction." They will seem excessive to those who refuse to consider the present situation, and the impossibility of survival for many branches of production without protection The tariff will yield much needed revenue. Some people object that it will permit no imports, and that therefore no duties will actually be paid. But this would hold true only if it were excessive, and it is not. The duties suggested

> are only compensatory, and we well know they will in no sense dry up foreign imports. They will only keep them in check: they will prevent the debasement of prices in our internal market, and we ask no more. . . .
>
> We are convinced that all impartial minds who will examine our work without prejudice will be obliged to recognize that

14 Kergall wrote: "This *volte face* of M. Méline will cause a profound disillusionment, and if our generation had as much courage [*sang*] as that of 1789, one would hear shouted in all the streets and on all the roads of France: *The great treason of M. Méline*, as one hundred years ago, *the great treason of M. de Mirabeau*." DR, March 7, 1891.

> we have modified our economic régime only insofar as absolutely necessary. We have made every effort to facilitate the transitions, and conciliate all the interests involved.[15]

In most instances, the agricultural rates (see tables, p. 174A), introduced by this statement of policy, and by a group of specific reports,[16] marked still another step along the road to high protection. The schedules of the Superior Council of Agriculture called for duties higher than those of the existing law, and the government bill went further. The Tariff Commission continued this upward process, but in some respects still failed to satisfy the *Société des agriculteurs.* The marquis de Dampierre declared that the high industrial duties and very moderate agricultural rates did not represent " the equality we have been demanding, the equality promised us." [17] Lavollée, chiefly responsible for drafting the *Société's* tariff proposals, was more outspoken and much more bitter.

> Thus, in effect, we asked that there be but one tariff: there are two. We asked that there be no more treaties of commerce: there will be, under another name. We asked, if it was necessary to have them, that at least agricultural products be not included: they propose to include them. We asked that customs equality be reestablished between agriculture and industry: it is not. We asked that all agricultural products be taxed: some, and among the most important, will continue to be admitted free according to the proposed tariffs.
>
> Such is the consideration they have given the demands of agriculture.[18]

Roche and Develle, for their part, had already indicated their disapproval of the increases made by the Commission. The former had insisted that hemp be kept on the free list: the latter, that his rates on meats be restored, and that oleaginous seeds,

15 For the foregoing, CDP, 1891, pp. 2-11.

16 Special reports are to be found in CDP, 1891 (see *Tables*).

17 CRSAF, vol. XXIII, 1891, pp. 21-22.

18 *Ibid.*, pp. 80-81.

for which he himself had proposed low duties, now be admitted free.[19] The Commission made only slight concessions to the Ministers,[20] but it was to face their renewed opposition on the floor of the Chamber, which tended to regain for it the support of the *Société des agriculteurs*.

The debate opened in the Chamber of Deputies on April 28th, following the Easter recess, and continued to July 18th, consuming forty-one sessions of the lower house. The summer recess then intervened, and the tariff was the subject of twenty-two sessions of the Senate between November 19th and December 18th. The bill then twice returned to the Chamber for adjustment of differences, and was finally passed on January 7, 1892.[21]

It cannot be said that either the art of oratory or the study of economics was greatly advanced by the proceedings in the Chamber. The most effective opposition speakers were Edouard Lockroy, of Paris, Aynard, of Lyon, and the economist Léon Say: the protectionist case was most competently presented by Viger, Deschanel and Méline.

Lockroy warned that the bill involved much more than a mere modification of certain duties. It was an effort to destroy the accomplishments of the republican assemblies:

> In fact, behind this great economic undertaking there is a political undertaking. It is the adversaries of the Republic who, after having failed in their efforts at restoration of the monarchy, try today to revive the aristocracy which formerly gathered about the throne of Louis-Philippe! [22]

From the economic standpoint, Lockroy declared that French soil was as poor that day as when it came "from the primordial ocean, thousands of centuries ago." It cannot feed the

19 BSAF, vol. XXII, 1890, p. 1109; vol. XXIII, 1891, p. 292.

20 It agreed to reduce its duties on meat extracts and jute.

21 CD, 1891, pp. 546, 641; Dijol, *op. cit.*, pp. 21-22.

22 CD, 1891, p. 714.

French people, and France should not be protectionist when there is nothing to protect. Besides, French industry and agriculture have actually prospered under the régime of 1860 and 1881. France is still not only the richest and most prosperous country in Europe, but also the country

> where social peace rules in the highest degree, that where social demands are least heard, where social antagonisms, where the hatred of classes are most soothed, and all this thanks to the régime of political liberty and commercial liberty.[23]

He attacked the proposed duties as an illogical conglomeration, which could only cost France her foreign trade, disrupt her economy and constitute a tax on the consumers.

> Yes, you vote duties on all things, for you pretend to protect everyone equally. Very well, let me tell you that that is a chimera, considering that it is the essence of protection to create privilege and inequality . . . and the day one wishes to protect everyone, one no longer protects anyone. . . .[24]

The protectionist folly, he argued, would drive the masses toward socialism, and would not help agriculture. There was no sense in pointing to Germany and the United States, for the former was near social revolution, and American agriculture was mortgaged to the financiers.[25] He concluded by urging France to adopt a policy of wise and moderate liberalism.

Aynard declared that while he and his friend Lockroy held certain theoretical views, they were not doctrinaires. Complete freedom of trade would be splendid for England, but it is because " we wish to husband the existing industries that we are not absolute free traders; we are 'temperate' free traders, we content ourselves with the *status quo.*" [26] Calling on the author-

23 *Ibid.*, pp. 712, 722.

24 *Ibid.*, p. 713.

25 *Ibid.*, pp. 717, 718, 723.

26 *Ibid.*, pp. 745-746, 755.

ity of J. B. Say, Aynard scorned Méline's views on a favorable trade belance as being either a play on words or senseless.[27] He then went on to attack agricultural protection. It could benefit only the great landowners: the small proprietor would produce barely enough for his own needs, or might even have to buy food, and thus suffer from protection.[28] He realized, however, that France was taking a road different from the one he favored. Protection was traditional in France, liberty was novel. Special interests could be advanced in the process of writing a tariff law: " our opponents have a tremendous superiority over us; they offer something, and we, we can only offer liberty and justice . . .".[29] Lastly, the *syndicats agricoles* had turned from their rightful tasks.

> These associations . . . are still in their infancy. They are of great help from the social point of view, when they perform, limit themselves to, their true rôle of improvement of all things agricultural about them; but . . . I shall add that they are in no way entrusted with creating the economic policy of France. Nevertheless, in large measure they have directed it, and they have certainly constituted a fertile soil for protection.[30]

The debate reached its high point in the address of Léon Say. Speaking as an avowed liberal economist, Say held that the principle of free trade had been deduced from observation, not from purely theoretical suppositions. It had a goal—to enable people to buy cheaply the things they need.[31] But from a larger standpoint, the struggle between free trade and protection was only an incident in

> the battle of the century, which will perhaps be the battle of the following century, the battle of those who fight either for

27 *Ibid.*, p. 749.

28 *Ibid.*, p. 752.

29 *Ibid.*, p. 748.

30 *Loc. cit.*

31 *Ibid.*, p. 833

> the individual or for the state, in that great combat of the individual against the state, and of the state against the individual.[32]

Flinging down the gauntlet to nationalist economics, challenging its most essential tenets, Say taunted Méline with being as much a theorist as himself. But what a theory! And he quoted Hume and Bastiat to contradict Méline's doctrines of the balance of trade.[33] He went on to show, in a very professorial way, how protection would raise the cost of living of the majority of the people, and redistribute income in favor of the large proprietors. The vaunted equality of protection was nowhere to be seen, he declared, referring to Lecouteux and Lavollée, for industry was obviously favored over agriculture. And even within the category of agriculture some districts would gain more than others, the great landowners would profit, but not the small.[34]

Finally he recommended that the grain duties be abolished, the existing general tariff maintained. It was low enough for foreign trade to continue, and the double tariff would fail in any event, for no country would negotiate for the minimum rates.[35]

> If I am moderate you tell me I abandon my principles. Not at all, I remain faithful to them: I shall try to apply them as far as I can, that's all. When I am against a wall, I turn back so as not to break my head; that's what all the ministries do, they withdraw so as not to break against a vote. (Laughter and applause.) [36]

And he concluded:

32 *Ibid.*, p. 843.

33 *Ibid.*, pp. 833–837.

34 *Ibid.*, pp. 838 ff.

35 *Ibid.*, pp. 849–850.

36 *Ibid.*, p. 837.

> I appeal to your sentiments of patriotism, and I ask you not to go too far along a disastrous road. I am not strong enough to ask you to come to me: but I can ask you to check yourselves.[37]

Viger, who opened for the protectionists, denied that he had any economic doctrine. He was "purely and simply a nationalist." He declared that his goal was the greatest possible prosperity for France, and that this could best be achieved by moderate protection. He rejected both the hypocrisy of free traders who excepted their own special interests, and the excessive demands of the *Société des agriculteurs* and the *Association de l'industrie française*. Taking up the situation of each branch of production in turn, he concluded that the proposals of the Commission were a fair answer to France's needs.[38]

Rising to attack the opposition, Paul Deschanel resorted to *ad hominem* arguments to prove that there were in the Chamber only "protectionists, under different forms, and in different degrees." [39] The representatives of the seaports believe in free trade for agriculture, but hold to the monopoly of the coastal trade. The Lyonnais favor free trade for raw silk, and protection for finished goods. Lockroy is a good free trader, but wants high duties on funeral wreaths. Deputy Berger of Paris firmly believes in free trade, but wants to protect electrical appliances, and

> of all the miracles electricity has performed in the course of this century, not the least prodigious is suddenly to have transformed our honorable friend from a fervent free trader to a convinced protectionist.[40]

Turning from his attack on "the ever growing family of protected free traders," Deschanel struck at liberal economic

37 *Ibid.*, p. 850. Other opposition speakers in the general debate were Charles-Roux, Raynal and Marius Martin.

38 *Ibid.*, pp. 728, 734, 735.

39 *Ibid.*, p. 824.

40 *Ibid.*, pp. 822-823.

theory, at the English school, which was unrealistic and narrow. "Thank the Lord," he said, "we have seen a new school arise which replaced the deductive method with that of observation, that of Carey in America and List in Germany. . . ."[41] He showed that France had not been the first to turn toward protection. Germany in 1879, Austria-Hungary in 1882, Italy in 1887 had preceded her. France was now obliged to defend herself.[42]

In some respects the most telling oratorical blow for the protectionist cause, Deschanel's address tended to weaken it in others. He warned against too narrow an interpretation of the French economy: "Gentlemen, the wealth of France is formed by two elements: first, her internal production, then her commercial expansion abroad." He warned that the problems of agriculture could not be solved simply by the imposition of customs duties, that it must exert every effort to become more scientific and more efficient. He pointed out that it was not the trade treaties in themselves, but their terms, that were harmful, and questioned the wisdom of the Parliament's substituting itself for the negotiator "up to a certain point," through the minimum tariff.[43]

Méline, who followed Léon Say on the rostrum, reiterated the arguments of his *rapport général*. He insisted on the justice of his views on the balance of trade, on the fact that low prices would result from increased domestic production, on the heavy charges borne by the French producer, on the great change in the general economic situation since 1860. Replying directly to Say's argument that protection increased the cost, and lowered the standard of living, Méline declared that middlemen were responsible for this, insofar as it was true. To have sought low prices abroad would have destroyed the French producer and

41 *Loc. cit.*

42 *Ibid.*, p. 832.

43 *Loc. cit.*; *Année politique*, vol. XVIII, 1891, pp. 117-118.

—"do you believe the foreigner would for long have sold to you at the same price!" [44]

Just before the general debate closed, Jules Roche spoke for the government. He outlined several reasons for adopting a system of moderate protection. The old national monopolies in particular lines of production were now broken, new lands, new techniques, new methods of transportation had been developed. Other nations had turned to protection and France must do likewise. But Roche favored the reasonable duties he and Develle had proposed, and regretted the increases made by the Commission (most of which related to agricultural products).[45] Without naming him, Roche attacked Méline's slurs on the middlemen who, he held, were both respectable and essential.[46] France, sociable and civilized France, could not live alone, he declared, stressing the importance of the export industries. She should guide her conduct by

> the necessity of maintaining a foreign commerce, and for this, of protecting, yes, of protecting our great export industry by means appropriate to its very nature . . . for you don't protect everyone in the same way. It is the necessity of establishing a régime of moderate tariffs . . . it is the necessity of maintaining our good relations with our foreign customers . . . it is the necessity of protecting the export industry by assuring it the freedom of its supplies, as we protect other industries which have to defend their products against foreign competition.[47]

On May 22nd, the Chamber proceeded to the examination of the articles of the bill. Of the hundreds of provisions the Chamber passed upon, it will be sufficient for the purposes of this study to consider its dispositions of the questions of the double

44 CD, 1891, p. 855. Turrel was another protectionist speaker in the general debate, pp. 786 ff.

45 *Ibid.*, pp. 925, 930.

46 *Ibid.*, p. 927.

47 *Ibid.*, p. 929.

tariff, the livestock duties, the duties on wool, hides, silk, oleaginous seeds and wines.

There was much uncertainty as to the exact significance of the minimum tariff. Did it imply that the government could not negotiate with foreign countries? Or did it mean that the government could merely offer other nations the concession of the minimum schedule? If either was the case, was there not a violation of the government's constitutional right to negotiate treaties? Could the government, on the other hand, by virtue of this right, inscribe in trade pacts duties lower than those of the minimum? If so, the minimum tariff was meaningless. Did it possibly mean that the government needed the prior consent of Parliament for such changes? The Chamber was perplexed. On May 22nd the matter was debated at length. In addition to several deputies, Roche, Méline and finally the Premier, Freycinet, took the floor. In a masterpiece of evasion, he declared that he would make no commitments which would in any way infringe the government's constitutional rights, but that he intended to carry out the provisions according to their spirit. Méline took the view that from the strictly legal standpoint the government could modify duties in the minimum schedule by treaty, but that it certainly would be voted out of office if the changes were unwelcome. The question recurred on December 21st, when the cabinet introduced a bill governing France's commercial relations until the new tariff should enter into effect. At the end of this second discussion, Clemenceau exclaimed "A while ago we understood a little: now we understand nothing." Méline's interpretation, unclouded by questions of constitutional prerogative, was generally accepted as the sense of the Chamber, although no precise elucidation was voted.[48]

48 CD, 1891, pp. 941 ff., 2763-2776; TN, vol. VII, 1890, p. 564; *Année politique*, vol. XVIII, 1891, pp. 128-129. At first the government was not seriously concerned over this matter, but in December 1891 a series of trade treaties were concluded among Germany, Austria-Hungary, Italy, Switzerland and Belgium. It became apparent that France could not afford to risk isolation. CD, 1891, p. 1825; Arnauné, *op. cit.*, p. 354.

On May 26th and 28th, Méline won two clear-cut victories over the government. Despite Develle's intervention, the Chamber voted the Commission's higher duties on cows and fresh meats (see table, p. 174A) by majorities varying from 307-265 on cows, to 359-146 on mutton.[49] With Méline's support, the government met no difficulty in securing the rejection of amendments providing for duties on raw hides, cocoons, raw wool and silk.[50] On June 18th, aided by a plea by J. Charles-Roux in behalf of the Marseille soap interests, Roche and Develle won a notable victory over Méline. By a tally of 328-208, the Chamber exempted oleaginous seeds.[51] This was but a temporary diversion of the protectionist current, however, for on July 2nd the deputies, by a vote of 307-218, adopted the Commission's wine duties over those of the government, despite Develle's strong protest.[52] On July 18th, the bill was sent to the Senate by a vote of 385-111.[53] Just before this division, Emile Leydet, of Aix, bitterly accused the anti-republican protectionists of burdening the people. This tariff, he said, will benefit only the great landowners and industrialists.

> I know what they'll say: in the end, the worker will receive his share; that is to say that the great proprietor will seat himself at table and deign to let fall some crumbs. (Exclamations at various benches.) *Bon appetit, messieurs!* (Noise.)

Méline rose to reply, blaming high prices on middlemen, insisting that prices could fall only as a result of increased production, pointing out that nearly all consumers were producers. "That is why," he said, "the great majority of the country called on us to defend the national endeavor [*travail national*]." [54]

49 CD, 1891, pp. 997 ff., 1032 ff.

50 *Ibid.*, pp. 1062-1063, 1100 ff., 1189, 1191. The government's majorities were: hides, 440-60; cocoons, 375-131; raw silk, 387-112; raw wool, 378-131.

51 *Ibid.*, pp. 1330 ff.

52 *Ibid.*, pp. 1527 ff., 1539.

53 *Ibid.*, pp. 1868-1870.

54 *Ibid.*, p. 1869.

The *Société des agriculteurs* was not enthusiastic over the results of the Chamber's deliberations. While the general debate was still in progress the *Société* declared that it would be satisfied only to the extent that its own figures were approached.[55] It resented the victory of Charles-Roux and the government in the matter of oleaginous seeds. On the whole, its reaction was that

> if the new tariff improved the situation of agriculture at several important points, it still sacrificed agriculture with regard to raw materials: it refused agriculture the guarantee we asked and hoped for with respect to commercial treaties and the definitiveness of the minimum tariff: finally, it did not reestablish customs equality between the products of the soil and those of industry. The friends of agriculture can only protest strongly.[56]

The proceedings in the Chamber, from the introduction of the bill to its first passage by the lower house, had given evidence of the basic difficulty in the question of protection for raw materials. Jules Delahaye, deputy of Indre-et-Loire, had attacked Méline in these terms:

> After having proclaimed the solidarity of agriculture and industry, he violently opposes one to the other, and, faced with the necessity of stating his position with respect to the only instances in which they are truly interdependent, truly in a state of solidarity, he fails . . . to serve both at the same time. For what reason? Because, says he, the dominant interest is on the side of industry.[57]

Agriculture, on the other hand, showed some reluctance to grant protection to *its* raw materials. When the Commission, against the wishes of the government, asked a low duty on

55 BSAF, vol. XXIII, 1891, p. 515.

56 *Ibid.*, pp. 728, 821.

57 CD, 1891, p. 976.

chemical fertilizer, Colonel baron de Plazanet, of Mayenne, declared " We ask only one thing! low prices!" [58]

Protection for raw materials had constituted the principal subject of negotiations between the *Société des agriculteurs* and the *Association de l'industrie française*. As early as 1888 the latter organization had accepted the principle of duties on raw materials, on two conditions: first, that provision be made for a drawback, the restitution of the tax paid on the raw material when the finished product was exported; second, that the duty on the manufactured article be raised to compensate for the increased cost to the producer.[59] The general assemblies of the *Association* in March 1890 and 1891 reaffirmed this position.[60] And its president, Aclocque, renewed his pledge of solidarity on numerous occasions, and condemned the opponents of agricultural protection.[61] The confidence of the *Société's* leaders was somewhat shaken, however. One remarked, with reference to an address by Aclocque to the *Société des agriculteurs,* that it was fitting and proper to applaud " the orator, his character, his good faith," but that no illusions should be held concerning his ability to produce adequate support. Another said that he, unhappily, could not share the illusions of the head of the *Association de l'industrie française*.

> In general, the industrialists are far from granting us the treatment to which we have the fullest right. Thus, for hides and wools . . . industry asks free entry, under the pretext that we

58 *Ibid*., p. 1594. This item proved a source of embarrassment to the *Société des agriculteurs*. In response to a request from the chemical trade association, the 12th section of the *Société* agreed not to oppose an increase in duties on chemical fertilizer. The *Société*, shortly thereafter, formally denied that this "opinion, which was not intended for publication," engaged the *Société des agriculteurs* as a whole. CRSAF, vol. XXIII, 1891, pp. 748-749; BSAF, vol. XXIII, 1891, p. 402.

59 CRSAF, vol. XXIII, 1891, p. 150.

60 BSAF, vol. XXII, 1890, p. 398; vol. XXIII, 1891, p. 407; TN, vol. VIII, 1891, p. 153.

61 TN, vol. VIII, 1891, pp. 146-149; CRSAF, vol. XXIII, 1891, pp. 20, 147.

> shall have obtained satisfaction with regard to livestock and meat.[62]

As we have seen, this was the attitude taken by Méline in his *rapport général,* and he considered the drawback impractical. Nevertheless, the alliance seemed threatened. The executive committee of the *Association de l'industrie française,* fearful of the possibility of revenge by the agricultural deputies, suggested that the industrialists should not be blamed for agriculture's reverses, any more than they blamed agriculture for the checks they had received. They realized that not all the agrarian leaders felt cheated, but were worried, and wished to dissipate any such feeling as did exist.[63]

The end of the summer recess of Parliament was now in sight, and attention turned from recriminations to the approaching consideration of the bill by the Senate. The Tariff Commission of the upper house, like that of the Chamber, was predominantly protectionist. Only nine of its thirty-six members were considered to lean toward economic liberalism.[64] Dauphin, the *rapporteur général,* expressed approval of the work of the Chamber. The usual trade treaties, he said, were of too long a duration for the rapid changes of modern times. The double tariff met all requirements: the general schedule, being aimed at no nation in particular, could not cause offense, the minimum would invite negotiations. The government's rights remained intact, but, as they could have effect

> only with the approval of Parliament, the vote of the two schedules will not be vain advice, but the expression of an actual will. This will will be a check on the government and an arm against the demands of other states.[65]

62 CRSAF, vol. XXIII, 1891, pp. 162-163.

63 TN, vol. VIII, 1891, p. 502.

64 BSAF, vol. XXII, 1890, p. 469.

65 SDP, 1891, p. 302.

If France is forced to follow other nations in adopting protection, Dauphin declared, it still remains true that there are difficulties between the home and export markets, agriculture and industry, production and commerce. The Chamber, in facing these problems, had adopted the following policy:

> To be resolutely protectionist for all the products of the soil, and the animals attached thereto.
>
> Protectionist also for manufactured objects.
>
> Free-trader for the materials necessary to industry.
>
> When there are clearly contradictory interests, give predominance to the most important of these interests, and indemnify the others.[66]

Thus, it could be said that the bill treated agriculture and industry equally. While some of the duties on manufactured articles were higher than the agricultural rates, "the national endeavor [*travail national*] must be protected in all the changes to which the [raw] material is subjected," and the duties increased at each step in the manufacturing process. The tax on the finished product must equal the sum of all the intermediary duties.[67]

The general debate in the Senate opened on November 9, 1891, and produced little that was new or different from the discussions in the Chamber. Suffice it to remark the attack of Challemel-Lacour, who opened for the opposition, on the protectionists' claim to respond to the country's wishes. This, he said, was the first time that north and south, agriculture and industry, spoke the same language. Nor was this a spontaneous development.

> They have made their voices heard, these organizations of recent date, they have loudly demanded protection, they have demanded it with an ardor that at times approached violence. Whence come they? Who brought them into the world?

66 *Ibid.*, pp. 302-303.

67 *Ibid.*, p. 309.

Where do they find their inspiration? I don't know; nevertheless I can say with certainty: (Smiles) from a powerful, active society, whose political opinions, notoriously hostile to republican institutions . . . are displayed in glaring letters in the names of those it has chosen for a general staff; from a society which has no equal for the strictness of its discipline, for the ardor of its propaganda . . . for the imperious tone of its communications, for the number of affiliated organizations, [no equal] except another society, which it seems to have taken as a model, and which history calls the Jacobins. (Ironical exclamations at the Right.)[68]

This attack on the *Société des agriculteurs* was inspired by a sense of the hopelessness of the opposition. Jules Roche, in taking the floor of the Senate, was cautious in speaking to the protectionist majority, and took a rather circuitous route to his usual plea for moderation. He spoke at length on the relative decline of the French population, and warned that

an industrial, agricultural people, whose population remains stationary, cannot content itself with its internal market; it is an essential condition of its existence to seek the foreign market, to turn to the new countries which enter into civilization.

Thus, he continued, it is necessary to exempt raw materials, to conclude agreements with other nations in the interest of commercial stability, and to understand that there is a limit which must not be exceeded.[69] His colleague Develle urged the need

68 SD, 1891, pp. 792-793. Other leading participants in the general debate were: for the opposition, Jules Simon, Poirrier, Tirard; for protection, Jules Ferry (president of the Tariff Commission), Dauphin and Fresnou. SD, 1891, pp. 805 ff.

69 *Ibid.*, pp. 852 ff. Roche declared: "We have obtained from the Chamber what it was possible to obtain. This mustn't be forgotten; let not those forget it who find that we have not gone far enough in the direction of free trade: a few months ago it would have seemed unlikely that the vote of the customs tariffs would leave exempt a considerable portion of the [raw] materials necessary to industry." He went on to credit the government with securing this exemption. *Ibid.*, p. 856.

for protecting agriculture—moderately. While there had been much criticism of the agricultural duties within Parliament on the ground that they were too high, many outside the legislature claimed they were too low.

> Perhaps you have in hand the protests of great agricultural societies which strongly reproach us for having maintained the exemption of the raw materials. I am not stirred by these reproaches, I even take pride in having incurred them, and I believe that in extending the increase in duties to certain products necessary to industry we would have committed a useless act, an imprudent act, an impolitic act.[70]

The Senate showed itself to be even more protectionist than the Chamber. It abolished the minimum, leaving only the general duties on meats. It defeated an effort, supported by Develle, to restore the government's duty on mutton. To the keen disappointment of Jules Roche, it voted the tariffs on oleaginous seeds proposed by the Chamber Commission, after having rejected even higher tariffs demanded by the Senate Commission. The government asked for restoration of its wine duties, and met with failure. Hides, raw silk and wool were, however, kept on the free list.[71]

On December 17th, by a vote of 210 to 10, with 66 abstentions (including many of the opposition leaders, such as Challemel-Lacour, Tirard and Jules Simon), the Senate returned the bill to the Chamber.[72] The lower house spent a week debating the Senate's revisions, and accepted one hundred forty-eight of the one hundred seventy-eight changes made.[73] It agreed to suppress the minimum duty on pork, but maintained the minimum rates on other meats. By a vote of 275-221 it again exempted oleaginous seeds, over the protest of the Cham-

70 *Ibid.*, p. 865.

71 *Ibid.*, pp. 874 ff., 899, 947, 969, 1004.

72 *Ibid.*, pp. 1236, 1238.

73 *Ibid.*, p. 1308.

ber Commission.[74] After a dispute with the Senate over petroleum duties, the Chamber passed the bill in its final form on January 7, 1892, by a vote of 384-100, and the law was promulgated four days later.[75]

The *Société des agriculteurs* had warmly approved the position of the Senate Tariff Commission, and the general attitude of the upper house. It particularly rejoiced when the latter voted to tax oleaginous seeds. But it realized that the government would oppose this step, and was not surprised at the final failure of the move.[76] Now that the bill had become law, however, the general tone of the *Société's* comments changed from complaint to reserved satisfaction. The marquis de Dampierre, observing that the *Société* had been constantly in the breach during the fight for the Méline Tariff, declared that

> if our influence was not sufficient to obtain complete justice for agriculture, it nevertheless contributed to results of real importance. The repudiation of the treaties of commerce . . . is of the greatest value for us. A duty averaging fifteen per cent on foreign agricultural products would sufficiently compensate for our charges, if they had not excepted from this protection what are so improperly called *raw materials*. . . .
>
> An even more grave reproach must be made against the new law: it has not admitted between agriculture and industry proper that great principle of equality which is deeply embedded in our customs and which dominates all our public law. . . .
>
> But, at least, we have had . . . a great consolation, that of seeing the spirit of equality in the most respected leaders of industry. . . . This happy concert of opinions leaves us for the future a battlefield which we shall not desert, for the greatest result we have obtained is that France remains master of her tariffs, and that she can correct them as good sense and experience require her to, from year to year.[77]

74 CD, 1891, pp. 2791-2813.

75 *Ibid.*, p. 2990; JO, Jan. 12, 1892.

76 BSAF, vol. XXIII, pp. 1073 ff., 1111, 1145; JAP, 1891, II, pp. 790-791.

77 CRSAF, vol. XXIV, 1892, p. 18.

This spirit of accepting gains and looking forward to new struggles was echoed at the 1892 banquet of the *Société des agriculteurs*. One of its leaders, M. Jacquemart, stated that it appeared wise to "accept provisionally the accomplished fact," without renouncing any claims for the future.[78] Thus bitter disappointment, at first expressed in disavowals of the Méline Tariff and renewed recriminations against industry, gave way to appreciation of the gains made.[79] Deputy Jean Plichon, of the Nord, declared

> The tariff schedule so laboriously prepared by the twelfth section and by the council of the *Société des agriculteurs* has just been applied. The struggle was sharp in Parliament, and it resulted in a state of affairs infinitely preferable for agriculture to that which previously existed. We note that this must be attributed to the valiant perseverance of M. Méline. . . .[80]

On February 22, 1892, a group of prominent agriculturalists headed by Josseau, vice-president of the *Société des agriculteurs,* tendered Méline a banquet, and gave him "a basket and two candelabra, in bronze embellished with gold." [81]

The tariff law which was given Méline's name was strongly protectionist. Levasseur estimates that its rates, applied to 1889 imports, would have yielded 259 million francs, an increase of 115 million, or about eighty per cent, over the actual 1889 custom receipts.[82] Dauphin, *rapporteur général* in the Senate, reached an estimate of 212 million francs, based on average

78 *Ibid.*, pp. 214-215.

79 *Ibid.*, p. 42; BSAF, vol. XXIV, 1892, I, pp. 135-136.

80 CRSAF, vol. XXIV, 1892, p. 686. The marquis de Dampierre said of Méline: "His talent, his perseverance, his energy triumphed over the obstacles which accumulated beneath his steps. We may have differed over the methods which were to lead us to the same goal, we were never at any moment unaware of his devotion to agricultural interests, which [devotion] never flagged in face of the greatest difficulties." CRSAF, vol. XXIV, 1892, p. 23.

81 BSAF, vol. XXIV, 1892, I, p. 311.

82 Levasseur, *op. cit.*, vol. II, p. 585.

imports in the period 1881-1889.[83] The duties, which in nearly all cases were specific, ranged up to twenty-five per cent *ad valorem* on agricultural commodities, up to sixty per cent on industrial products.

Beyond this, however, we may well ask, and attempt to answer, several questions: what groups or interests met in conflict over this law? to what extent was their existence evident in the passage of the bill? which of them gained most? to what degree does the Méline Tariff reflect the prescriptions of nationalist economics?

We have seen organizations of industry and agriculture campaign for protection, but it should not be thought that the field was theirs alone. True, there was little evidence of a real free-trade movement. As Levasseur remarks, the extreme terms free trade and prohibition did not define the opposing groups. At most, he says, they " indicated theoretical tendencies: in reality, the debate was between the *status* quo of 1860 or 1881 and increases in duties. . . ." [84] A denial of doctrinaire economic liberalism has been observed in the Parliamentary speeches of the opposition, and it was reaffirmed by Lockroy in a letter to Kergall's paper, *La Démocratie rurale*. At a banquet at Pau, Basses-Pyrénées, in May 1891, Léon Say expressed his satisfaction with the moderate tendencies of Parliament and the country. Even the *Syndicat économique agricole* and " my good friend Kergall " were moderates, he said. Kergall, who was present, thanked him, and asked him to certify to the country, as only he could, that the agricultural forces were not prohibitionist and were not in league to raise the cost of foodstuffs to the consumer. " M. Léon Say bowed in sign of agreement, and raised his glass toward M. Kergall. The gathering applauded frantically. . . ." [85]

83 SDP, 1891, pp. 308-309.

84 Levasseur, *loc. cit.*

85 DR, May 10, 1891.

If the opposition did not bear the authentic stamp of the Manchester School, it was, however, none the less real. It was some time after the elections of 1889 that the opponents of protection began to organize for pressure purposes. Committees springing from the Chambers of Commerce had been formed in such cities as Paris, Lyon, Marseille, Bordeaux and Reims. Over the signatures of Senator Poirrier, former head of the Paris Chamber of Commerce, deputies Charles-Roux of Marseille, Berger of Paris and Aynard of Lyon (president of the Chamber of Commerce of that city), these committees were invited to join in a *Union pour la franchise des matières premières et la défense de l'exportation.* This organization held its first meeting at Paris on November 5, 1890.[86] A *Ligue des consommateurs contre le renchérissement de tous les objets nécessaires à la vie* was formed at Bordeaux. Shortly after this, the same city saw the birth of a *Ligue pour la défense du commerce d'importation et d'exportation Bordeaux-Sud-Ouest.*[87] The president of the Paris Chamber of Commerce headed the *Société d'encouragement pour le commerce français d'exportation.*[88] Under the leadership of Edouard Lockroy, a *Comité de défense de l'exportation française et de l'alimentation nationale* held its greatest meeting in Paris on July 25, 1891 (after the Chamber had passed the bill).[89] Labor leaders and men of arts and letters joined business men in this belated protest.[90]

The regional basis of the opposition to protection is evident. It was above all in the great centers, such as Paris, Marseille, Lyon, Bordeaux, that the supporters of the *status quo* raised their voices. The mayors of Lyon and Bordeaux were associated with many of their constituents in protests against the

86 JEC, 1890, pp. 261 ff., 307.

87 *Ibid.*, pp. 433, 497-498; 1891, pp. 112, 460 ff.

88 TN, vol. VII, 1890, p. 597; JEC, 1891, pp. 420-421.

89 TN, vol. VIII, 1891, p. 401; JEC, 1891, p. 311.

90 BSAF, vol. XXIII, 1891, p. 191; JEC, 1891, pp. 112 ff., 146, 460 ff.; TN, vol. VIII, 1891, pp. 194, 258.

tariff bill.[91] The strongest reaction, however, occurred in Marseille. Here, in April 1891, a large meeting voted a resolution calling on the deputies of the Bouches-du-Rhône to resign if the bill became law.[92] The Mayor of Marseille, many leading citizens and most of the senators and deputies of the department wrote to Freycinet, Roche and Develle that if Parliament should reject the respectful requests of the people of Marseille,

> we solemnly declare that we decline all responsibility with regard to the feelings which will not fail to be aroused by such a denial of justice in response to the testimony of ardent devotion which they [the Marseillais] have at all times given to the Republic.[93]

As the protectionists well knew, therefore, their adversaries were to be found in urban districts where commerce and production for export were dominant.[94] We have seen, in connection with the Agricultural Group of the Chamber, that Rightist protectionist strength centered in western France. Further light on this matter will be obtained, however, in seeking the answer to our second question: to what extent was the existence of these opposing groups evident in the passage of the bill? In considering this question we shall examine three votes taken by the Chamber of Deputies: the first to indicate the nucleus, or extreme of protectionism; the second, to show wider protectionist strength (when government and Commission were at odds, a condition favorable to the opposition), and the power of the opponents when supported by the cabinet; the third, to illustrate full protectionist strength and the heart of the opposition. By thus observing the size, and the regional and political distribution of the opposing groups, we shall be able better to understand the nature of the tariff law.

91 JEC, 1891, pp. 110-111.

92 TN, vol. VIII, 1891, p. 205.

93 JEC, 1891, pp. 264 ff.

94 *Cf.* Aclocque, CRSAF, vol. XXIII, 1891, p. 97.

Map I—Geographical Distribution of the Protectionist Vote against the Viger Bill to Reduce Grain Duties

Rightists 63 Republicans 66

The first vote was that in opposition to the Viger proposal to authorize temporary reduction of the grain duties. This bill, which had the full backing of Roche, Méline, the Tariff Commission, and the somewhat hesitant support of Develle, was inspired by a fear that the temporarily high price of wheat and further prospects of poor crops might lead to a widespread reaction against protection. The measure was opposed by 129 deputies, about one-third of the entire Rightist representation accounting for 63 of the noes. The opposition to Viger's bill centered in western France, Brittany alone furnishing 29 votes. Picardy and the department of the Nord, in the North, and Gascony in the South were other foci of protectionist—and Rightist—strength.[95]

The second vote to be considered was on an amendment (to the bill as passed by the Senate) exempting oleaginous seeds. It was carried by 275-221. The majority was composed of 217 Republicans and 58 Rightists, the minority of 114 Republicans and 107 Rightists. While the former voted almost two to one for exemption, the latter voted almost two to one for maintenance of the duties. The regional distribution was similar to that in the vote on the Viger Bill, with protectionist strength spreading from the centers mentioned.[96]

The third vote, of December 29, 1891, was on the bill as a whole, which passed by 386-105.[97] The protectionist majority was composed of 242 Republicans and 144 Rightists, the minority of 80 Republicans and 25 Rightists (including 12 from

95 CD, 1891, pp. 952, 965; *Année politique*, vol. XVIII, 1891, pp. 131 ff. There were 49 abstentions, 40 absences by leave. Viger quoted the following prices per quintal: Jan. 1891, 26 frs.; Feb., 27 frs.; March, 28 frs.; April 1, 28 frs.; April 26, 32.50 frs. He admitted that these prices were not exceptional, but feared they might rise out of hand. This vote, rather than one on the bill proper, was selected for this purpose because grain duties were rather symbolic of agricultural protection. Hence the vote reflects a general attitude rather than local interests.

96 CD, 1891, pp. 2832, 2833. There were 38 abstentions, 36 absences by leave.

97 *Ibid.*, pp. 2917, 2918. There were 44 abstentions, 36 absences by leave.

Map II—Geographical Distribution of the Vote on an Amendment Exempting Oleaginous Seeds

Against (protectionist)	For
Rightists 107	Rightists 58
Republicans 114	Republicans 217

the department of the Seine).[98] The deputies belonging to the cabinet were prominent among those who abstained: Roche, Develle, Foreign Minister Ribot, Finance Minister Rouvier. While the Republicans voted for the Méline Tariff in the proportion of less than four to one, the Right supported the measure in the ratio of almost six to one. The centers of protectionist strength were, as before, in the west, north-west and south-west, although, in the case of this larger protectionist vote, the spread from these foci was more extensive. Of the 105 opposition votes, 42 came from the departments of the Seine, Rhône and Bouches-du-Rhône, containing the cities of Paris, Lyon and Marseille. Diversification of crops makes it difficult to correlate areas of agricultural specialization with protectionist votes. About two-thirds of the latter came, on the Viger bill and oleaginous seeds amendment, from what may be called wheat, wine and cattle regions (Chapter II, note 37. Industrial protectionism appeared in full strength on the final vote, rendering a similar analysis impossible.) But, while Rightist cattle districts in the west were consistently protectionist, the Republican cattle areas of Savoy and Jura supported the government on these two tests.

From the foregoing, as well as from the general trend of the study, it is safe to say that the nucleus of protectionism was the agrarian Right, the nucleolus the *Société des agriculteurs* and its affiliated organizations. Alone, the influence of these elements would have been inadequate for victory, and it was their alliance with Republican protectionists, agricultural and industrial, that made possible their success.

This conclusion indicates that the answer to our third question, which reduces itself to whether agriculture or industry gained most in the bill, is not simply to be determined by comparing the duties enacted. Lecouteux felt that agriculture had fallen into a trap, that in exchange for the increases it had received, it had given so much to industry that the latter could be

98 Paris was the center of the Boulangist element of the National Coalition of 1889.

MAP III—GEOGRAPHICAL DISTRIBUTION OF THE FINAL VOTE ON MÉLINE TARIFF

For (protectionist)	Against
Rightists 144	Rightists 25
Republicans 242	Republicans 80

said to have "*donné un oeuf pour avoir un boeuf*." He declared that a new system of inequalities had been created which would only continue the march from farm to factory.[99] Develle had frankly stated that in the matter of oleaginous seeds the government had committed itself to the special interests of Marseille, in opposition to those of agriculture.[100] It should not be forgotten, however, that the great majority of agricultural products were protected by the Méline Tariff. Animal products, such as hides, wool, fats; cocoons and raw silk, oleaginous seeds, raw flax and hemp had been kept on the free list as raw materials essential to industry. But even here agriculture received aid when Parliament voted subsidies for the cultivation of flax, hemp and cocoons.[101] And, as a representative of the *Association de l'industrie française* had pointed out to the *Société des agriculteurs*, acceptance by industry of the agreement they had reached on raw material duties involved a double conversion. First, the industrialists had to be persuaded to accept the introduction of tariffs in a field free for over thirty years. Second, they had to be convinced of the efficacy of a drawback.[102] Once the latter had been rejected by the government and Méline, the whole scheme was doomed to failure. If we consider the proposals of the *Société des agriculteurs* as maximal, a glance at the table on page 174A will suffice to show in how large a part they received satisfaction. It is not surprising to find the agrarian leaders incompletely satisfied. But when we consider the extent to which their demands were met, and the fact that from the political standpoint they were incapable of any success alone, they could logically have hardly expected much more.

Our last question concerned the theoretical factor in the Méline Tariff. The economist Truchy writes

99 JAP, ser. 6, vol. XLV, 1890, I, pp. 401, 432. "... given an egg to get an ox."

100 BSAF, vol. XXIV, 1892, I, p. 16.

101 *Principales mesures*, p. 90; Perreau, *op. cit.*, p. 333.

102 CRSAF, vol. XXII, 1890, p. 644.

> It would be an exaggeration to say that the reform of 1892 is the translation of a doctrine into practice, for in all questions of commercial politics, whatever be the tendency, liberal or restrictive, in which they are resolved, it is basically less a matter of doctrines than of interests. . . . But, at the very least, the reform of 1892 has doctrinal conceptions of systematic and coherent character; it is a whole whose parts are closely linked; it is capable of being expressed in theoretical formulae.[103]

Protection of agriculture (but not where it would clearly undermine existing industries), its rationalization on the basis of productivity theory and the necessities of national independence and defense; denial of any desire for autarky; willingness to accept higher commodity prices as the inevitable corollary of the defense of productive capacity; state stimulation when protection would involve serious conflicts between branches of national production: all these tenets of nationalist economic theory are evident in both speeches and reports and in the terms of the act itself. The relationship between the Méline Tariff and the economies of Cauwès may be further observed in the provisions regarding colonies. The bill introduced by the government had called for no important changes in the colonial customs system. The Chamber Commission, however, adopted the policy of tariff assimilation, or customs union.

The colonies were divided into two groups. Imports into the first (including Martinique, Guadeloupe, Guiana, St. Pierre-Miquelon, Réunion, Mayotte, Gabon, Indo-China and New Caledonia) were brought under the metropolitan tariff, subject to modifications made by the Paris government on recommendation of the colonial authorities. Colonial products, with important exceptions, were to enter France free. Exotic commodities, such as coffee, tea, spices, were to be admitted to France at half the general tariff (there was no minimum schedule for these products). Sugars and their derivatives were only given

103 H. Truchy, "Étude sur le commerce de la France," *Revue d'économie politique*, vol. XVIII, 1904, pp. 543 ff.

the benefit of exemption from the surtax levied on European sugars, or those shipped by way of European ports. Imports into the second group, of non-assimilated colonies (comprising French west African possessions except Gabon; Tahiti, French India, Obock, Diego Suarez, Nossi-Bé and Sainte-Marie de Madagascar) were regulated by special decrees of the home government. Assimilation was to be the rule: these exceptions arose from the distance, the lack of development, or the peculiar conditions of these colonies.[104]

The policy of assimilation, begun with Algeria in 1884, answered the demand for protection of, and the need for assistance in developing, these new export markets. It responded to a widespread feeling that France's great sacrifices in winning the colonies should be repaid with advantages in colonial trade. Beyond this, however, assimilation harmonized with protection in the nationalist economic vein, and with longstanding traditions. Cauwès declared that, given sufficient flexibility to meet local conditions,

> customs union, like the colonial compact, has the advantage of tightening the bonds between the metropolis and the colonies, of justifying the sacrifices which the former continues to assume, without creating tyrannical exploitation of the latter. Customs union does not suppress the freedom of the colonies to develop on their soil all the industries which can be acclimatized, and to export their products where they wish, but it creates for colonies and metropolis a system of preference in harmony with the political bonds and the institutions which unite them.[105]

104 Girault, *op. cit.*, pp. 81 ff.: "Le nouveau régime douanier des colonies et ses résultats," *Revue d'économie politique*, vol. VIII, 1894, pp. 858 ff.; see Sémars, *op. cit.*; CDP, 1891, pp. 113 ff. On earlier colonial policy see above, ch. I, pp. 58 ff. Bajkić, *op. cit.*, p. 467, writes: "Colbert's colonial policies were merely a postulate of his economic policy; the colonial enthusiasm of the Third Republic had to satisfy a political necessity, but it is incompatible with its economic policy." This may be true of its empire building, but the policy of tariff assimilation seems rather to correspond with the development of mercantilism into nationalist economics.

105 Cauwès, *Cours*, vol. II, pp. 129, 629-630.

Chapter IV opened with the assertion that there is a theoretical element in all economic legislation, sometimes stated, more often implicit. The theory behind the Méline Tariff was openly set forth in Parliament, and the question before us is not so much the theoretical nature of the law, as the degree to which this theory served merely as a rationalization of particular interests. While the Méline Tariff was certainly not the product of an economics seminar, it would be incorrect to consider its relation to nationalist economics as incidental or fortuitous. Nationalist economics served, it is true, as an apology for special desires, but it also influenced the direction of these desires, and gave them a degree of coherence and an explicit rationale. Without examining the innermost minds of the participants in the campaign for protection, it is impossible to say more than that economic fact and theory interacted. Agrarian and industrial leaders joined in alliance under the banner of nationalist economics, and, during and after the elections of 1889, skimmed over the waves of politics to victory.

The passage of the Méline Tariff, however, settled neither the economic problems which formed so great a part of its background nor the struggle over protection and nationalist economics. By way of epilogue and an attempt at evaluation, therefore, we may turn to the story of the years following 1892.

CHAPTER VII

THE PROGRAM IN OPERATION

THE policy of agricultural protection enshrined by the Méline Tariff continued throughout the life of the Third Republic, but changing economic and political conditions required frequent adjustments of the duties enacted in 1892. The first general tariff revision, however, was that of the law of March 29, 1910, and the debates preceding its adoption provided an opportunity for renewed theoretical discussion and for evaluation of the Méline Tariff itself. In general, the debates were similar in character to those of 1891. The liberals disclaimed any doctrinaire notions of free trade, the protectionists insisted that they were not systematic protectionists. The liberals, aware of their parliamentary weakness, and activated by particular interests, called for maintenance of the existing tariff structure, and the protectionists, similarly activated, held that the old duties were no longer adequate, and had to be raised. As in 1891, however, theoretical considerations were introduced, especially when the Parliamentary orators reflected on the results of the Méline Tariff. It was attacked as having raised the cost of living of the French masses, and defended as having saved French agriculture from the destructive competition which threatened it. The protectionists, arguing along the theoretical lines discussed in previous chapters, claimed that increased production had prevented any charge on non-agricultural income. The liberals, who, for patriotic and other reasons, could not say that French agriculture was dying, contended that it was, on the contrary, quite healthy. Jaurès, the great socialist leader, conceded that agriculture might possibly have needed protection in years past, but declared that the tariff was now preventing it from realizing its true possibilities, by maintaining the uneconomic production of grain and limiting the development of an export trade in the special lines in which it excelled.[1]

The questions raised in these debates furnish the framework for our attempt at evaluation of the Méline Tariff: what were the major social and economic trends in French agriculture under this protectionist régime? how effective were the duties? how did they affect the standard of living of the non-agricultural French population? what general conclusions can be reached? In seeking the answer to these questions we may, as before, turn to the available statistical data.

THE AGRICULTURAL ECONOMY

Population

The downward trend in agricultural population and the general movement to the cities continued, at a slow and steady pace, in the period 1891-1911. Recalling that urban population was defined as that living in communes of 2,000 persons or more, and rural as that in communes with less than 2,000 inhabitants, the fall in rural population may be observed in the following figures (in thousands):[2]

	Rural pop.	% Total	Urban pop.	% Total
1891	24,032	62.6	14,311	37.4
1896	23,492	60.9	15,026	39.1
1901	23,005	59.1	15,957	40.9
1906	22,715	57.9	16,537	42.1
1911	22,093	55.8	17,509	44.2

The ratio of those engaged in agricultural occupations to all occupied persons (excluding soldiers, sailors, fishermen and personal servants) fell from .47 in 1896 to .44 in 1911. In-

1 CD, 1909, pp. 1646-1925, *passim*, for the general debate, Jaurès, p. 1914. Brief summaries of the debates are given in Arnauné, *op. cit.*, pp. 340 ff., Levasseur, *op. cit.*, vol. II, pp. 590 ff.

2 Statistique générale de la France, *Résultats statistiques du recensement général de la population effectué le 5 mars 1911*, Paris, 1913, vol. I, part I, p. 33.

creased mechanization in agriculture may, of course, partly account for this decline. The number active in agriculture actually rose from 8,429 thousand to 8,517 thousand, but the increase was entirely in women; the number of men fell. It is hard to say to what extent this represents a social change or a change in methods of census classification.[3] In any event, our previous generalizations with respect to population are still applicable: agriculture continued slowly to give ground to industry in French society.

Division of the Land

A similar conclusion, continuation of previous trends, can be drawn from the somewhat fragmentary data on size of farms and land tenure. There are no statistics for the first decade of the twentieth century as trustworthy as those of the *enquête* of 1892. In 1909 the Minister of Agriculture, Ruau, presented the following figures, furnished him by the Ministry of Finance, in an address before the *Musée social*:[4]

NUMBER OF FARM UNITS (in thousands)

		1892	*1908*
Very small	(less than 1 ha.)	2,235	2,088
Small	(1 to 10 ha.)	2,618	2,524
Medium	(10 to 40 ha.)	711	746
Large	(40 to 100 ha.)	105	118
Very large	(over 100 ha.)	33	30

These figures would indicate a clear tendency toward concentration of land ownership and the decline of the small peasant farmer. But Ruau insisted on the strength of this traditionally French group, and maintained that this was illustrated by data concerning the areas occupied by the various sizes of farms.

3 *Ibid.*, part III, p. 12, *Résultats . . . du recensement . . . 1906*, vol. I, part II, p. 58. Compare with *Résultats statistiques du dénombrement de 1891*, pp. 269 ff.

4 JO, 1909, pp. 2704 ff. Ministère des finances, direction générale des contributions directes, *Tableau présentant la répartition du nombre des exploitations agricoles d'après la superficie exploitée.*

HECTARES IN THOUSANDS

	1892	*1908*
Very small	1,243	1,229
Small	10,383	11,559
Medium	12,946	14,825
Large and very large	18,580	16,271

Small and medium sized farms would appear to have grown in total area, very small farms to have declined moderately, and large and very large farms to have fallen significantly while continuing to occupy a large proportion of French soil. Unfortunately, the accuracy of these figures is open to question. The Ministry of Finance, which did not itself publish them, stated that no actual *enquête* had been undertaken, but that data had been gathered by a process of sampling.[5] Augé-Laribé demonstrates that they are not strictly comparable with those of 1892.[6]

In 1908-1909, however, the Ministry of Agriculture conducted an *enquête* on small property. No classifications in terms of area were established, but the Departmental Professors of Agriculture were asked what they considered small, medium and large holdings, according to crops and regions, and which types seemed to be rising or falling in number. While no quantitative results could be obtained for the nation as a whole by this procedure, the following conclusions did result: over a period of twenty years, small holdings had increased in number in forty-two departments, in area in fifty-two departments; they had diminished in number in thirteen departments, in area in five departments; their number had been stationary in seventeen departments, their area in nineteen departments; no conclusions as to number could be drawn in fifteen departments, as to area in eleven departments.[7] The general impression left by these

5 *Ibid.*, p. 2704 note. "*Il n'a été procédé à l'enquête que par vérifications ou recensements par épreuves.*"

6 Augé-Laribé, *Evolution*, pp. 103 ff.

7 Ministère de l'agriculture, office de renseignements agricoles, *La petite propriété rurale en France: enquêtes monographiques* (*1908-1909*), Paris, 1909, pp. 290 ff.

data is that small holdings increased somewhat in number and more significantly in size, as peasant proprietors acquired the lands of those who left their farms for the city, or parcels of large farms, whose number was declining. These data are in agreement with Ruau's figures as to the greater area occupied by small farms. In 1892, however, it seemed that small holdings were growing in number and falling in size, and that medium holdings were falling somewhat in number. Yet we can say that no sharp changes had appeared since 1892. It must be remembered that under the *enquête* of 1908-1909 a farm of ten hectares might be classed as small, medium or large, depending on its location and on the type of crop grown, and that, in any event, such changes as did occur were of small amplitude.[8]

There are no adequate data regarding types of tenure after 1892.[9] The quinquennial censuses classify the agricultural population as "*patrons*", employes, workers, families and servants, and also as proprietors, cash tenants and sharecroppers, horticulturists and truck farmers, and lumbermen. But the census categories are complicated and rather confused, and there are no comparable data between 1891 and 1911.[10] The *enquête* of 1908-1909 reported that non-ownership tenure was progressing in twelve departments, regressing in thirty departments, stationary in fourteen departments and without import-

According to the report Ruau presented, the number of small owners and the area of their property rose in 36 departments; the number fell and the area remained the same in 4 departments; both number and area were stationary in 13 departments. Medium sized property rose in number in 4 departments and in part of Calvados. No clear statement was given regarding the remaining departments.

8 See Augé-Laribé, *op. cit.*, p. 113.

9 Such subjects were covered by the decennial *enquêtes*, but not by the annual agricultural statistics.

10 See Augé-Laribé, *op. cit.*, p. 131. Compare, for example, the census of 1891, pp. 436 ff., with that of 1906, vol. I, part III, pp. 54 ff.

ance in thirty-one departments.[11] In 1912 the Ministry of Agriculture conducted an *enquête* on wages of agricultural laborers. The reports it received from the different departments varied greatly in quality: in some an actual census was taken, in others the reports were given in the most general terms on the basis of superficial examination. This study, therefore, provides the basis for only a rough comparison with the figures of 1892.[12]

AGRICULTURAL LABORERS (in thousands)

	1892	*1912*
Laborers also owning small properties	509	563
Laborers not owning small properties	701	619

It would appear from these scattered indications that ownership of small properties was progressing at the expense of very small and large holdings, and that, owing to mechanization in agriculture and the attraction of urban employments, an agricultural proletariat had failed to develop. In general, therefore, the agrarian social structure maintained a character consistent with the aims of the authors and proponents of the Méline Tariff.

CROPS AND LIVESTOCK

The diversified character of the crops grown on most French farms, evidence of resistance to the specialization which would result from the extension of mature capitalism to agriculture, was maintained in the first decade of the twentieth century. The Ministry of Agriculture's failure to conduct the decennial *enquêtes* in 1902 and 1912 forces us to rely on its regular annual statistics, which are less reliable than the special studies.

11 Ministère de l'agriculture, *La petite propriété*, pp. 300-302.

12 Ministère de l'agriculture, office de renseignements agricoles, *Enquête sur les salaires agricoles*, Paris, 1912. Pierre Régnier, *L'Ouvrier agricole*, Paris, 1924, p. 42, gives the following totals for the same study: Landowning laborers, 506,087; non-landowning, 537,039. Because of the many differences between reports, and numerous inconsistencies, the total arrived at depends in large part on the reader.

In general, the *Statistique agricole annuelle* for 1909 shows little departure from previously observed trends.[13]

AREAS IN THOUSANDS OF HECTARES

	Wheat	All grains	Garden crops	Potatoes	Sugar beets	Other Ind. crops
1882	7,191	15,090	344	1,338	240	260
1892	7,166	14,827	320	1,474	271	180
1909	6,596	13,642	434	1,547	237	95

	Vineyards	Woods, forests	Fodders, pastures
1882	2,197	9,455	8,697
1892	1,800	9,522	9,326
1909	1,687	9,329	10,328

PRODUCTION IN THOUSANDS

	Of Hectoliters			Of Quintals			
	Wheat	All grains	Wine	Potatoes	Beets	Hemp, flax	Fodders
1882 ...	129,339	295,254	33,582	100,994	88,504	758	223,321
1892 ...	117,449	268,549	29,038	154,190	72,519	424	226,673
1909 ...	125,522	297,939	54,446	166,844	62,542	274	424,501

Rising grain production on a smaller area, the continued growth of potato cultivation and a striking advance of fodder crops are made evident by these figures. The most specialized crops, sugar beets, flax, hemp and rape seed (included among "other industrial crops") declined sharply, and the vineyards, which had with difficulty overcome the scourge of phylloxera, were now faced with the problem of low prices, as we shall see.

Despite the sharp increase in fodder production, there was no significant change in the numbers of livestock on French farms. In 1909 there were more cattle and horses, fewer sheep,

13 *Enquête*, 1892, tables. Ministère de l'agriculture, office de renseignements agricoles, *Statistique agricole annuelle*, 1909, Paris, 1911. Figures relating to "other industrial crops," fodder areas and production are not comparable with those given in Chapters I and II, owing to differences between the *enquêtes* and the 1909 data. The "other industrial crops" include: tobacco, hops, flax, hemp, rape (colza and *navette*) and poppy. Fodder production comprises: fodder beets and cabbage, clover, sainfoin and alfalfa. Fodder acreage includes, in addition to this group, *prés naturels* and *herbages*.

hogs and goats than in 1892, but the general situation remained much the same. (Figures in thousands).

	Cattle	Sheep	Pigs	Horses	Goats
1892	13,709	21,116	7,421	2,794	1,845
1909	14,298	17,358	7,306	3,236	1,418

RENTS AND LAND VALUES

In a series of over one hundred monographic studies of institutional properties in various parts of France, the economist Zolla demonstrated a steady decline in rents. Four of his studies are of particular interest, as they cover most of the period under consideration, (unfortunately they are not well distributed geographically).[14] In the following table incomes from rent of four *Hospices* are reduced to relatives:

	H. de Dijon	H. de Nevers	H. de Clermont-Ferrand	H. de Riom
1876–1881	100	100	100	100
1881–1886	102	110	95	101
1886–1891	94	113	88	96
1891–1896	84	95	82	87
1896–1901	76	98	76	84
1901–1906	70	97	72	69

Such scattered evidence can hardly furnish the basis for accurate generalization, but it is of value in conjunction with broader studies. One such was the evaluation of unbuilt properties for tax purposes conducted by the *Direction générale des contributions directes* in 1908-1911.[15]

14 Zolla, *Blé et céréales*, pp. 80 ff. The Dijon and Clermont-Ferrand series are dated 1876-1881, 1881-1886, etc. The Nevers and Riom series are dated 1876-1880, 1881-1885, etc. The Dijon series starts with 1871-1876 = 100, 1876-1881 = 104, etc., and the relatives were reduced to 1876-1881 = 100 for the sake of uniformity.

15 Ministère des finances, Direction générale des contributions directes, *Evaluation des propriétés non bâties prescrite par l'article 3 de la loi du 31 décembre 1907: Rapport de M. Charles Dumont, Ministre des finances, sur l'ensemble des opérations (3 novembre 1913)*, Paris, 2 vols., vol. I, pp. 264 ff.

RENTAL VALUE

	Per Class (000 francs)			Per Hectare (francs)	
	1879	*1908*		*1879*	*1908*
Orchards, gardens, etc.	145,517	123,015		104	108
Tillable lands[a]	1,485,098	1,195,621		57	49
Pastures, meadows, etc.	483,159	447,649		97	65
Vineyards	301,546	114,610		130	76
Woodlands	188,910	144,841		23	17
Wastelands, etc.	41,275	31,213		6	4
Total	2,645,506	2,056,950	Average[b]	53	41

With the exception of the first category the decline is marked and incontestable, but Zolla's data show that the first evaluation occurred during a period of rising, or at least high rents, and that the fall became accentuated about 1891.

A similar picture results from a consideration of gross value of land. Edmond Théry, the distinguished editor of *l'Économiste européen,* estimated that the sale value of unbuilt property had fallen from 77,847 million francs in 1892 to 75,500 million francs in 1908, a decline of about 3%.[16] The evaluation of 1908 indicates a fall from 91,584 million francs in 1879 to 61,757 million francs in 1908, about one third.[17] Here again it would appear that the decline became significant in the last decade of the nineteenth century and continued into the twentieth, but at a slower pace. In his study of land values, Caziot suggests that a plateau had been reached, at a far lower level than in the period 1860-1880, and that some signs of a rise were discernible.[18]

[a] Unfortunately the figures for this class are not strictly comparable. The 1879 evaluation included the ground on which rural buildings stood, courtyards etc. (*Ibid.*, p. 292 note.) The names of all classifications were changed in 1908, and those used here are summaries.

[b] Weighted by the area of each category.

16 Edmond Théry, *La fortune publique de la France*, Paris, 1912, p. 242.

17 Direction générale des contributions directes, *op. cit.*, vol. I, p. 293.

18 P. Caziot, *La valeur de la terre en France*, Paris, 1914, p. 10.

Combining rent and sale values to determine the rate of return, the evaluation of 1908 shows the following results:[19]

	1879	*1892*	*1908*
Orchards, gardens, etc.	3.08		3.58
Tillable lands	2.58	2.75	3.31
Pastures, meadows, etc	3.26	3.41	3.45
Vineyards	4.38	4.60	3.76
Woodlands	3.02		2.90
Wastelands	2.96		2.73
Overall average	2.89		3.33

With sale values and rentals falling, a rising rate of return indicates that sale prices fell more rapidly than rents. For all classes, the former declined by about 32% and the latter by about 22%. Several possible explanations for this phenomenon suggest themselves. First, more rapidly falling sale prices may represent a discounting of an expected fall in returns. Second, rents may be held above sale prices by long term leases, ignorance or financial weakness on the part of tenants which would prevent them from moving. In the case of orchards, gardens, etc., rentals per hectare actually rose.[20] The second hypothesis seems valid for tillable lands, pastures, meadows, etc., where tenancy was most prominent. A third possible explanation is that in these, the vast majority of all lands, and the least specialized, buyers were wanting as capital was transferred to far more liquid urban or industrial investments.[21] For vineyards, woodlands and wastelands, however, the rate of return fell. We may ignore the last category, as too small to be significant. Vineyards, as we have seen, were predominantly operated by

19 Direction générale des contributions directes, *op. cit.*, vol. I, p. 264. The 1892 figures were arrived at by adjusting the figures given in the agricultural *enquête* of that year by the percentage by which the 1882 agricultural *enquête* data varied from those of the tax evaluation of 1879.

20 *Loc. cit.*

21 In this connection Caziot emphasizes the high legal fees for transfer of real property. *Op. cit.*, p. 48.

small owners,[22] who might be expected to retain their properties as long as possible even in the face of falling income. Forest lands, large areas of which were part of estates held for other than economic reasons, saw their situation complicated, in the years preceding 1908, by serious labor difficulties.[23] Assuming the validity of the third hypothesis, that agriculture was at a disadvantage in competing with industry for capital, variation in the rate of return, especially when deduced from tax valuations, does not necessarily connote similar variation in farm income.

Considered only in relation to its own past, French agriculture in the first decade of the twentieth century seemed to be continuing to progress very slowly. Per hectare yields had risen, land ownership had gained somewhat over tenancy. But the dominant note was one of maintenance of traditions, of resistance to change rather than progressive change. If a rise in truck farming indicated a slight tendency toward specialization, the decline of so-called industrial crops indicated a return to diversified farming. Such progress as there was becomes less impressive when we compare yields with other countries,[24] and within French society, industry and commerce advanced rapidly relative to agriculture, if slowly relative to industry and commerce in other lands.

THE SYNDICATS AGRICOLES

The *syndicats agricoles* were one progressive element in French agriculture, contributing to technical improvement and economic strength. Evidence of both the need for economic defense and of the vitality existing to provide it, the *syndical* movement continued to grow, if at a slow and unspectacular pace. The *enquête* of 1892 listed 863 *syndicats,* with 313,800

22 See Chapter II, note 33.

23 See p. 229 below.

24 JO, 1911, p. 57. Among thirteen countries of Europe, France was tenth with respect to wheat, eighth with respect to barley and seventh with respect to oats.

members.[25] In a survey conducted in 1898 the *Musée social* reported 2,016 *syndicats agricoles.* For the year 1910, the *Annuaire silvestre,* an agricultural association yearbook, listed 4,629 *syndicats,* the *Annuaire des syndicats agricoles* of the Ministry of Agriculture listed 5,058 *syndicats,* 2,392 of which belonged to 55 unions; in a study based on both these sources, the comte de Rocquigny estimated 5,827 *syndicats.*[27] Augé-Laribé declares that no definitive calculation can be made, because of lack of replies and erroneous replies to questionnaires, dormant organizations, etc. He suggests an approximation of somewhat over 5,000 *syndicats* in 1910. But, as he points out, there were 847 with a membership of 25 or less, and it could not be said that these weak organizations were generally strengthened by membership in unions of *syndicats.* For, as we have seen, only somewhat over half were so affiliated. Of the 778,189 members of *syndicats,* according to the *Annuaire des syndicats agricoles,* 341,258 belonged to *syndicats* affiliated with unions.[28] The number of *syndicats* had increased six times since 1892, the number of members only two and one half times. As Augé-Laribé points out, only about twenty per cent of the possible membership actually belonged to these organizations.[29]

The *syndicats* continued their varied program of services, and advanced their social attitude, as before. They were naturally subject to a tendency to extend the range of their commercial operations, and thereby incurred the enmity of local merchants. In 1907 the *Syndicat agricole* of Consenvoye, in Lor-

25 *Enquête,* 1892, tables p. 436.

26 Musée social, *Etat général des syndicats agricoles classés par départements,* Paris, 1898, pp. 1-80.

27 Ministère de l'agriculture, *Annuaire des syndicats agricoles,* Paris, 1911, pp. 42 ff. Rocquigny, "La statistique des associations agricoles," *Le Musée social: Annales,* 1911, pp. 263 ff.

28 *Annuaire des syndicats agricoles, loc. cit.* Augé-Laribé, *Evolution,* pp. 192 ff.

29 Augé-Laribé, *op. cit.,* p. 200.

raine, was charged with owning and operating a "general store," and with buying other than agricultural goods without previous order by its members. It was fined heavily and ordered to dissolve. The *Union centrale* appealed the case for the *syndicat,* but the appellate bench at Nancy upheld the verdict of the court of first instance. The case was carried to the Court of Cassation, which, although sustaining the decision, and warning *syndicats* to remain strictly within the limits of the law of 1884, reduced the penalties considerably.[30] This judicial defeat resulted in a special assembly of the *Union centrale,*[31] and in the introduction in the Chamber of Deputies of several measures designed to remedy the situation. The first was a bill introduced by Minister of Agriculture Ruau, providing for the creation of an economic *syndicat* beside each *syndicat agricole.* The leaders of the movement felt, however, that to make the *syndicat* a purely professional society, without economic functions, would destroy its influence.[32] A bill introduced in 1909 was more satisfactory. It confirmed the right of *syndicats* to buy and sell professionally necessary goods, and extended this right to unions of *syndicats.* This bill was not enacted, however, and the upshot of the matter was that the *syndicats* continued on their way, buying and selling to their members goods needed in agriculture (sometimes under a very broad interpretation of this phrase), and without previous specific orders. They were protected by a ministerial policy of not prosecuting except in flagrant cases of exceeding the limits of the law.[33]

We have emphasized the fact that the leaders of the *syndical* movement regarded it as a defense against agrarian socialism through the maintenance of peasant proprietorship, and this reasoning was given point by a series of agricultural laborers'

30 *Annuaire des syndicats agricoles,* pp. 14-18.

31 *Bulletin de l'Union des syndicats des agriculteurs de France,* December, 1908 and supplement.

32 Lécolle, *Les associations agricoles,* pp. 30 ff.

33 Marcillac, *Syndicats,* pp. 207-209, 253.

strikes in the first decade of the twentieth century. As early as 1891 woodsmen's strikes had occurred and unions had been formed.[34] But in 1903 vineyard workers in Languedoc struck, and organized, later affiliating with the *Confédération générale du travail*. Sharecroppers in the Bourbonnais region of central France organized in 1904.[35] Horticultural workers, mushroom gardeners, woodsmen and day laborers in various regions struck in 1906-1907, and more organizations were formed. At the end of 1910 the various unions belonging to the Federation of Agriculture of the *Confédération générale du travail* numbered 628, with 61,613 members.[36] Even this small scale movement worried the conservative agrarian leaders, and inspired some conciliatory counter measures, but Augé-Laribé points out that trade union organization of agricultural laborers was effective only when there was a close similarity of tasks and a common salary level.[37] There were no large units, as in industry, to furnish a common ground for different types of workers, nor were there generally large numbers of the same type of worker in a single area. Unionization of agrarian labor along lines similar to that of industrial labor was evidence of the industrialization of agriculture and of its entry further into the framework of modern capitalism, and the slightness of this evidence bespeaks the resistance of French agriculture to both industrialization and modern capitalism.

CREDIT

It was through the collective medium of association that French agriculture made its closest approach to capitalist techniques. One possible explanation for the more rapid rise, noted

34 See p. 108 above.

35 This was a district of large estates, leased to agents at fixed rentals, subleased by the latter on a crop-sharing basis.

36 R. Garmy, *Histoire du mouvement syndical en France des origines à 1914*, Paris, 1933, p. 163. Augé-Laribé, *Problème du socialisme*, pp. 279 ff.

37 Augé-Laribé, *Evolution*, pp. 255, 262 ff.

above, of the number of *syndicats* than of members was the growth of auxiliary societies and services, especially loan and insurance associations whose formation was facilitated by the prior organization of *syndicats*. In Chapter III we indicated the early beginnings of mutual credit in the society of the *syndicat* of Poligny and in the *caisses Durand*. Both types had serious limitations. The first was subject to the complicated corporation law of 1867, and since it discounted its paper with the Bank of France, it had to require a co-signer and limit loans to three months renewable up to a year. The second, which drew its loan funds from deposits and profits, was not capable of significant expansion of credit.[38]

A new type of credit institution was authorized by a law of November 5, 1894, introduced in the Chamber by Jules Méline. This provided that the members of a *syndicat agricole* could form a mutual credit bank exempt from the *patente*, or business license, and from the tax on securities. Shares could be held only by members, and were to receive a fixed return. All profits after payment of necessary expenses were to be placed in a reserve fund.[39] In 1897, on the occasion of the renewal of the charter of the Bank of France, it was provided that the Bank was to give the state 2,000,000 francs each year, and lend it 40,000,000 francs repayable in 1920. These sums were to be used for the promotion of agricultural credit, and in 1899 nine regional banks were created to aid the local societies by discounting their paper and giving them direct loans. The capital funds of the regional banks were provided by the local units, and the government was empowered to lend them up to four times their capital sum.[40] The principle of loans to a *syndicat* as an entity, enacted in 1894, was extended in 1906 by a law providing for long term loans to agricultural cooperatives, all

38 See p. 91, above. Sagnier, *Le crédit agricole*, p. 11.

39 Ministère de l'agriculture, *Dix ans de crédit agricole (1900-1909)*, Paris, 1911, pp. 1 ff. Sagnier, *op. cit.*, pp. 32-33.

40 Sagnier, *op. cit.*, pp. 59-60, 65. Rocquigny, *Syndicats*, p. 310.

of whose members belonged to *syndicats*. A law of 1910 made possible the extension of long term credit to individuals.[41]

This policy of stimulating agricultural credit bore results. According to the Ministry of Agriculture, in 1900 the state advanced 612,250 francs to nine regional banks; eighty-seven local banks lent 1,910,456 francs to borrowers among their 2,175 members. In 1909 the state advanced 46,231,456 francs to ninety-five regional banks; 2,983 local banks lent 105,026,-740 francs to borrowers among their 133,382 members.[42] In the ten years 1900-1909 a total of 442,751,696 francs had been lent to individuals. But, unfortunately, these figures are open to question. To the total of loans granted in each year was added loans current at the end of the previous year, and no distinction was made between renewals and new borrowings. Augé-Laribé therefore estimates the total lent as 160,000,000 francs and, in any event, not more than 200,000,000 francs. In his study of agricultural credit, Henry Sagnier reaches an estimate of 313,097,000 francs. In view of the seriousness of the credit problem in the nineteenth century, even at the lowest figure the results were notable.[43]

Agricultural mutual insurance has a longer history than credit, but was slower to receive state support.[44] At the end of 1897 there were 1,484 societies, of which almost half were in the single department of Landes. Méline, who was Minister of Agriculture at the time, secured an appropriation of 500,000 francs in the budget of 1898 for the purpose of aiding the development of insurance societies, and from 1898 to the end of

41 *Annuaire des syndicats agricoles*, p. 3. Sagnier, op. cit., pp. 99 ff. Augé-Laribé, *op. cit.*, p. 182. The full story of the legislation on agricultural credit between 1894 and 1910 would require far too much space to be given here. See Sagnier, *op. cit.*

42 *Dix ans de crédit agricole*, p. xvi. Rocquigny, *op. cit.*, *Musée social: Annales*, 1911, p. 265, declares that there were, in addition about seven hundred *caisses Durand*.

43 Augé-Laribé, *op. cit.*, p. 213. Sagnier, *op. cit.*, pp. 88, 96.

44 See p. 91 above.

1910, 9,240 such organizations were established.[45] About four-fifths of these mutuals insured against loss of livestock. In September, 1910, they had 438,216 members, and had issued policies insuring livestock worth 532,807,990 francs. Unfortunately, only 3,055 out of 8,428 of these local societies had their policies underwritten. Fire insurance, with 2,187 mutuals (of which 2,096 were affiliated with underwriters), and 53,110 members held second place; hail insurance, with 25 societies and 44,677 members held third place, and accident insurance brought up the rear with 7 societies and 3,478 members.[46] In 1909 the *Union centrale* established a central underwriting agency to support both regional underwriters and local societies.[47]

In insurance, as in credit and the *syndicats* proper, the agrarian leaders could find satisfaction only in glancing back over the road they had traveled: the road ahead was far longer. They could report progress, but could not diminish their efforts. And they were faced with a serious threat. The tradition of recourse to the state was strong in France, and in a parliamentary democracy demands for governmental asistance, presented in the name of a major interest among the population, are rarely resisted. Thus, as we have seen, the resources of the treasury were more and more often called upon. And yet the old leaders of the *syndical* movement knew that this tendency ran counter to free association, to corporatism *within* the state.[48] Given the character of the French state and the old tradition of centralization, and the ascendancy of middle class political groups, pursuance of direct intervention rather than through the agency of independent, voluntary associations was almost inevitable. The failure of agricultural association, under the lead-

45 Ministère de l'agriculture, *Principales measures*, p. 15. Blanchoin, *Assurances*, p. 33.

46 JO, 1911, *Annexes*, pp. 1-10. *Sociétés d'assurances mutuelles agricoles: Rapport au Président de la République.*

47 Marcillac, *Syndicats*, pp. 142-143.

48 For example, *ibid.*, pp. 118 ff.

ership of the *Société des agriculteurs de France,* its affiliates and allies, to grow into an agrarian mass movement organizing the majority of the farm population meant that while many objectives had been secured, and the opposition to outright *étatisme* (whether socialist or middle class) had been strengthened, victory had not been achieved. Movements, efforts and issues, therefore, were hurled into the cauldron of the war years of 1914-1918, to emerge, changed, into a strange, unhappy world.

CONCLUSIONS

If we may regard the complex of association and protectionism as the defense elaborated by conservative agrarian leaders against the rise of industry and its corollary society, a society in which socialist *étatisme* was at least a threat, we may risk the conclusion that this defense was a stubborn, hard fought retreat.[49] But it was, in a larger sense, a sub-complex: the basic social complex into which we have delved unevenly and partially was the tenacious rear guard defense of the French social structure that had grown with the Third Republic. This defense was built around nationalist economics.[50] It could not succeed in maintaining French political primacy against the competition of nations overwhelmingly greater in territory and population, such as the United States, Russia (in the long run) and, to a lesser extent, Germany. It can be asserted, however, that this rear guard action postponed and mitigated the symptoms of a long run trend of relative decline. And, with regard to the more limited field we have surveyed, it can be asserted that the adoption of nationalist economic policies for agriculture attenuated and slowed the decline of agriculture within French society. To test this assertion, to attempt to answer the questions raised by the tariff debate of 1909 which introduced this chap-

49 Augé-Laribé, *op. cit.*, p. 300, writes: "... the impression is that the growth of cities and industry is already out of proportion to the total population of the country, to the rural element, and that, should this tendency continue, we shall some day have to regret it."

50 Clough, *op. cit.*

ter, to try to evaluate the degree of success of the Méline Tariff remains our final task.

TARIFF REVISIONS

As a preliminary step, however, it is necessary to list the tariff revisions enacted between 1892 and 1910 which continued the policy laid down in 1892 and are essential to any consideration of the effectiveness of this policy. There were some thirty major legislative modifications of the tariff structure in this period, and many of these affected agriculture. A law of February 22, 1894, raised the wheat duty from 5 to 7 francs per hundred kilograms, and carried corresponding increases for bread, spaghetti, etc. The law of December 13, 1897, the *Loi du cadenas,* provided that the government might raise or lower by decree, subject to subsequent parliamentary ratification, duties on grains, flours, breadstuffs, wines, livestock and meats. The purpose of this measure was to prevent speculation in anticipation of tariff changes. A law of February 4, 1902 abolished temporary free admission for grains for milling and reexport, and substituted a system of drawbacks. It had been found that under the old regulations some of the grain imported duty-free eventually found its way into domestic markets instead of being processed and exported. The new law eliminated the loopholes. The law of April 9, 1898 sharply raised the duties on horses and mules and also created minimum rates: the tax on horses under five years of age was raised from 30 francs per head to 200 francs in the maximum, and 150 in the minimum schedule; the duty on mules was raised from 5 francs per head to 50 and 30 francs. A law of August 9, 1903, brought cattle and sheep into the minimum schedule, but raised duties as follows: oxen, cows and bulls, from 10 francs per hundred kilograms live weight (1892) to 30 and 20 francs; heifers and sheep from 12 and 15.50 francs, respectively (1892) to 40 and 25 francs; hogs from 12 francs (1898) to 25 and 15 francs. Subsidies for production of flax, hemp and silkworms were continued and extended by laws of April 9, 1898, and March 31, 1904, and April 2, 1898 and June 11, 1909.

The Méline Tariff had taxed wine by alcoholic content and by volume, 10% wines paying 12 francs per hectoliter on the maximum schedule and 7 francs on the minimum. A law of February 4, 1899 changed the duties to 25 and 12 francs per hectoliter for wines of up to 12% alcoholic content, and a duty equal to the internal tax on alcohol was added for each degree above 12. The purpose of this was to stop the practice of importing strong wines for dilution. A law of December 29, 1900, raised the internal alcohol tax from 156.25 francs per hectoliter to 200 francs, and the law of July 18, 1906, raised the maximum duty on 12% wines from 25 to 35 francs per hectoliter. The complicated sugar legislation, in which direct and indirect subsidies had followed one upon the other as in many other countries, was greatly simplified by the International Sugar Conference at Brussels in 1902, which abolished all subsidies. In addition to the tariff changes enumerated, there were others affecting fruits, coffee, spices and other colonial products.[51]

These various revisions, with the exception of sugar, constituted an upward course in agricultural duties. They responded to a demand articulated, as before, by the *Société des agriculteurs,* and by such newer organizations as the *Association de l'industrie et de l'agriculture françaises,* founded in 1893 by Méline and directed by Domergue, editor of *la Réforme économique.*[52] This rise in duties proves, at the very least, that the law of 1892 did not give protection that seemed adequate to the agrarian leadership.

51 JO, dates following those of laws; *Principales mesures,* pp. 90 ff., and on sugar, 111. Summaries in Arnauné, *op. cit.,* pp. 338 ff.; Perreau, *op. cit.,* pp. 55 ff.; Lamy, *op. cit.,* pp. 31 ff.; Levasseur, *op. cit.,* vol. II, p. 588. On the Brussels sugar convention see René Romanet, *La Conférence de Bruxelles de 1901-1902 sur le régime des sucres,* Poligny, 1904, pp. 105 ff.

52 See BSAF and *la Réforme économique, passim.* Augier and Marvaud, *op. cit.,* p. 193.

FOREIGN TRADE

A likely reason for the demand for increased protection appears when we examine French foreign trade in agricultural commodities. In all but three of the nineteen years 1891-1909 agricultural net imports exceeded total net imports, outweighing French industry's export surplus. Grain imports, which averaged 333.3 million francs in 1891-1899 (295.8 million francs excluding the exceptional year 1898), fell to an average of 159.4 million francs in 1900-1909. Wine imports, which averaged 266.4 million francs in 1891-1899, fell to an average of 124.9 million francs in 1900-1909; an average import surplus of 35.4 million francs in the first period gave way to an average export surplus of 88.8 million francs in the second.[53]

SPECIAL COMMERCE IN MILLIONS OF FRANCS

	1	2	3	4	5	6	7	8
	Agri. Imp.	Agri. Exp.	1–2	Total Imp.	Total Exp.	4–5	Grain Imp.	Wine Imp.
1891	1935	796	1139	4768	3570	1198	532	401
1892	1670	770	900	4188	3461	727	487	306
1893	1388	727	661	3854	3236	618	307	183
1894	1506	693	813	3850	3078	772	363	145
1895	1269	623	586	3320	3373	–53	162	212
1896	1304	707	597	3799	3401	398	123	294
1897	1365	778	587	3956	3598	348	247	280
1898	1843	734	1109	4473	3511	962	632	310
1899	1434	825	619	4518	4153	365	144	267
1900	1284	836	447	4698	4109	589	127	155
1901	1209	800	409	4369	4013	356	185	85
1902	1199	843	356	4394	4252	142	148	111
1903	1412	796	616	4801	4252	549	174	182
1904	1211	863	348	4502	4451	51	111	160
1905	1272	897	375	4779	4867	–88	152	109
1906	1495	889	606	5627	5265	362	221	103
1907	1663	927	736	6223	5596	627	226	104
1908	1323	867	456	5641	5051	590	97	117
1909	1629	1067	562	6246	5718	528	153	124

53 The items composing these lists are given in Chapter I note 57. Cocoons were omitted from the import list, as imports of this commodity became negligible. This accounts for the slight difference between the figures given for 1891 here and on p. 68 above. *Tableau décennal* until 1896, *Tableau annuel* therafter.

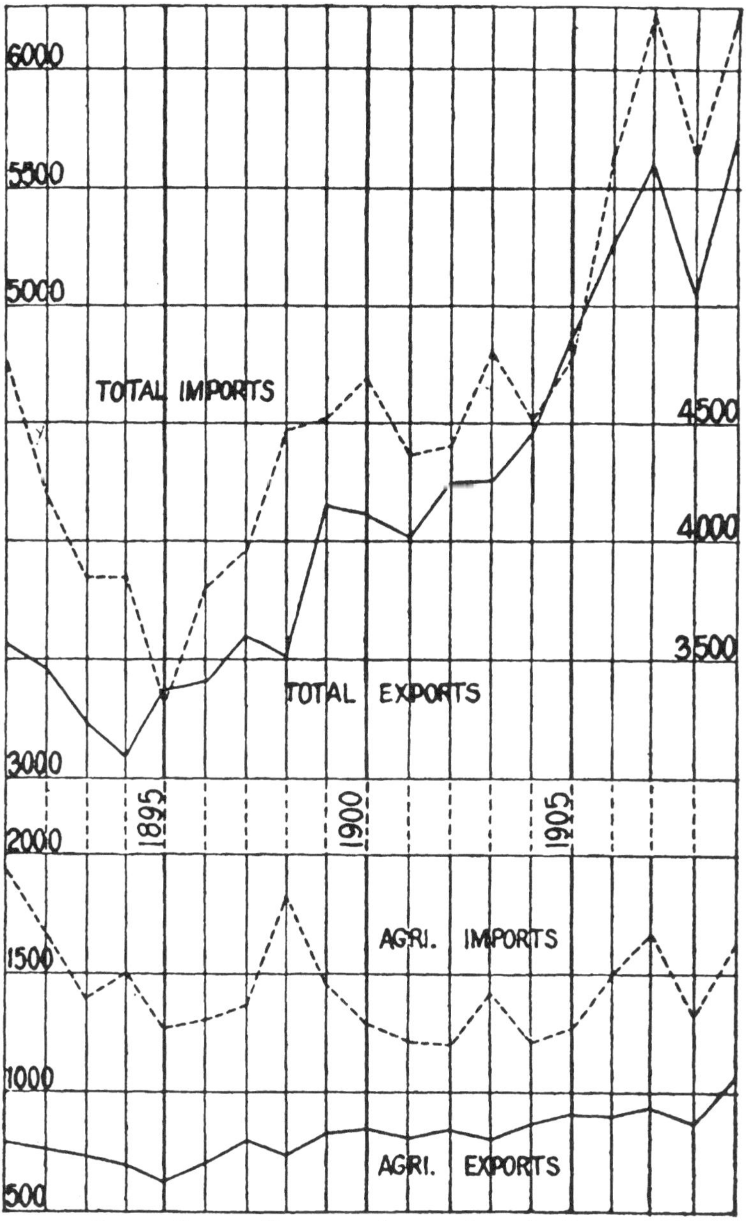

Fig. 5. Special Commerce (000,000 francs), 1891-1909

Increased imports of such commodities as wool, oleaginous seeds, vegetable oils and flax, domestic production of which had declined, in large part explain the maintenance of the import surplus at a high level; but it should be noted that net imports of grain still averaged 141.8 million francs in 1900-1909.

PRICES

The adverse agricultural commodity balance shows that domestic production was unable to meet the demands of the French consumer. It does not necessarily prove, however, the ineffectiveness of protection. Combined with falling prices the adverse balance would be evidence of destructive competition. In the face of stable prices the import surplus might be taken to reflect the List thesis that imports should take a share of the annual increase in consumption.[54] This thesis may be modified to read that imports should provide that portion of domestic needs which cannot economically be produced at home. The test of the effectiveness of duties would therefore be sought in price trends rather than foreign trade.

For the purpose of this inquiry a French and an English price index have been constructed. They are weighted averages of relatives, and the value weights are the same for both series: French prices (1891) times French production (*enquête* of 1892). This procedure is designed to illustrate the influence of protection on French agricultural prices. Although absolute differences between French and English prices in 1891, and therefore the influence of French duties enacted before the Mélin Tariff, are ignored by this method, it has the important advantage of eliminating the factor of qualitative differences between English and French commodities. These indexes do not offer a comparison of absolute French and English prices. They do offer a comparison of degrees of change in French and English agricultural prices.[55]

54 List, *Introduction*, in Hirst, *op. cit.*, pp. 313-314.

55 These series are composed of the following items: wheat, maize, oats, barley, flax, hemp, rape seed oil, sugar, butter, beef, mutton, pork, veal,

In the case of wine increased domestic production (from an average of 37.4 million hectoliters in 1891-1899 to 50.6 million hectoliters in 1900-1909) depressed prices despite the imposition of higher duties. An added factor was that production of wine in other countries had risen greately during the phylloxera period, and thus tended to lower prices when French production resumed.[56] In monetary terms there was an average difference

cheese, potatoes, edible oil (olive oil for England, *huile à manger* for France).

French prices for the following commodities were taken from the tables in Ministère du travail et de la prévoyance sociale: Statistique générale de la France, *Salaires et coût de l'existence à diverses époques jusqu'en 1910*, Paris, 1911:

Wheat, rape seed oil: (*Bourse du Commerce de Paris*), p. 386.

Beef, veal, mutton, pork: (*Halles centrales*), p. 388.

Butter, cheese, potatoes, wine, sugar: (Prices paid by *Assistance publique à Paris*), pp. 391-393.

Prices for maize, oats, barley, flax and hemp were taken from the market reports of the *Journal d'agriculture pratique*. From 1897, flax and hemp prices were drawn from the data of the *Commission des valeurs en douane* (*Annuaire statistique*, 1937, p. 137*) and were adjusted to the JAP prices. The prices paid by the *Assistance publique* followed official market prices closely, sometimes going below wholesale averages. Butter, cheese and potatoes were purchased at the *Halles*, wine from the *cave centrale*, sugar from the *magasin central*. These were bid prices, and since uneveness owing to the circumstances of bidding might be expected to adjust over the course of a year, they may be regarded as equivalent to wholesale prices.

All English prices with the exception of cheese, veal and rape seed oil were taken from Saurbeck's articles in the *Journal of the Royal Statistical Society*, vol. 66, 1903, pp. 97 ff.; vol. 75, 1911, pp. 420 ff. Edam cheese (selected for continuity), rape seed oil and veal prices were taken from the market quotations of *The Economist*. Until 1906 the price of middling quality veal was used (because of continuity), from 1906 to 1909 it became necessary to use first quality veal prices, and these were adjusted on the basis of the ratio between the two prices in 1905. Similar adjustments were made in the French series in changing from *avoine ordinaire* to *avoine blanche* in 1903, and from *orge de Brie* to *orge de Beauce* in 1904.

The value weights are as follows: wheat, 2499; barley, 173; oats, 777; maize, 122; potatoes, 1022; beef, 730; mutton, 217; pork, 646; butter, 813; sugar, 658; flax, 15; hemp, 17; edible oil, 23; rape seed oil, 14; veal, 269; cheese, 179.

56 See *Annuaire statistique*, 1911, p. 188*.

PRICE INDEXES, 1891 = 100

	Wheat						
	1 France	2 England	3 1–2	4 France	5 England	6 4–5	Wine France
1891	100	100	—	100	100	—	100
1892	93	93	—	84	82	2	102
1893	92	88	4	76	71	5	93
1894	94	81	13	69	60	9	86
1895	91	78	13	69	62	7	86
1896	88	77	11	70	71	-1	86
1897	95	84	11	92	81	11	92
1898	99	90	9	92	91	1	88
1899	93	83	10	72	69	3	87
1900	92	88	4	72	72	—	80
1901	95	88	7	73	72	1	45
1902	94	88	6	79	76	3	41
1903	97	86	11	83	72	11	56
1904	94	88	6	80	77	3	60
1905	95	89	6	85	81	4	40
1906	97	88	9	85	77	8	38
1907	100	93	7	86	82	4	40
1908	98	94	4	82	87	-5	45
1909	97	98	-1	88	100	-12	44

of 6.12 francs per quintal of wheat between French and English prices, with a maximum of 8.40 francs in 1897 and a minimum of 3.58 francs in 1909.[57] The wheat duties, therefore, were largely effective. In general, it may be said that protection stemmed the fall of agricultural prices, but did not prevent it.[58] To this partial extent, therefore, nationalist economic policy aided French agriculture: to this partial extent, it produced a burden for the non-agricultural consuming public, since their costs for agricultural commodities fell, but not as much as they might have fallen.

COST OF FOODSTUFFS TO THE URBAN CONSUMER

Closer consideration of this question is greatly facilitated by studies of typical budgets and costs of living by the English

57 Zolla, *Blé et céréales*, p. 129, finds an average difference of 5.71 francs for 1891-1900, lower by .41 than the figure given here. He does not indicate the source of his price data.

58 See Ashley, *op. cit.*, p. 332.

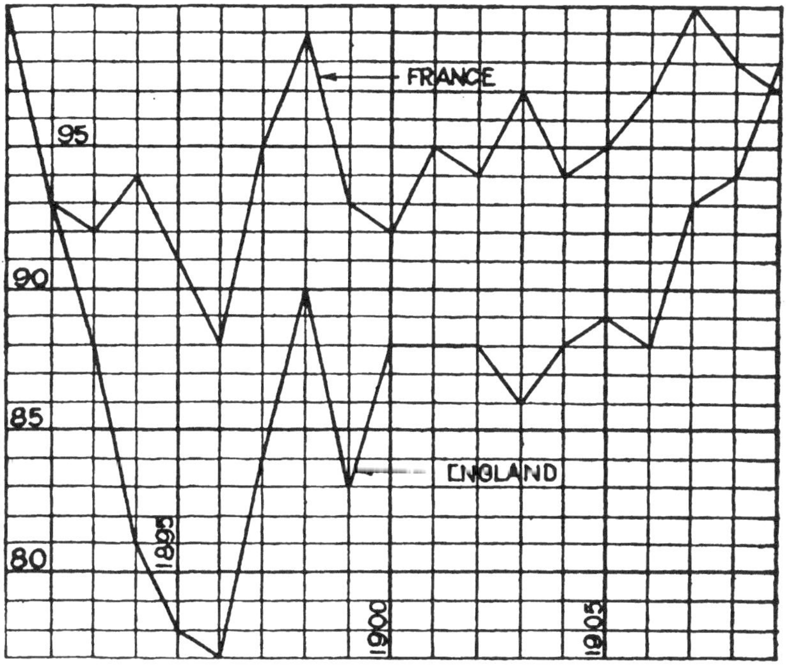

FIG. 6. PRICE INDEXES, 1891-1909. Base 1891 = 100

Board of Trade and by the French *Bureau de la statistique générale*.[59] According to the former, a typical English workingman's family food budget, taken as 100, would have cost 111 in France as of October 1905. A typical French workingman's family budget, taken as 100 in English prices, would have cost 106 in France.[60] The greatest differences were on wheat flour,

59 *Cost of Living in French Towns. Report of an Enquiry by the Board of Trade into Working Class Rents, Housing and Retail Prices together with the Rates of Wages in certain Occupations in the Principal Industrial Towns of France. With an introductory Memorandum and a Comparison of Conditions in France and the United Kingdom*, Cd. 4512, London, 1909. *Salaires et coût de l'existence*. See also *Receuil statistique de la Ville de Paris*, 1910, pp. 29 ff.

60 *Cost of Living in French Towns*, pp. xli-xlii. The items used in this calculation were: sugar, butter, potatoes, wheat flour, white bread, milk, beef, mutton, pork.

	Carpenter				*790 Paris workers*		*Bourgeois Family*					
	Commissary		*Ass. pub.*		Commissary		Commissary			*Ass. pub.*		
	A	B	A	B	A	B	A	B	C	A	B	C
1891 ...	100	100	100	100	100	100	100	100		100	100	
1892 ...	99	100	94	93	99	98	98	97		96	94	
1893 ...	94	94	91	91	96	94	94	92		94	93	
1894 ...	94	95	94	96	96	98	94	94		97	100	
1895 ...	92	95	93	95	94	98	94	95		96	99	
1896 ...	89	91	92	92	91	93	91	93		86	93	
1897 ...	88	89	92	93	92	91	91	91		92	93	
1898 ...	93	96	93	94	94	97	94	95		93	94	
1899 ...	94	95	90	91	95	97	94	94		92	93	
1900 ...	89	91	90	93	92	92	92	93		93	96	
1901 ...	89	92	83	91	91	94	93	95	93	85	95	92
1902 ...	85	93	82	91	84	95	87	95	93	83	94	90
1903 ...	88	96	91	98	87	99	89	97	95	91	100	97
1904 ...	88	95	89	95	87	96	87	95	93	88	98	95
1905 ...	86	97	83	92	84	100	87	96	92	84	96	91
1906 ...	85	96	82	91	84	101	82	95	88	81	93	87
1907 ...	89	101	88	98	87	105	87	99	93	86	100	93
1908 ...	91	104	89	99	88	107	88	101	94	88	101	94
1909 ...	90	101	88	98	87	104	87	99	93	87	100	94

(In column C of the third series 0.19 franc was added to the price of wine. This represents the *octroi* and internal revenue duties abolished from 1901.)

pork and sugar. Wine was not included in these calculations.

In the French study, the quantities purchased by a Parisian carpenter, calculated in 1856 and 1890, the quantities determined by the Board of Trade,[61] and the quantities used by a bourgeois Parisian family of nine (estimated in 1895) were applied to prices paid by railway commissaries and by the *Assistance publique.*[62] In the above table total expenses are

61 *Salaires et coût de l'existence*, p. 57, refers merely to a study conducted in 1907 among eight hundred Paris working class families, but there is little question that it was the study conducted by the Board of Trade.

62 The word *économat* is translated as commissary. As was noted above, the prices paid by the *Assistance publique*, a quasi-official charitable agency, could be regarded as equivalent to wholesale prices.

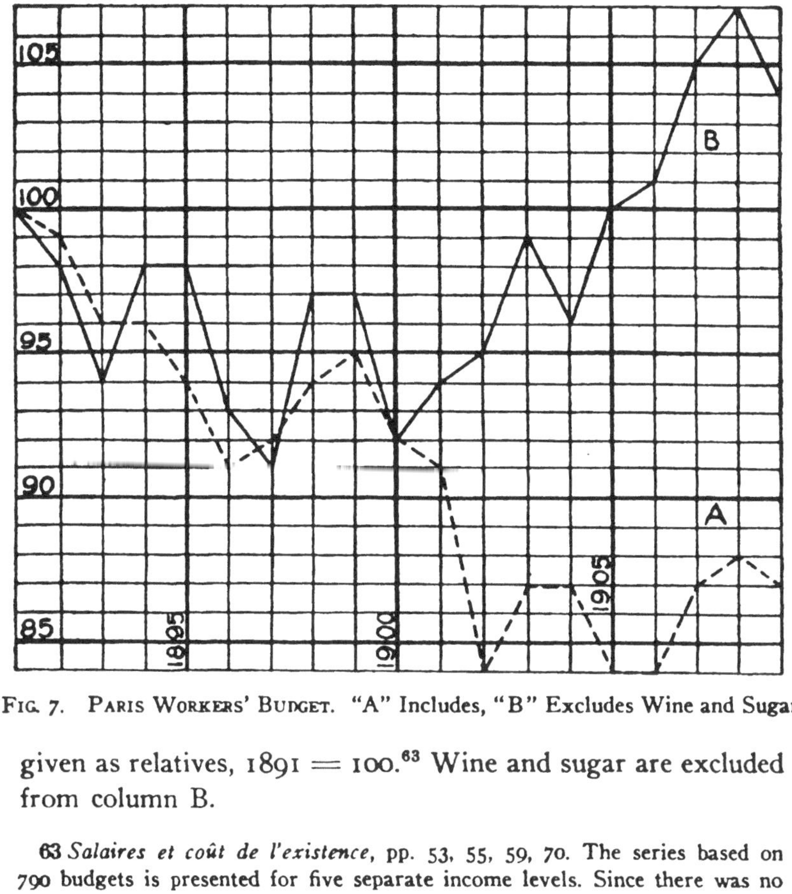

FIG. 7. PARIS WORKERS' BUDGET. "A" Includes, "B" Excludes Wine and Sugar

given as relatives, 1891 = 100.[63] Wine and sugar are excluded from column B.

63 *Salaires et coût de l'existence*, pp. 53, 55, 59, 70. The series based on 790 budgets is presented for five separate income levels. Since there was no statement as to the number in each group, the five series were averaged arithmetically. The greatest price rise appeared in the highest income level. See R. H. Hooker, "The Course of Prices at Home and Abroad, 1890-1910," *Journal of the Royal Statistical Society*, vol. LXXV, 1911-1912, pp. 1-36. Hooker indicates that French food prices generally fell more than English (table, p. 16; Table II, p. 30). His failure to employ weights (attacked by J. M. Keynes in the discussion following presentation of the paper) led to results in contradiction to those presented here. Although, in considering the data of *Salaires et coût de l'existence*, Hooker notes the importance of falling wine and sugar prices in producing low French index numbers, he seems insufficiently critical of the methods used in this study of the *Ministère du travail*.

Little difference arises from the fact that two types of prices and three sets of quantities were used. All series indicate that the consumer was able to pay less for foodstuffs through 1904, but that his savings arose, in large part, from declining sugar and wine prices. In three of the five columns "B" prices reached or passed 100 in 1907. The series based on the typical budget of 790 Paris workers reached 100 in 1905. For the greater part of the period, however, foodstuffs cost less than in 1891 despite agricultural tariffs.

Thus both antagonists and protagonists of agricultural protection were partly right. This policy did constitute a tax on the non-agricultural consuming public, to the extent that French prices remained above the English level, but not so great a tax as the liberal orators of 1891 predicted. The best defense of the policy rests on other grounds, however. From the standpoint of nationalist economics Méline and his successors could claim that the tax-subsidy was justified, for it had saved French agriculture from rapid decline, preserved national independence with regard to foodstuffs (especially wheat) and many other raw materials, helped to maintain the balanced, varied economy they considered essential to a rich, thriving national culture. This defense rests, of course, on a hypothesis which cannot be tested or proved, that in the absence of protection French agriculture would indeed have fallen. History cannot be reversed, but the indications are that the hypothesis is valid. Considering the geographic location and the natural resources of France, the technical skill and traditions of the French people, and the nature of the French empire, it is likely that the long existing trend from agrarian to urban, industrial life would have accelerated in the absence of agricultural protection. If this trend was not reversed, it was at least retarded.

The whole policy of agricultural protection is nevertheless open to the accusation of timidity. Augé-Laribé writes that a nation courageous and conscious of its strength would have entered the competitive world market of the late nineteenth and twentieth centuries, and accommodated itself to the necessities of a new day.[64] But this transcends economic policy and raises a question of national attitudes. The economist Truchy writes:[65]

> We risk little, we gain little; we are prudent and thrifty; we seek in money not the opportunities it affords but the interest coupons it assures. In these tranquil ways in which sons are led by fathers and in which they, in their turn, will lead their children, we perhaps find happiness, but certainly these are not the ways by which modern peoples march to greatness or a historic rôle. Threatened by the competition of more adventurous and more energetic nations, we prudently sought shelter. We judged it better to content ourselves with the untroubled possession of the domestic market than to risk the hazards of the world market, and we built a solid fortress of tariffs. Within the boundaries of this limited, but assured market, the French live calmly, comfortably enough, and, leaving to others the torment of great ambition, are no more than spectators in the struggles for economic supremacy.
>
> There is the entire philosophy of the Tariff of 1892. It is perfectly suited to our present social and economic status; it is a manifestation of this state, and at the same time one of its supports. It is one of the reactions of this social condition to the pressure of the environment and to the changes this pressure was tending to compel. In consolidating the interests which created it, to their own advantage, in blocking or restraining the tendencies which would have weakened or eliminated them, it continually creates for itself new reasons to be perpetuated.

---

64 Augé-Laribé, *op. cit.*, p. 21. It may be argued that if not for the Méline Tariff and continuing legislation, France might have been better equipped to withstand the shock of the Second World War, but at this writing it seems unlikely that greater industrialization would materially have changed the situation. It was not so much a lack of resources or equipment as their improper utilization that brought France to defeat.

65 H. Truchy, "Etude sur le commerce de la France," *Revue d'économie politique*, vol. XVIII, 1904, p. 564. See also R. G. Tugwell, "The Agricultural Policy of France," reprinted from *Political Science Quarterly*, vol. XLV, nos. 2, 3, 4, 1930, pp. 220, 547.

The troubled and strenuous life of the Third French Republic began at a time when the major economic institutions of the western world were bringing astounding material progress, but were failing, more and more, to achieve security; a time when the nation-state was becoming more active and ambitious, when world politics were unstable. In France, as elsewhere, instability and insecurity helped to build the strength of Marxian socialism. And in France, where middle-class, generally anti-clerical elements came to dominate the political machinery of the state, conservative agrarian leaders could not enthusiastically turn to government alone for defense against socialism. In response to this situation, two strong elements, deeply rooted in the past, came increasingly to the fore. One was the Social Catholic philosophy, which sought to overthrow economic and political liberalism, and replace them with an organized society based on Christian tenets of justice. The other was nationalism, inspiring and at the same time serving as an apology for many groups and interests; striving to establish the idea of national interest, with which these groups identified their own.

As an expression of both these elements rose the *syndicats agricoles*. They campaigned with ardor and ability for the conservation of the existing social order, while trying to modify it by strengthening its more traditional aspects. And they campaigned for protection of their own interests along nationalist lines. In and among these factors played the ordinary, everyday practices of political barter as well as important constitutional questions. The interaction of all these elements of the complex climaxed in 1892 with the adoption of the Méline Tariff. Nationalist economic policy was enshrined, but the problems it was called upon to eliminate persisted, although modified by the conditions it imposed.

In a field in which no all-embracing natural laws have been discerned, owing to the existence of human, subjective standards rather than physical, objective ones, we can reach no absolute conclusion as to the value of nationalist economic policy in this particular application. All we can say is that from the standpoint of cosmopolitan, liberal economics, the policy was, as foredoomed, a failure. From the standpoint of nationalist economics it achieved considerable success. Thus the debate must necessarily revert to standards and value judgments, social philosophies and ethics. It cannot be resolved in terms of economics alone, if by economics we mean something like Professor Robbins' "science which studies human behavior as a relationship between ends and scarce means which have alternative uses." [66] It is for this reason that a synthetic treatment of the subject seemed valid, and, in a larger sense, that the search for and the development of a synthetic philosophy of history must continue.

66 Lionel Charles Robbins, *An Essay on the Nature and Significance of Economic Science*, London, 1932, p. 15.

BIBLIOGRAPHY

A. Works of General Interest

Augé-Laribé, Michel, *L'Evolution de la France agricole*, Paris, 1912.

Bainville, Jacques, *La troisième république*, 93rd ed., Paris, 1935.

Charléty, S., *La Restauration (1815-1830)*, vol. iv of E. Lavisse, ed., *Histoire de la France contemporaine depuis la révolution jusqu'à la paix de 1919*, Paris, 1921.

Clough, Shepard Bancroft, *France: a History of National Economics 1789-1939*, New York, 1939.

Dansette, Adrien, *Du boulangisme à la révolution dreyfusienne: le boulangisme (1886-1890)*, Paris, 1938.

Hanotaux, Gabriel, *Histoire de la France contemporaine (1871-1900)*, 4 vols., Paris, 1903-1908.

Sagnac, P., *La Révolution (1789-1792)*, vol. I of E. Lavisse, ed., *op. cit.*, Paris, 1920.

Sée, Henri, *Esquisse d'une histoire économique et sociale de la France depuis les origines jusqu'à la guerre mondiale*, Paris, 1929.

——, *Fransösische Wirtschaftsgeschichte*, 2 vols., Jena, 1930-1936.

Seignobos, Charles, *L'Evolution de la 3e république (1875-1914)*, vol. VIII of E. Lavisse, ed., *op. cit.*, Paris, 1921.

Siegfried, André, *Tableau politique de la France de l'ouest sous la troisième république*, Paris, 1913.

Simond, Emile, *Histoire de la troisième république de 1887-1894: présidence de M. Carnot*, Paris, 1913.

Tugwell, Rexford G., *The Agricultural Policy of France*, rep. from *Political Science Quarterly*, vol. XLV, 1930, New York, 1930.

Zévaès, A., *Au temps du boulangisme*, 6th ed., Paris, 1930.

——, *Histoire de la troisième république*, Paris, 1938.

B. Economic History

Aconin, Maurice, *Le prix des objets de première nécessité depuis cinquante ans*, Paris, 1912.

Aftalion, Albert, *Les crises périodiques de surproduction*, Paris, 1913.

Allix, Edgard, *Les droits de douane; traité théorique et pratique de législation douanière*, 2 vols., Paris, 1932.

Amé, Léon, *Etude sur les tarifs de douane et les traités de commerce*, Paris, 1876.

Arnauné, Auguste, *Le commerce extérieur et les tarifs de douane*, Paris, 1911.

Ashley, Percy, *Modern Tariff History: Germany—United States—France*, New York, 1904.

Augé-Laribé, Michel, *Grande ou petite propriété?*, Montpellier, 1902.

Augier, C., and Marvaud, A., *La politique douanière de la France dans ses rapports avec celle des autres états*, Paris, 1911.

Bajkić, Wellimir J., *Der Französische Handelspolitik 1892-1902*, Stuttgart and Berlin, 1904.

Beaurieux, Noël, *Le prix du blé en France au XIXème siècle*, Paris, 1909.

Blanchoin, Albert, *L'Assurance mutuelle agricole; essai sur l'assurance coopérative*, Paris, 1935.

Block, Maurice, *Statistique de la France comparée avec les divers pays de l'Europe*, 2nd ed., 2 vols., Paris, 1875.

Boissevain, G. M., *The Monetary Question*, A. T. Warner, trans., London, 1891.

Boizard, E. and Tardieu, H., *Histoire de la législation des sucres*, Paris, 1891.

Caziot, P., *La valeur de la terre en France*, Paris, 1914.

Chevallier, Emile, *Exposition universelle internationale de 1900 à Paris: Rapports du jury international: class 104—grande et petite culture—syndicats agricoles—crédit agricole*, Paris, 1902.

Dijol, Marcel, *Le tarif douanier de 1892 et la situation économique de la France*, Montpellier, 1910.

Dunham, Arthur Louis, *The Anglo-French Treaty of Commerce of 1860 and the Progress of the Industrial Revolution in France*, University of Michigan Publications: History and Political Science, vol. IX, Ann Arbor, 1930.

Foville, Alfred de, *Le morcellement*, Paris, 1885.

Franke, Bernhard, *Der Ausbau des heutigen Schutzzollsystems in Frankreich*, Leipzig, 1903.

Girault, Arthur, *The Colonial Tariff Policy of France*, Carnegie Endowment for International Peace, Division of Economics and History, Oxford, 1916.

Imbart de la Tour, comte Joseph, *La crise agricole en France et à l'étranger*, Nevers, 1901.

Lamy, A., *La révision du tarif douanier actuel de la France*, Paris, 1909.

Layton, Walter T., *An Introduction to the Study of Prices: With special Reference to the History of the Nineteenth Century*, London, 1920.

Lescure, Jean, *Des crises générales et périodiques de surproduction*, 5th ed., 2 vols., Paris, 1938.

——, *Hausses et baisses de prix de longue durée*, Paris, 1933.

Levasseur, Emile, *Histoire du commerce de la France*, 2 vols., Paris, 1911-1912.

——, *La population française: histoire de la population avant 1789 et démographie de la France comparée à celle des autres nations au XIXe siècle*, 3 vols., Paris, 1889-1892.

Meredith, H. O., *Protection in France*, London, 1904.

Michel, Edmond, *La propriété*, Paris, 1908.

Moras, Adrien, *La crise du blé*, Paris, 1902.

Perreau, Pierre, *La révision du régime douanier de 1892*, Paris, 1910.

Régnier, Pierre, *L'Ouvrier agricole*, Paris, 1924.

Risler, G., *Le travailleur agricole français*, pref. by J. Méline, Paris, 1923.

Romanet, René, *La conférence de Bruxelles de 1901-1902 sur le régime des sucres*, Poligny, 1904.

Ronce, P., *La crise agricole*, pref. by E. Levasseur, Paris, 1900.
Sée, Henri, *Esquisse d'une histoire du régime agraire en Europe au XVIIIe et XIXe siècles*, Paris, 1921.
Sémars, Fernand, *Relations économiques des colonies avec la métropole*, Nancy, 1905.
Seulliet, Fernand, *Le métayage*, Paris, 1905.
Souchon, A., *La crise de la main d'oeuvre agricole en France*, Paris, 1914.
——, *La propriété paysanne*, Paris, 1899.
Spengler, Joseph J., *France Faces Depopulation*, Durham, N. C., 1938.
Théry, Edmond, *Les progrès économiques de la France: bilan du régime douanier de 1892*, pref. by P.-L. Cauwès, Paris, 1909.
——, *La fortune publique de la France*, Paris, 1912.
Vernaison, Paul, *Le métayage en France*, Paris, 1902.
White, Harry D., *The French International Accounts 1880-1913*, Harvard Economic Studies, vol. XL, Cambridge, 1933.
Zolla, Daniel, *L'Agriculture moderne*, Paris, 1913.
——, *Le blé et les céréales*, Paris, 1909.
——, *La crise agricole dans ses rapports avec la baisse des prix et la question monétaire*, Paris, 1903.
———, *Etudes d'économie rurale*, Paris, 1896.

C. THE *Syndicats agricoles* AND SOCIAL CATHOLICISM

Augé-Laribé, Michel, *Le probème agraire du socialisme*, Paris, 1907.
——, *Syndicats et coopératives agricoles*, Paris, 1926.
Blum, Léon, *Les congrès ouvriers et socialistes français*, 2 vols., Paris, 1901.
Boullaire, J. and Le Conte, P., *Manuel des syndicats professionnels agricoles suivi d'un formulaire à l'usage spécial des syndicats agricoles*, Paris, 1888.
Caziot, P., *La terre à la famille paysanne*, Paris, 1919.
Colliez, André, *Les associations agricoles de production et de vente*, Paris, 1905.
Coulet, Elie, *Le mouvement syndical et coopératif dans l'agriculture française*, Montpellier, 1898.
Courtin, A., *Les congrès nationaux des syndicats agricoles*, Paris, 1920.
Dop, Louis, *Le Crédit foncier de France dans le rôle de banque centrale*, Paris, 1901.
Dufourmantelle, Maurice, *Agricultural Credit*, P. C. Biddle, trans., Philadelphia, 1912.
Durand, Louis, *Le crédit agricole en France et à l'étranger*, Paris, 1891.
Durousseau-Dugontier, L., *Evolution du métayage en France*, Paris, 1905.
Flour de Saint-Genis, V.B., *Le crédit territorial en France et la réforme hypothécaire*, 2nd ed., Paris, 1889.
——, *La propriété rurale en France*, Paris, 1902.
Gailhard-Bancel, H. de, *Petit manuel pratique des syndicats agricoles*, 8th ed., Paris, 1908.
——, *Quinze années d'action syndicale*, Paris, 1900.
Garmy, R., *Histoire du mouvement syndical en France des origines à 1914*, Paris, 1933.

Gaumont, J., *Histoire générale de la coopération en France*, 2 vols., Paris, 1923-1924.

Genin, Maurice, *Les associations agricoles dans l'ancienne France et sous le régime de la loi du 21 mars 1884*, Lyon, 1893.

Gide, Charles, *Les associations coopératives agricoles*, Paris, 1925.

Glotin, Hyacinthe, *Etude historique, juridique et économique sur les syndicats professionnels*, Paris, 1892.

Justin, Emile, *Les sociétés royales d'agriculture au XVIIIe siècle (1757-1793)*, Saint-Lô, 1935.

Launay, Maurice, *Etude sur les unions des syndicats agricoles*, Paris, 1900.

Lécolle, Gabrielle, *Les associations agricoles, syndicats, coopératives, mutualités, et les nouvelles lois sociales agricoles*, pref. by comte de Rocquigny, Paris, 1912.

Lecomte, Antoine, *Les associations agricoles professionnelles et mutuelles*, Paris, 1907.

Lestapis, Samuel de, *Notions élémentaires d'organisation professionnelle agricole*, Paris, 1922.

Luçay, comte de, and Sénart, P., *Voeux de l'assemblée générale de la Société des agriculteurs de France*, 2nd ed. rev., Paris, 1894.

Marcillac, marquis de, *Les syndicats agricoles: leur action économique et sociale*, Paris, 1913.

Martin Saint-Léon, Etienne, *Histoire des corporations de métiers suivie d'une étude sur l'évolution de l'idée corporative de 1791 à nos jours et sur le mouvement syndical contemporain*, 3rd ed., Paris, 1922.

Moon, Parker Thomas, *The Labor Problem and the Social Catholic Movement in France: a Study in the History of Social Politics*, New York, 1921.

Musée social, *Le concours entre les syndicats agricoles au Musée social*, Paris, 1897.

Noël, abbé L., *Le syndicat agricole mixte paroissial: par un curé de campagne*, Arras, 1895.

Roblin, L. H., *Les bûcherons du Cher et de la Nièvre: leurs syndicats*, Paris, 1903.

Rocquigny (Henri du Fayel) comte de, *La coopération de production dans l'agriculture: syndicats et sociétés coopératives agricoles*, Paris, 1896.

——, *Les syndicats agricoles et leur oeuvre*, 2nd ed., Paris, 1906.

——, *Les syndicats agricoles et le socialisme agraire*, Paris, 1893.

Sagnier, Henry, *Le crédit agricole en France: ses origines, son essor, son avenir*, pref. by J. Méline, Paris, 1911.

Souchon, A., *Agricultural Societies in France*, report to San Francisco Exposition, San Francisco, 1915.

Toussaint, Adrien, *L'Union centrale des syndicats agricoles, ses idées directrices*, Paris, 1920.

Vogüé, comte L. de, with the collaboration of Marius Pelud, *Emile Duport, la leçon de ses oeuvres*, Lyon, 1909.

Weill, Georges, *Histoire du catholicisme libéral en France 1828-1908*, Paris, 1909.

D. Nationalist Economic Theory

Angell, James W., *The Theory of International Prices, History, Criticism and Restatement,* Harvard Economic Studies, vol. XXVIII, Cambridge, 1926.
Boissonade, P., *Colbert, le triomphe de l'étatisme, la fondation de la suprématie industrielle de la France, la dictature de travail (1661-1683),* Paris, 1932.
Bouvier-Ajam, Maurice, *Frédéric List, sa vie, son oeuvre, son influence,* Paris, 1938.
Brocard, Lucien, *Principes d'économie politique nationale et internationale,* 3 vols., Paris, 1929-1931.
Cantillon, Richard, *Essai sur la nature du commerce en général,* H. Higgs, ed., London, 1931.
Carey, Henry Charles, *Principles of Political Economy,* 3 vols., Philadelphia, 1837-1840.
——, *The Past, the Present and the Future,* Philadelphia, 1848.
——, *Harmony of Interests, Agricultural, Manufacturing and Commercial,* Philadelphia, 1850.
——, *Principles of Social Science,* 3 vols., Philadelphia, 1858-1859.
——, *The Unity of Law as Exhibited in the Relations of Physical, Social, Mental and Moral Science,* Philadelphia, 1872.
Cauwès, Paul-Louis, *Cours d'économie politique: contenant avec l'exposé des principes l'analyse des questions de législation économique,* 3rd ed., 4 vols., Paris, 1893.
——, *Précis du cours d'économie politique professé à la Faculté de droit de Paris,* 1st ed. of preceding, 2 vols., Paris, 1878.
Cole, Charles W., *Colbert and a Century of French Mercantilism,* 2 vols., New York, 1939.
——, *French Mercantilist Doctrines before Colbert,* New York, 1931.
Cournot, Antoine Augustin, *Principes de la théorie des richesses,* Paris, 1863.
——, *Recherches sur les principes mathématiques de la théorie des richesses,* G. Lutfalla, ed., Paris, 1938.
——, *Revue sommaire des doctrines économiques,* Paris, 1877.
Domergue, J., *La comédie libre-échangiste,* Paris, 1891.
——, *La réforme économique,* pref. by J. Méline, Paris, 1890.
Dubois, A., *Précis d l'histoire des doctrines économiques,* vol. I, Paris, 1903.
Dupont-White, Charles Brook, *Essai sur les relations du travail avec le capital,* Paris, 1846.
——, *L'Individu et l'état,* Paris, 1857.
——, *La centralisation,* Paris, 1860.
Ferrier, F. L. A., *Du gouvernement considéré dans ses rapports avec le commerce,* 3rd ed., Paris, 1822.
——, *De l'enquête commerciale,* Paris, 1829.
Forbonnais, François Véron-Duverger de, *Principes économiques,* Collection des principaux économistes, Paris, 1847.

Ganilh, Charles, *Dictionnaire analytique d'économie politique*, Paris, 1826.

——, *Des systèmes d'économie politique*, 2 vols., Paris, 1909.

——, *Théorie d'économie politique*, 2 vols., Paris, 1815.

Gide, C. and Rist., C., *A History of Economic Doctrines from the Time of the Physiocrats to the Present Day*, R. Richards, trans., London, 1915.

Gonnard, René, *Histoire des doctrines économiques*, 3 vols., Paris, 1921-1922.

Harsin, P., *Les doctrines monétaires en France du XVIe au XVIIIe siècles*, Paris, 1928.

Heckscher, Eli, *The Continental System: an Economic Interpretation*, Oxford, 1922.

——, *Mercantilism*, 2 vols., London, 1935.

Hirst, Margaret E., *Life of Friedrich List and Selections from his Writings*, New York and London, 1909.

Horrocks, J. W., *A Short History of Mercantilism*, London, 1925.

Jenks, J. W., *Henry C. Carey als Nationalökonom*, Jena, 1885.

Johnson, E. A. J., *Predecessors of Adam Smith: the Growth of British Economic Thought*, New York, 1937.

Kaplan, A. D. H., *Henry Charles Carey. a Study in American Economic Thought*, Johns Hopkins University Studies, series XLIX no. 4, Baltimore, 1931.

Lachapelle, Georges, *Le ministère Méline*, Paris, 1928.

Lestiboudois, G.-T., *Economie pratique des nations*, Paris, 1847.

List, Friedrich, *National System of Political Economy*, S. S. Lloyd, trans., London, 1885.

Méline, Jules, *Le retour à la terre et la surproduction industrielle*, Paris, 1905, trans. as *The Return to the Land*, New York, 1907.

——, *Le salut par la terre*, 2nd ed., Paris, 1920.

Morini-Comby, J., *Mercantilisme et protectionnisme: essai sur les doctrines interventionnistes en politique commerciale du XVe au XIXe siècle*, Paris, 1930.

Pirou, Gaëtan, *Les doctrines économiques en France depuis 1870*, Paris, 1925.

Rastel, Georges, *Les controverses doctrinales sur le bimétallisme au XIXe siècle*, Paris, 1935.

Raymond, Daniel, *Elements of Political Economy*, 2 vols., Baltimore, 1823.

Robbins, Lionel Charles, *An Essay on the Nature and Significance of Economic Science*, London, 1932.

Say, Louis, *Considérations sur l'industrie et la législation sous le rapport de leur influence sur la richesse des états et examen critique des principaux ouvrages qui ont paru sur l'économie politique*, Paris, 1822.

——, *Etudes sur las richesse des nations et réfutation des principales erreurs en économie politique*, Paris, 1836.

——, *Principales causes de la richesse ou de la misère des peuples et des particuliers*, Paris, 1818.

——, *Traité élémentaire de la richesse individuelle et la richesse publique et éclaircissements sur les principales questions de l'économie politique*, Paris, 1827.

Sommer, Arthur, *Friedrich Lists System der politischen Okonomie*, Jena, 1927.

Teilhac, Ernest, *Pioneers of American Economic Thought in the Nineteenth Century*, E. A. J. Johnson, trans., New York, 1936.

E. Articles and Pamphlets

Augé-Laribé, Michel, " La petite propriété rurale en France d'après une enquête officielle," *Revue d'économie politique*, vol. XXIV, 1910, pp. 69 ff.

Bouchié de Belle, A., " Le nouveau régime douanier des colonies," *Journal des économistes*, vol. XII, 1892, pp. 19 ff., vol. XVI, 1893, pp. 161 ff.

Cauwès, Paul-Louis and Gide, Charles, " Bauernbefreiung in Frankreich," *Handworterbuch der Staatswissenschaften*, 2nd ed., Jena, 1899.

Cauwès, Paul-Louis, " L'Economie politique nationale," *Revue d'économie politique*, vol. XII, 1898, pp. 97 ff.

——, " Les nouvelles compagnies de colonisation privilégiées," *Revue d'économie politique*, vol. VI, 1892, pp. 1 ff.

Charles-Roux, J., " La question des sucres," *Revue politique et parlementaire*, vol. II, 1894, pp. 246-ff.

Cournault, " Jules Méline," *Bulletin de l'Union des syndicats agricoles vosgiens*, June 1938.

Dunham, Arthur Louis, " The Attempt of President Thiers to Restore High Protection in France (1871-1873)," *Journal of Economic and Business History*, vol. I, 1928-1929, pp. 302 ff.

Duport, Emile, *Les engrais et les syndicats agricoles*, pamphlet, Lyon, 1888.

Durand, Louis, *La caisse rurale, la caisse ouvrière*, pamphlet, Paris, 1907.

——, *Les caisses rurales, leurs origines, leur avenir*, address to *Congrès de l'Union catholique de la Gironde*, Bordeaux, 1896.

Ernle, (R. E. Prothero) Lord, " Farming Partnership in France," *Nineteenth Century*, vol. LXXXVII, 1920, pp. 439 ff.

Flux, A. W., " Price Movements in Foreign Trade of France," *Journal of the Royal Statistical Society*, vol. LXIII, 1900, pp. 480 ff.

Foville, Alfred de, " Le morcellement depuis dix ans," communication to *21e congrès de l'Association française pour l'avancement des sciences*, Paris, 1892, pp. 1085 ff.

Gailhard-Bancel, H. de, *Les syndicats agricoles et l'union des classes*, address to 1897 *Congrès national catholique*, Valence, 1898.

Gimel, C., " De la nouvelle évaluation du revenu foncier des propriétés non bâties," *Journal de la Société de statistique de Paris*, vol. XXV, 1884, pp. 299 ff.

Girault, Arthur, " Le nouveau régime douanier des colonies et ses résultats," *Revue d'économie politique*, vol. VIII, 1894, pp. 854 ff.

Hanotaux, Gabriel, " Jules Méline," *Revue des deux mondes*, 7th ser., vol. xxi, 1926, pp. 440 ff.

Henry, René, " Le parti rural organisé et mobilisable," *Revue politique et parlementaire*, vol. XIII, 1897, pp. 14 ff.

Hitier, Henry, "A propos de nos statistiques agricoles," *Journal d'agriculture pratique*, ser. 7, vol. LXII, 1926, pp. 150 ff.

Hooker, R. H., "The Course of Prices at Home and Abroad, 1890-1910," *Journal of the Royal Statistical Society*, vol. LXXV, 1911-1912, pp. 1 ff.

Kergall, *L'Impôt démocratique sur le revenu*, pamphlet, Paris, 1896.

——, *Du rôle social des syndicats agricoles*, report to *3e congrès national des syndicats agricoles*, Paris, 1897.

——, *Rapport sur la doctrine sociale des syndicats agricoles français*, to *Congrès international de sociologie*, Genoa, 1899, pamphlet, Paris, n. d.

Lamane, Henri, "La dette hypothécaire en France," *Journal de la Société de statistique de Paris*, vol. XXVI, 1895, pp. 216 ff.

Levasseur, Emile, "Enquête sur le prix des denrées alimentaires en France," *Revue économique internationale*, 6th year, 1909, vol. II, pp. 205 ff.

——, "Les périodes de l'histoire des prix en France au XIXe et au XXe siècle," *Revue économique internationale*, 7th year, 1910, vol. IV, pp. 239 ff.

——, *Les populations urbaines en France comparées à celles de l'étranger*, extract of proceedings of *Académie des sciences morales et politiques*, Paris, 1887.

Levermore, C. H., "Henry C. Carey and his Social System," *Political Science Quarterly*, vol. V, 1890, pp. 553 ff.

Maunier, René, "Les économistes protectionnistes en France de 1815-1848," *Revue internationale de sociologie*, vol. XIX, 1911, pp. 485 ff.

Musée social, *Etat général des syndicats agricoles classés par départements*, pamphlet, Paris, 1898.

Musset, René, "Les statistiques agricoles officielles françaises," *Annales d'histoire économique et sociale*, vol. V, 1933, pp. 285 ff.

Rocquigny (Henri du Fayel) comte de, "La statistique des associations agricoles," *Le Musée social: Annales*, 1911, pp. 263 ff.

Sauerbeck, Augustus, "Prices of Commodities in 1902," *Journal of the Royal Statistical Society*, vol. LXVI, 1903, pp. 87 ff.

——, "Prices of Commodities in 1911," *ibid.*, vol. LXXV, 1911-1912, pp. 412 ff.

Sée, Henri, "Les progrès de l'agriculture en France de 1815 à 1848," *Revue d'histoire économique et sociale*, vol. IX, 1921, pp. 67 ff.

Société des agriculteurs de France, *Les Agriculteurs de France*, pamphlet, Paris, n. d.

Teilhac, E., "H. C. Carey," *Revue d'histoire économique et sociale*, vol. XIII, 1925, pp. 418 ff.

Truchy, H., "Etude sur le commerce de la France," *Revue d'économie politique*, vol. XVIII, 1904, pp. 543 ff.

F. Periodicals (*dates are for volumes used in this study*)

L'Année politique: avec un index raisonné, une table chronologique, des notes, des documents et des pièces justificatives, A. Daniel, ed., vols. XVI-XVIII, 1889-1891, Paris.

Annuaire de l'agriculture et des associations agricoles, 1902-1910, Lyon (known as *Annuaire Silvestre*).

Annuaire des syndicats agricoles et de l'agriculture française, 1890-1895, Paris, L. Hautefeuille ed.

Association catholique, Paris, 1876-1892.

Bulletin de la Société des agriculteurs de France, Paris, 1869-1910.

Bulletin de l'Union des syndicats et du Syndicat central des agriculteurs de France, Paris, 1887-1892.

Comptes rendus des travaux de la Société des agriculteurs de France, Paris, 1869-1910.

Corporation, Paris, 1883-1892.

Démocratie rurale, Paris, 1889-1892.

Journal des économistes, Paris, 1888-1892.

Travail national, Paris, 1883-1892.

G. Official Publications

France:

Journal officiel de la République Française:

Journal officiel;

Compte rendu in extenso *des séances du Sénat*;

Annexes du Sénat: Projets de loi et Rapports des Commissions;

Compte rendu in extenso *des séances de la Chambre des Députés*;

Annexes de la Chambre des Députés: Projets de loi et Rapports des Commissions.

Ministère de l'agriculture (name varies):

Annuaire des syndicats agricoles établi à l'aide de documents réunis par le Ministre de l'agriculture, Paris, 1911.

Dix ans de crédit agricole (1900-1909), Paris, 1911.

Office de renseignements agricoles (of Ministère de l'agriculture):

Enquête sur les salaires agricoles, Paris, 1912 (summarized by Lucien March, *Bulletin de la Statistique générale de la France*, vol. II, 1912-1913, pp. 155 ff.)

La petite propriété rurale en France: enquêtes monographiques (1908-1909), Paris, 1909.

Principales mesures législatives et administratives prises en faveur de l'agriculture sous le gouvernement de la 3e république, Paris, 1914.

Statistique agricole annuelle, for 1909, 1918, Paris, 1911, 1920.

Syndicats professionnels agricoles existants au 1er janvier 1904, Paris, 1904.

Statistique de la France. Agriculture: Résultats généraux de l'enquête décennale de 1862, Strasbourg, 1868.

Statistique agricole de la France (Algérie et colonies): Résultats généraux de l'enquête décennale de 1882, Nancy, 1887.

Statistique agricole de la France: Résultats généraux de l'enquête décennale de 1892, Paris, 1897.

Statistique de la France: Agriculture, 4 vols., Paris, 1838-1842.
Statistique de la France: Agriculture, 2 vols., Paris, 1858-1860.
Tisserand, E. *Rapport sur l'enseignement agricole en France publié par l'ordre de M. Viger, Ministre de l'agriculture*. 2 vols., Paris, 1894.

Ministère du commerce: Direction générale des douanes,
Tableau décennal du commerce de la France avec ses colonies et les puissances étrangères, 1877 à 1886, and *1887-1896* (annual thereafter) Paris, 1888, 1898.

Ministère des finances:
Bulletin de statistique et de législation comparée, esp. vol. XIII, 1883-I, and vol. XXIV, 1888-II, Paris.
Direction générale des contributions directes (of Ministère des finances):
Annuaire des contributions directes, esp. 1897, Paris.
Evaluation des propriétés non bâties prescrite par l'article 3 de la loi du 31 décembre 1907: Rapport de M. Charles Dumon, Ministre des finances, sur l'ensemble des opérations (3 novembre 1913), 2 vols., Paris, 1913.
L'Evaluation des propriétés non bâties, Paris, 1910.
Tableau présentant le répartition du nombre des exploitations agricoles d'après la superficie exploitée, in *Journal officiel*, 1909, pp. 2704 ff.

Ministère de la justice:
Compte général de la justice civile et commerciale en France, Paris, 1873-1891.

Ministère du travail (name varies):
Bulletin de la Statistique générale de la France et du Service d'observations des prix, Paris, especially;
Dugé de Bernonville, L., "Essai d'un indice pondéré des prix de gros en France," vol. XVII, 1927-1928, pp. 201 ff.
March, Lucien, "Le mouvement des prix et l'activité productrice," vol. I, 1911-1912, pp. 63 ff.
Sauvy, A. de, "Indice annuelle des prix de gros en France de 1820 à 1857 et aperçu sur le mouvement des prix depuis 1790," vol. XVII, 1927-1928, pp. 309 ff.
Statistique générale de la France: Annuaire statistique, esp. vol. XXX, 1910, Paris, 1911.
Résultats généraux du dénombrement de 1876, Paris, 1878.
Résultats statistiques du dénombrement de 1891, Paris, 1894.
Résultats statistiques du recensement général de la population effectué le 4 mars 1906, 3 vols., Paris, 1908-1911.
Résultats statistiques du recensement général de la population effectué le 5 mars 1911, 2 vols., Paris, 1913-1917.
Résultats statistiques du recensement général de la population effectué le 7 mars 1926, 4 vols. in 3, Paris, 1928-1932.

Salaires et coût de l'existence à diverses époques jusqu'en 1910 (Lucien March), Paris, 1910.

Service de la statistique municipale:

Receuil de statistique municipale de la ville de Paris (1910), Paris, 1911.

Germany:

Statistisches Jahrbuch für Elsass-Lothringen, Strasbourg, 1907.

Great Britain:

Cost of Living in French Towns. Reports of an Enquiry by the Board of Trade into Working Class Rents, Housing and Retail Prices together with the Rates of Wages in certain Occupations in the Principal Industrial Towns of France. With an introductory Memorandum and a Comparison of Conditions in France and the United Kingdom, Cd. 4512, London, 1909.

United States:

Department of Commerce and Labor, Bureau of Statistics:

Transportation Routes and Systems of the World, Washington, 1909.

Department of Commerce, Bureau of Foreign and Domestic Commerce:

Wolfe, A. J., *Commercial Organizations in France; with a Summary of Governmental Activities in Promoting Commerce*, Special Agents, No. 98, Washington, 1915.

INDEX

Bei Fragen zur Produktsicherheit wenden Sie sich bitte an:
If you have any questions regarding product safety,
please contact:

Walter de Gruyter GmbH
Genthiner Straße 13
10785 Berlin
productsafety@degruyterbrill.com